SOME PRINCIPLES OF
MORAL THEOLOGY

SOME PRINCIPLES OF
MORAL THEOLOGY
AND THEIR APPLICATION

BY

KENNETH E. KIRK

SOMETIME BISHOP OF OXFORD AND HON. FELLOW OF
ST. JOHN'S AND TRINITY COLLEGES, OXFORD

LONGMANS, GREEN AND CO.
LONDON ◆ NEW YORK ◆ TORONTO

LONGMANS, GREEN AND CO LTD
6 & 7 CLIFFORD STREET LONDON W I
THIBAULT HOUSE THIBAULT SQUARE CAPE TOWN
605–611 LONSDALE STREET MELBOURNE C I

LONGMANS, GREEN AND CO INC
55 FIFTH AVENUE NEW YORK 3

LONGMANS, GREEN AND CO
20 CRANFIELD ROAD TORONTO

ORIENT LONGMANS PRIVATE LTD
CALCUTTA BOMBAY MADRAS
DELHI HYDERABAD DACCA

First Edition . . . *October* 1920
New Impressions, November 1921, *April* 1926,
April 1930, *June* 1934, *December* 1939,
March 1944, *January* 1946, *May* 1948,
March 1954, *August* 1957

Printed in Great Britain
SPOTTISWOODE, BALLANTYNE & CO. LTD.
London & Colchester

TO

THE VEN. H. ARMSTRONG HALL, C.B.E., B.D.

CHAPLAIN TO THE KING
ARCHDEACON OF RICHMOND

IN GRATEFUL ACKNOWLEDGMENT OF THE INFLUENCE
WHICH BY HIS ENTHUSIASM, ADVICE, AND EXAMPLE
HE HAS HAD UPON THE LIVES OF THE CLERGY WHO
HAVE KNOWN HIM

THIS BOOK IS DEDICATED

1106106

PREFACE

THE present book is an attempt to bring together, from the Bible and from Christian experience, the principles which have guided the Church in dealing with individual souls; to test those principles by the light of modern knowledge; and to apply them to present-day conditions and needs. Some of the traditional terminology of moral theology has been discarded; much has been retained, either because it seemed the best medium for expressing what had to be expressed, or because it would have been impossible otherwise to indicate the development and formulation of Christian thought on the subject. Thus the book may prove of interest not merely to the clergy and others who are confronted by the practical problems of conduct and morality, but also to students entering upon the study of moral theology for its own sake.

The Church of England affords her clergy singularly little expert guidance in this matter of the direction of souls. Two branches of the subject—those which go by the names of 'Christian ethics' and the 'theory and practice of the confessional' respectively—have indeed been systematically and fully treated by recent writers; and there is a wealth of practical experience to be drawn both from manuals of 'pastoral theology' and from biographies. Moral theology, however, as will appear, comprises much more than the two topics just mentioned. Yet within the last fifty years, apparently, only three books have attempted to present the whole content of moral theology in such a form as should guide the theory and practice of the Church of England, and all three are out of print and consequently difficult of access.

The three in question are the following :

James Skinner, 'Synopsis of Moral and Ascetical Theology' (London, 1882).

J. J. Elmendorf, 'Elements of Moral Theology based on the Summa Theologiae of St. Thomas Aquinas' (first edition, New York, 1892 ; second edition, New York, 1895).

W. W. Webb, 'The Cure of Souls' (first edition, New York, 1892).

Of these three, Skinner's 'Synopsis' is by far the greatest ; though by reason of its being a synopsis alone it is at the same time the least useful to the general reader. The fruit of many years' patient study of patristic and later writers, it was intended to give the clergy 'a *conspectus* of the whole subject, arranged in a scientific form, with direction to authorities which they may consult for themselves' ; and the Committee at whose request it was compiled had in view the further possibility that it might serve as a basis for the 'construction of a " Manual of Moral Theology " suited to the growing needs of the English priesthood.' Unfortunately this hope was never fulfilled. Mr. Skinner died before his 'Synopsis' was actually published ; and the whole edition, all but a few hundred copies, was accidentally destroyed by a warehouse fire. For these reasons, therefore, the 'Synopsis' never exerted the influence its great authority deserved. But it remains an indispensable book for the student ; and if ever the study of moral theology in the Church of England reaches a point at which the task of compiling a 'manual' becomes possible, the value of Mr. Skinner's vast researches will be widely recognised.

Elmendorf's 'Moral Theology' and Bishop Webb's 'Cure of Souls' are by comparison slighter books, though each is the outcome of careful study—the former of the 'Summa Theologica,' the latter of patristic, Eastern and Anglican writers. Both of them assume, however, as does the 'Synopsis,' a considerable acquaintance with the principles and terminology of moral theology on the part of their readers. It is just this acquaintance which seems to be lacking in the Church to-day. I have tried, therefore, in the chapters which follow, to provide a general outline of the subject to serve as an introduction both to the books in question, as well as to other and older authorities.

There is a close agreement between the authors mentioned on one point of fundamental importance. Whilst recognising that the theology of St. Thomas Aquinas has a value for the Christian student of morals second only to that of the Bible and the Fathers, they agree in never using later Roman Catholic writers except with the utmost possible caution. The present book follows them in that respect. This attitude towards the developments of moral theology in post-scholastic Roman thought is due to no ecclesiastical prejudice, but to what is itself a vital matter of principle. The point is of such importance for a clear understanding of the subject that it is not inappropriate to deal with it here at some length.

The standing problem of all ethics is the reconciliation of two apparently opposed principles, which may be called respectively the principles of law and liberty, or of authority and individualism. Particularly is this the case with Christian ethics. A society which has its roots in a divine revelation once given (however much expanded under the later guidance of the Spirit)—a society, moreover, of which it is a fundamental principle that no member lives to himself alone—cannot dispense with authority and law. Limits must be set to the freedom of the individual. Yet they must not interfere with his *true* freedom; he must be free to develop every part of his personality to its utmost in the service of God and his neighbour. Christian theology then, above all other thought, is called to the task of solving this problem—the reconciliation of authority with freedom.

It is the great and abiding merit of St. Thomas Aquinas that he attempted to effect such a reconciliation. From Aristotle he drew the twin conceptions of free speculative thought and of conduct based upon the principle of the fullest self-expression; from the Church that of an authority and revelation beyond whose limits such conduct and speculation—to remain Christian—must not step. Believing that the two could be combined without loss to either, he attempted to hold them in combination. Widely different opinions have been expressed as to the success which attended this attempt. Some of his critics accuse him of going too far in the direction of freedom—Albertus Magnus was called upon to defend his memory against the charge of unorthodoxy within a few months of his death. Others regard the liberty which he appears to allow to the individual as no more than a phantom concession, and believe that they can trace in the 'Summa' the outlines of all modern Roman Catholic authoritarianism. The most popular and plausible criticism of his work is that, perhaps, which regards him as *holding together* indeed, but by no means *reconciling*, the two principles in question. According to this view, he speaks now as a dogmatist and now as a philosopher ; but finds no way of combining the two points of view in a single consistent system. He never, that is, escapes from the dualism which is the abiding problem of ethics.

It is beside the mark to inquire which of these estimates —if any of them—is the true one. The crucial fact for us is that St. Thomas made the attempt, whatever its outcome may have been. And in this respect he has had few followers.

The Roman Church as a whole has certainly not profited by his example. If Protestant thought, as is usually held to be the case, has erred on the side of liberty and individualism, Roman Catholic theology has lapsed into an almost complete authoritarianism. Some of the causes and results of this lapse are briefly indicated upon a later page ; its principal outcome must be that for the student who is attempting to solve the problem of the relation between law and liberty, whether in the matter of conduct or in that of thought, there is little to be learnt from Rome. The practice, therefore, of providing for the use of Anglican clergy handbooks of moral theology which are little more than translations of St. Alphonso Liguori or his imitators, is one which can scarcely be deprecated too strongly. Should such a practice become at all common, it would give to Anglican moral theology a bias in the direction of legalism which might well be considered almost fatal. Even where it is fully understood that the scope of these manuals is limited to the discussion of a single problem only—the problem of *when and when not* to absolve (a fact which their sponsors and their detractors alike too often ignore) —their tendency is too authoritarian to render them either safe or desirable guides.

The only successors of St. Thomas who can fairly be said to have attempted to carry out his ideal of combining the principle of authority with that of freedom are the little group of Anglican divines of the seventeenth century— Hooker, Jeremy Taylor, Sanderson, Hall, and their fellows. Their mistakes and limitations are obvious, even on the most casual reading ; yet it is clear that they grasped and held fast the true ideal. They had no doubts whatever as to the authority and divine commission of the Church, yet they rejected with finality the tendency of the Roman communion to push that authority to extremes. One of the great needs of the Church of England to-day is renewed and detailed study of her great theologians of the Caroline period.

The 'Summa Theologica' and the writings of Sanderson and Jeremy Taylor have therefore been freely drawn upon in what follows. Modern Roman Catholic writers have indeed been consulted on matters of principle, but rarely quoted. Freer use has been made of them, however, in matters of *practice* ; for the Roman communion has collected a vast accumulation of practical experience of the utmost value. In particular, the genial but garrulous 'Directorium' of Scaramelli is full of observations of real insight and importance, which will be found in singular agreement with the conclusions of modern psychology. The principles of casuistry, of course, have been drawn in the main from Roman Catholic writers, but not without a considerable degree of caution.

Some surprise may perhaps be occasioned by the amount of space devoted in this book to what is known as *ascetic theology*—the science, that is to say, of the methods and rules of Christian progress. In the strict sense, no doubt, this branch of the subject is only subsidiary to moral theology proper. But—quite apart from the present-day need of the Church of England for a proper understanding of the prin-

ciples of Christian progress—it is important in this matter
to emphasise that theory and practice are very closely
allied, and cannot be considered separately without great
detriment to both.   Mr. Skinner was very emphatic on this
point in the preface to his ' Synopsis.'   ' Whether a manual
of moral theology for the use of priests in the English Church
shall ever be compiled,' he wrote, ' remains to be seen.   But
if ever it is undertaken, it must, in the largest sense, include
spiritual and mystical theology.   Otherwise we shall but
protract, among ourselves, the mischief of which the learned
Benedictine, Martin Gerbert, complained in the middle of
the last century : "Huic enim divortio puto labem maximam
theologiae debere : separationi quidem positivae a schol-
astica corruptiones theologiae theoreticae seu speculativae,
separationi moralis a mystica corruptiones theologiae prac-
ticae tribuimus, *ubi mores Christiani sejuncti a virtutibus
Christianis fuerunt.*"   The whole end of our manual must be
practical, not speculative ; and therefore the wide field of
ascetic theology must be open to us from which to draw for
the building up of souls. . . . The ancient Fathers and
English divines of every school of thought would be all
but excluded if we should restrict ourselves to the pure
scholastics.' [1]

[1] The best Roman Catholic thought of recent times echoes this opinion.
' Moral theology has two branches.   The first is occupied with the right
judgment of sins ;   the second aims at the *practice of virtue*.   As a science
the former is much more developed than the latter ;   the former enables
the priest to become a judge ;   it deals with the commandments of God,
the duties of individual classes ;   it draws a line between what is sin and
what is not sin, what is of obligation and what is not of obligation.   This
is moral theology ;   if its rules are applied to individual cases, we have
casuistry.   The second science is called the science of the saints, asceticism,
and it makes the priest a guide of souls *on the road to perfection*.   While
the first is more cultivated in the schools, the latter is left more to the
individual's zeal and devotion.   Yet the *science* of perfection is necessary ;
for that which is known in scientific form makes a deeper impression.
There is great danger in cultivating the former without the latter.   If
in the discharge of his office as judge, a man does not cast his eyes upward,
he judges of sin and duty according to the standard of lawfulness and
not according to the light of perfection which must guide us.'—Dr. Ulla-
thorne, Roman Catholic Bishop of Birmingham, in 1873 ;   quoted, Schieler-
Heuser, *Theory and Practice of the Confessional*, p. 428.   How little
the admonition has been regarded by Roman Catholic writers may be
inferred from the statement in Fr. Slater's *Cases of Conscience* (vol. i. p. 36),
that the object of moral theology ' is not to place high ideals of virtue before

The reader must bear in mind that it is the *principles* of moral theology and their general application, not the detailed systems of ecclesiastical law which with widely differing emphasis have been built upon this foundation by different branches of the Church, that form the subject of this book. This will account for omissions which would otherwise be indefensible. Thus the general principles upon which a solution of the problem of authority and liberty must be sought for are repeatedly indicated throughout the book, as also some of the points at which the Church of England fails, in current practice, to apply those principles ; but the question of the organised forms and channels through which that authority should express itself has not been discussed. Again, confession of sin is treated throughout as a necessary principle of the spiritual life ; and confession in the presence of man as well as of God is put forward as a practice which a vast preponderance of Christian experience has found essential to any great advance in holiness. But the problem of the *degree of obligation* which binds a member of the Anglican communion to the practice of sacramental confession is not discussed. Such discussions at the present moment are indeed more in the province of textual critics, historians and canonists ; and a far greater consensus of opinion on their part is necessary before moral theology, in the Church of England, can hope to speak with a clear voice on these and kindred subjects.

The present generation is witnessing great advances in researches of this character, and it is not too much to hope that conclusions of sufficient cogency will be reached to make the compilation of a *manual* of Anglican moral theology, such as Mr. Skinner wished for, a practical possibility. Till that time we must be content to enunciate principles based, as far as possible, solely upon the great Biblical and Catholic doctrines which the Church has proclaimed throughout history with comparatively few dissentient voices. Such

the people and train them in Christian perfection. . . . Its primary object is to teach the priest how to distinguish what is sinful from what is lawful. . . . It is not intended for edification nor for the building up of character,' even though it is also not intended ' to teach people how to shake off the burden of the moral law, or to minimise its obligations.'

doctrines will always be the mainstay of moral theology, rather than the variations or peculiarities of this or that period or branch of the Church. In the present book the references in the footnotes, together with the bibliography, will perhaps provide the student with some slight indication as to sources in which he can study such disputed questions more fully.

One purpose of this book is to indicate in general terms the extent of agreement which exists between modern psychological practice—as evidenced, for example, in educational methods—and the ' ascetic ' principles of the Church. It is sometimes urged, on insufficient grounds, that Catholic methods of dealing with souls are antiquated or mistaken ; and it is consequently important to recognise that, so far from this being the case, there is a quite extraordinary degree of identity between the methods, on the one hand, of Scaramelli and Jeremy Taylor, and, on the other, of Starbuck, James, Welton, and their colleagues. The great Catholic directors of souls based their practice, no doubt, on experience rather than on scientific knowledge. But they brought to bear upon their experience an insight and power of criticism of exceptional truth and acuteness ; and psychology is daily vindicating the accuracy of their teaching.

In this connection, it may come as a surprise to the reader that no account has apparently been taken of the phenomena of psycho-therapy. Some justification for this may be found in the fact that psycho-therapeutic methods are, on the whole, directed to the cure of the abnormal, whilst the scope of the present book does not extend beyond the direction of normal souls.[1] But an investigation into the relation between psycho-therapy and spiritual direction is urgently required ; and it is to be hoped that it will before long be undertaken by experts competent to deal with both sides of the question. Among the principles

[1] It might perhaps be a truer differentiation to say that psychotherapy deals mainly with disorders of which the patient or penitent is *unconscious*, whilst moral theology is concerned with repressed sins of which he is *conscious*.

which may be established as the result of such a comparison will probably be the following :

(a) Sin *for practical purposes* (see *infra*, p. 223) must be regarded mainly in the light of a disease to be cured rather than of a fault to be punished.

(b) The Catholic principle of ' confession for all mortal sin ' is wholly in accord with the psycho-therapeutic ideal of ' getting up a repressed (or dissociated) complex.' Absolution, in its psychological aspect, is clearly a form of ' re-association,' for it enables the penitent to regard his sin as something which has been forgiven instead of as something which involves punishment and estrangement from God.

(c) The great stress which has rightly been laid, in Catholic teaching, upon the importance of *conscious effort* in the formation of character requires to be supplemented and to a certain extent modified by a recognition of the immense power of influences of which the penitent is *unconscious*—suggestion, environment, and the like ; and the training of the *will* must be given a less isolated position in the development of character than has hitherto been the case. Conversely, where a penitent can be led to see the extent to which tendencies against which he has struggled in vain may have been intensified by group-suggestion, unconscious imitation of parents and others, occurrences and influences which have over-stimulated or given a perverted direction to certain fundamental instincts, his power to resist or re-direct them will be correspondingly strengthened.

(d) The relation between spiritual and nervous disorders is extraordinarily close. The priest should never undertake the treatment of abnormal spiritual conditions without taking expert medical advice.

(e) The tracing of disorders to the misdirection of one of the basic instincts, and the principle of healing them not by ' repression ' but by ' sublimation,' i.e. by redirection of the instinct into beneficent channels (*infra*, p. 264), is wholly confirmed by modern therapeutic experience.

(f) The possibility of a *forgotten* emotional shock or crisis being the root cause of mental and spiritual disorder has been fully established by the analytic method of the Freudian school, and the value of ' analysis '—with or without hypnotic treatment—in bringing to light and ' reassociating ' such complexes is being more and more widely recognised. It seems probable that in cases of serious disorder which are not amenable to the ordinary methods of question, answer, and advice, whether employed by priest or physician, patients should be recommended to submit themselves to analytic treatment.

(*g*) On one point there will be, for the present, considerable divergence of opinion. Catholic practice, on the whole, regards a regular habit of sacramental confession as a helpful and laudable rule of life. The psycho-analyst, on the other hand, aims at curing his patients so completely that they will be in no further need of treatment ; and might well deprecate their continuing to consult priest or physician as likely to lead to morbidity or even to a recurrence of the disorder. It is clear that any medical man who deprecated the *habit* of sacramental confession on these or similar grounds would be in agreement, not merely with much Anglican thought on the subject, but with the teaching and practice of the primitive Church. Cases undoubtedly occur in which dependence upon sacramental confession must be admitted to have a deleterious effect upon character ; it is only open to question, in such cases, whether the root of the evil does not lie rather in *faulty direction* than in the *habit* itself. Are we forced to admit that the Catholic principle is psychologically unsound ?

Several solutions of the difficulty are possible. It may be that those who urge that ' every confession should be regarded as a last confession ' will prove to be in the right ; though the experience of the Church throughout many centuries tends to the opposite opinion. Or, again, it may appear that sacramental confession can rightly be regarded —as it is regarded in most Catholic teaching—no less in the light of *regulating the spiritual life in general* as in that of *remedying specially serious falls from grace*. Finally, it is possible that ' spiritual convalescence ' (the point of view from which moral theology regards Christian progress, see *infra*, p. 136) is far slower in operation than physical or nervous convalescence ; and that it requires, in consequence, direction by the expert practically throughout life. Further investigation of the psychology of the confessional is needed before the question can be settled on *scientific* grounds ; in the meantime the experience of the Church should be sufficient support for the Catholic principle.[1]

It is impossible to mention by name all those to whom I am indebted for advice, guidance and criticism in the preparation of this book. One or two obligations, however, cannot go unacknowledged. To Dr. Darwell Stone, Principal Librarian of the Pusey House, and the Rev. A. E. J. Rawlinson, Student of Christ Church, my warmest gratitude is due for the care with which they read and criticised the manuscript. Most, if not all, of the suggestions and illustrations which they contributed have been incorporated in the text, and in deference to their criticism a number of passages have been altered or re-written. Fr. L. S. Thornton, of the Community of the Resurrection, Mirfield, showed equal kindness in reading the proofs. I have not consciously retained anything to which these advisers took exception ; but of course they are not to

[1] These observations on the relation of psycho-therapy to spiritual direction are the outcome of a private conference between Canon B. H. Streeter, the Rev. S. F. Hawkes, the Rev. A. E. J. Rawlinson, Dr. J. A. Hadfield, and the writer. Dr. Hadfield has also been kind enough to contribute the following note as to his own conclusions, as a psycho-analyst of great experience, on the question discussed above : ' The crux of the difference [between the methods of the confessor and the psycho-analyst] is this. Assuming that the character is very largely influenced by *un*conscious complexes, the psycho-analyst gets down to these and roots them out. This is not done in the routine work of the priest, who in the nature of his work deals almost entirely with *conscious* troubles. This is not so radical as the psycho-analytic method, and therefore not so permanent in its effect. Of course the priest gives what the analyst cannot give—a new and inspiring ideal : but here again the " patient " needs constantly to be kept up to the ideal, and therefore the more regular " confession " is necessary. Thus if possible the " treatment " should be so radical that periodic " treatment " should not be necessary ; but if (because it deals with conscious troubles only) the confessional is *not* going to be radical, then periodic confession *may* be necessary. It is a similar case to the difference between treatment by " suggestion " and that by " analysis." The former often needs to be repeated : the latter properly done should be radical, complete and permanent.'

B

be held responsible for any statements or opinions which occur in the following pages.

The book has grown out of a series of lectures delivered during 1918 to successive ' courses ' of temporary Chaplains to the Forces at the Chaplains' Training Schools at Ripon and Catterick Camps. Not one of the hundreds of chaplains who attended those schools will forget how much they owed to the interest, oversight and personal teaching of the Archdeacon of Richmond, at that time Deputy-Assistant-Chaplain-General of the Northern Command. Without his constant encouragement and advice, I should never have made this attempt to present in systematic form the principles of the Church of England in the matter of conduct. There must be much in this book which his ripe experience would reject as immature or ill-advised ; nevertheless, it is with a very real sense of gratitude for his constant guidance and friendship that I avail myself of his permission to dedicate it to him.

OXFORD,
August 1920.

NOTE TO SECOND IMPRESSION

IN this impression a few misprints and errors in references have been corrected, and some sentences re-written to prevent misinterpretation of their meaning. The writer's thanks are due to the numerous friends and reviewers who have brought the need for these alterations to his notice.

OXFORD,
October 1921.

CONTENTS

CHAPTER III

PENITENCE

CHAPTER IV

FAITH

CHAPTER V
ZEAL

CHAPTER VI
THE EDUCATION OF THE SOUL

CONTENTS xxiii

CHAPTER VII

THE EDUCATION OF THE SOUL (continued)

CHAPTER VIII

CONSCIENCE, LAW AND CASUISTRY

CHAPTER IX

THE HEALING OF THE SOUL

CONTENTS

CHAPTER X

SIN

CONTENTS

CHAPTER XI

THE TREATMENT OF SIN

SOME PRINCIPLES OF MORAL THEOLOGY

AND THEIR APPLICATION

CHAPTER I

THE NATURE AND SCOPE OF MORAL THEOLOGY

1. *The Purpose of Moral Theology*

' COMMON sense, kindliness, manliness, and good intentions,'
in the words of a recent pronouncement, ' will no more
solve the problems of religion than they will solve the
problems of strategy or economics.'[1] The problems of
religion are manifold, but the greatest of them, perhaps,
are those which lie around the shepherding of individual
souls; the calling of them into the fold; the tending,
feeding, healing them once they are there. This, in St.
Gregory's words, is the 'art of arts.'[2] Every priest at
his ordination hears the same solemn charge, ' See that you
never cease your labour, your care and diligence, until you
have done all that lieth in you, according to your bounden
duty, to bring all such as are or shall be committed to your
charge, unto that agreement in the faith and knowledge of
God, and to that ripeness and perfectness of age in Christ,
that there be no place left among you, either for error in
religion, or for viciousness in life.'

But if common sense, kindliness, manliness and good
intentions will not solve the problem, ' our bounden duty '

[1] *Report of the Archbishop's Committee on the Teaching Office of the
Church*, p. 25.
[2] Gregory, *De Past. Cur.* i. 1.

must include the acquisition of something more than these. And indeed we know how liberally the clergy have given of these four qualities to the service of the Church, and yet how many of God's people thay have failed to reach and guide. What else is needed ? Many things, no doubt ; not least among them that the ' art of arts ' should once more, like every other art, have its science ; that those who practise it may grow from amateurs into experts.

This science in the past was called *Moral Theology*, and it formed an essential part of Christian doctrine. It gave the priest an outline first of all of the ideal of Christian character for which he was to work ; then of the internal dispositions of that character without which its virtues cannot flower ; then, too, of the means and motives by which its growth can best be fostered ; lastly, of the hindrances that threaten to spoil the work, and the ways in which they can be met and neutralised. ' Since the days of Peter Lombard,' wrote Bishop Webb, ' every great treatise of systematic theology has had at least a third of its space given up to a treatment of morals '—yet English clergy are still hard put to it to find any text-book on the subject, and the demand for one grows more insistent every year. Parts of the subject, no doubt, have often and admirably been handled ; but the Church of England still waits for the evolution of a full system of moral theology which will recognise the peculiar status of her clergy—so different, in fact, from that obtaining in the Roman communion ; which will express itself in terms of present-day thought, and not in the forgotten categories of a system that can never be revived ; and which will deal with the spiritual problems of to-day, rather than with those of yesterday.

It may be urged that the scholastic system of moral theology signed its own death-warrant by attempting to regard the deepest things in life as susceptible of rigid and detailed classification ; by applying to the living phenomena of personality, human and divine, the methods of abstract mathematics. To a large extent this is true, and therefore it would be futile to try to revive the categories of mediæval theology, in spite of their perpetuation by Roman Catholic writers. Human nature is infinitely too vast, complex and surprising a thing to be confined within the limits of strict and exhaustive analysis and definition ; and what is true, in this respect, of human nature is infinitely more true of divine. The variety of endowments, impulses, inconsistencies, which go to make up even the most normal man, is more than the most detailed observation can ever take account of. 'Caesar, Richelieu, Napoleon, were well-defined types; but at certain points of their lives they ceased to be themselves. . . . Cromwell was by turns an illuminated mystic and a practical joker.' [1] The springs of action lie deeper than human thought can plumb. Any attempt to formulate them exhaustively is doomed to failure from the outset. If the attempt is persisted in, or pushed beyond those limits of accuracy and truth of which the subject allows, we are left with lifeless categories, satisfying perhaps to the requirements of an abstract science, but wholly unlike the things and persons of real life, or even actually dangerous if used as infallible guides to action.[2]

A philosophy or an art which would reduce everything to strict rule and type is therefore doomed to failure. It may attract attention for a moment, because it has succeeded in fixing in clear outline some passing mood or shade of thought ; once let the conditions alter and its value becomes purely antiquarian. Such works as 'John Inglesant' or 'Robert Elsmere,' which were welcomed at their birth with enthusiasm, are half-forgotten to-day, for the simple reason that the characters they depict are not so much human beings as animated points of view. At the time of their publication, indeed, they were faithful representations and criticisms of contemporary currents of thought; but the popular shibboleths and questionings have changed, and books which at one time roused widespread attention are falling, in consequence, into neglect.

On the other hand, and for the opposite reason, the

---

[1] T. Ribot, *Psychology of the Emotions* (English trans.), p. 409.

[2] Cp. J. H. Newman, *Grammar of Assent*, p. 284 : ' Science in all its departments has too much simplicity and exactness, from the nature of the case, to be the measure of fact. In its very perfection lies its incompetency to settle particulars and details.'

' Pilgrim's Progress ' has never lost its popularity. Bunyan,
as Robert Louis Stevenson once pointed out, was too good
an artist to be bound down by his allegory. He gives
his characters names which show that he means them
to represent types of Christian life ; but the story he tells
and the people he depicts are so real to him as to break
down his strict moralising. Touch after touch of human
nature is introduced, sometimes no more than superfluous
and unmeaning to the allegory, but sometimes actually
inconsistent and contradictory to its purpose. ' The
mere story and the allegorical design enjoyed perhaps
his equal favour. He believed in both with an energy of
faith that was capable of moving mountains. And we have
to remark in him, not the parts where inspiration fails and
is replaced by cold and merely decorative invention, but
the parts where faith has grown to be credulity, and his
characters become so real to him that he forgets the end of
their creation.'

' We can follow him,' continues Stevenson, ' step by
step into the trap which he lays for himself by his own entire
good faith and triumphant literality of vision, till the trap
closes and shuts him in an inconsistency. . . . Christiana
dying " gave Mr. Standfast a ring," for no possible reason
in the allegory, merely because the touch was human and
affecting. Look at Great-Heart, with his soldierly ways,—
garrison ways I had almost called them ; with his taste for
weapons ; his delight in any that he found " a man of his
hands " ; his chivalrous point of honour, letting Giant Maul
get up again when he was down, a thing fairly flying in the
teeth of the moral ; above all with his language in the
inimitable tale of Mr. Fearing : " I thought I should have
lost my man "—" chicken-hearted "—" at last he came in,
and I will say that for my Lord, he carried it wonderfully
lovingly to him." This is no Independent minister ; this is
a stout, honest big-busted ancient ; adjusting his shoulder-
belts, twisting his long moustaches as he speaks. Last and
most remarkable : " My sword," says the dying Valiant-
for-Truth, he in whom Great-Heart delighted, " My sword
I give to him that shall succeed me in my pilgrimage, and
my courage and skill to him that can get it." And after this

boast, more arrogantly unorthodox than was ever dreamt of by the rejected Ignorance, we are told that " all the trumpets sounded for him on the other side." ' [1]

In exactly the same way, the method of exact and formal classification has proved itself, both in theology and in psychology, to be inadequate to the phenomena with which they have to deal.   There was a time, for example, when psychology divided human nature into ' faculties ' as a grocer divides sugar into parcels—each of them complete, independent, unyielding.   There was much value in the classification, but since Herbart's time it has fallen into disrepute. It is recognised that emotion, reason, will, are not three disconnected units, but aspects under which every phase of consciousness, every human act, can severally be regarded; not component parts of a mosaic personality, but interdependent, inseparable tendencies, never to be distinguished from one another by any definition so strict and logical as this.

So too with theology.   The clear-cut classifications of scholastic theology about virtue, vice, stages of progress, operations of grace and the like, proved inadequate to the delicate phenomena they were intended to define; to-day they are half-forgotten and wholly inoperative. On the other hand, the inconsistent, undifferentiated poetry of St. Paul's theology touches the heart as triumphantly as ever with its unconquerable realism.   He can tell us at one moment that love believeth all things and hopeth all things, and at the next that faith and hope are separate virtues, equal or almost equal to love, and no less abiding ; he can appeal now to faith and next to hope as the ground of salvation ; he can substitute sobriety for hope in his list of these three virtues; and it matters nothing to the truth of what he says.[2]   His theology is true to life rather than to thought ; it admits the inconsistency and undefinableness of human nature, and glories in it ; and we sympathise with a charity which does not attempt to reduce the

---

[1] R. L. Stevenson, *Essay on Bagster's Edition of the ' Pilgrim's Progress.'* Lord Macaulay, in his *Essay on Southey's Edition of the ' Pilgrim's Progress,'* notices the same characteristic in almost identical terms.

[2] See 1 Cor. xiii. 7, 13 ; Rom. viii. 24 ; Eph. ii. 8 ; 1 Tim. ii. 15.

mysteries of personality to strict rules and limitations, but rejoices in their depth and strangeness.

The theologian must therefore be on his guard against the temptation to press his analyses of character and its parts to conclusions of a mathematical accuracy. To do so is to regard the phenomena of life in the light of dead matter; to be true perhaps to the letter, but wholly to neglect the spirit, of the inquiry. Human conduct and divine grace are fields which admit only of the widest generalisations, and to every such generalisation there must be innumerable exceptions.

Yet we must not conclude that moral theology, on this account, is a superfluous study. Rather it is important to emphasise the fact that the principal danger of modern religious thought is not over-analysis, but vagueness. The reaction from over-exact definition has gone so far that to-day we are faced by an almost total want of definition in spiritual matters. This *failure to define* is no less disastrous than the opposite extreme of over-description. It finds its natural outcome in a prevailing indifference both as to the truths of doctrine, pure and simple, and as to those of morals. It has resulted in a widespread abandonment of any ideals of absolute truth or of absolute goodness; in an individualism according to which each man may believe what he likes and do what he likes without reference to any external criterion except a vague social convention that is entirely unable to justify its own standards. That this is the prevailing tone of mind of the English laity, at all events, cannot be denied. ' It doesn't much matter what a man believes,' and ' Every man must decide for himself what is right for him to do and what is wrong,' are the only rules commonly regarded as final in faith and morals; and the result is naturally enough that neither truth nor morality is any longer considered a matter in which God has revealed, or man can discover, an absolute standard.

This prevailing vagueness can only be counteracted in the matter of conduct—which is our special concern—by a new investigation into the principles of human action, the nature of conscience, the character of divine law, the distinction between virtue and sin; and a reassertion of whatever certainties can be discovered as to the nature and rules of Christian life. Such an investigation must start from the teaching and life of our Lord and the experience of the Church, and be corroborated, wherever possible, by any ascertained principles of natural cause and effect to which science has given an unqualified assent. Points will be found where religion and science still seem to give divergent answers ; to these points the theologian must devote special attention. It may be that, in such matters, either religion has claimed as revealed what in fact is no more than pious speculation, or that science has expressed a certainty unjustified by the evidence. Whichever be the case, the theologian who is assured that the Holy Spirit uses the slow processes of natural reason as at least one channel of divine revelation, will not falter in his belief that sooner or later the divergent claims of the two will be reconciled.

Moral theology must therefore steer a course between over-rigidity of definition on the one hand and the vagueness of individualism or unthinking piety on the other. It requires such a degree of exactness as will ensure to the priest clear guidance in dealing with the problems that beset human conduct, without giving him the arrogance and obstinacy which are bred by a sense of absolute rightness. It must emphasise the value of revealed truth and of fully substantiated experience without denying the possibility of further revelation or new experience. It must neither be a slave to precedent,[1] nor yet an opportunist deciding each new question without reference to the dictates of faith and history. Such is its ideal character : the combination of certainty as to some things with an open mind as to others. But for the present day the certainty is more needed than the open mind ; and we should turn again to Scripture, Christian experience, and the agreed results of

[1] The type of theologian whose thought is wholly dominated by the authority of the past is well indicated by the description which Anthony Trollope gives of one of his political characters : ' He was a great reader . . . working through an enormous course of books, getting up the great subject of the world's history—filling himself full of facts—though perhaps *not destined to acquire the power of using those facts other than as precedents.'—Small House at Allington*, chap. 23.

C

free inquiry into human character, to re-establish for the guidance of conduct truths whose validity has not so much been questioned as forgotten.

2. *The Scope of Moral Theology*

The aim of moral theology is therefore to accumulate from every available source [1] whatever information will be of use to the priest for his task of shepherding individual souls. Its *scope* therefore must comprise the following subjects :—

(*a*) The natural endowments of the human soul and the laws of responsible action.

(*b*) The ideal of character to which God desires each man to conform.

(*c*) The means by which God enables the soul to progress towards that ideal.

(*d*) The means by which the priest can co-operate with God in stimulating or fostering such progress.

(*e*) The hindrances, natural or acquired, to spiritual progress, and the means by which they can be eradicated or their influence counteracted.

To these should be added :—

(*f*) A discussion of the principles by which actions whose legitimacy or morality is doubtful, or which do not seem to be referable to any rules of morality at all,[2] are to be regulated.

(*g*) The qualifications demanded of the priest in his capacity as a spiritual director, or guide of souls.

Something must be said about the branches of study comprised under the first six of the above heads :—

(*a*) *Natural endowments and laws of action.*

The description and formulation of these is the work of

---

[1] ' Read the Bible, the *Ethics*, and good novels,' is said to have been Bishop King's advice to inquirers who wished for guidance in the study of moral theology.

[2] Cases of which at first sight it is natural to say that ' advice is good or bad only as the event decides ' (Jane Austen, *Persuasion*).

Psychology. It may fairly be said that the Christian Church has no divinely-revealed psychology. The Bible indeed contains a variety of indications on the subject, but no formal account of the organisation or composition of personality ; though on two points, to which special reference must be made, its witness is absolutely clear. Scholastic philosophy adopted almost without question the Aristotelian psychology which, in its garbled Latin dress and with certain later developments, had come down to it ; and Roman theologians still think in Aristotelian terms under the influence of St. Thomas Aquinas. The English student may therefore believe himself free to employ in his account of the soul and its properties both the terms and the conclusions of modern psychological research, *provided always that these do not, either implicitly or explicitly, run counter to the two fundamental postulates of Scripture and Christian doctrine,* without which a *Christian* science of morality is impossible.

These two fundamental postulates are as follows :—

(i) *The soul is free to choose between good and bad, right and wrong, in all its actions :* it has what is technically known as *free-will.*

(ii) *The soul, however tainted or corrupted by sin, retains an innate power both of perceiving what is good and right, and of aspiring to it*—a *conscience,* in short ; though that power may be grievously weakened and perverted, and *in the end* may be altogether inhibited by a constant life of vicious habits.

The task of establishing the truth of these two assumptions rests not with moral theology but with Christian apologetics.[1] As we shall see, they are only two of many assumptions which the moralist receives from the apologist. This is not to say that the individual priest need not consider carefully the evidence upon which they are

---

[1] Both these assumptions are deducible more from the general tenor of Scripture than from particular statements ; but it is clear that the constant emphasis upon *human responsibility* for sin (e.g. Rom. ii. 1–16, iii. 9–18 ; Phil. iii. 19 ; Col. iii. 6, 7 ; John i. 11, iii. 19, v. 40 *et pass.*) would be a mockery unless the freedom of the will and the fact of conscience were indisputable.

based; it merely asserts that in his capacity as director of souls he assumes them to be true and acts upon them.

(b) The Christian ideal of character.

The elaboration of this ideal, both for the individual and for the community—for it must extend to both—is usually conducted under the name of *Christian Ethics*.[1] It may be developed either along *a priori* or *a posteriori* lines. In the former case, the Christian ideal is expressed mainly in terms of *duty*; or regarded (as in modern Roman theology) as a system of divine law, having for its original sanction the teaching of our Lord. In the latter it is developed in terms of *virtue* or *excellence*; the Christian ideal, that is to say, is regarded as the finest manifestation of character which human nature can produce—the fullest realisation of its possibilities. To this end, the various natural endowments are considered, and a picture drawn of a character in which each is manifested in its greatest perfection.[2] The first of these two methods recognises the *absolute standard* of the Christian ideal; the second, its *infinite demands*. Any analysis of Christian duty based upon the decalogue (interpreted in the light of the New Testament) or the Sermon on the Mount belongs to the former type; the cardinal and theological virtues belong to the latter. Both methods are obviously legitimate, and Christian ethics usually combines the two, by this means reaching a fuller truth than either method separately could attain; though, as will be seen in the next chapter, the greatest

---

[1] 'Christian ethics' is a term with a double meaning. It is taken above in a sense which constitutes it a *part* of moral theology; but it is also used frequently to express a branch of study *preliminary* to moral theology—an inquiry into the general principles of all ethics (the nature of happiness, of the voluntary and involuntary, of the moral consciousness and the moral criterion) undertaken with the object of establishing the truth of the Christian doctrine on these points. In other words, 'Christian ethics' may be applied either to the *positive* or the *apologetic* statement of Christian moral doctrine. Cp. H. Martensen, *Christian Ethics*, §§ 11, ff.

[2] Cp. St. Thomas Aquinas, *Summa Theologica*, i. 2, q. 24, a. 3—human excellence varies in proportion as it extends to 'more things appertaining to man.'

Christian writers have with good reason preferred the second.[1]

(c) *The means by which God forwards the progress of the soul.*

These again can be studied either *a priori* or *a posteriori*. In the former case they are expressed in the doctrine of *Grace and the Sacraments*, deduced from the eternal principles of the nature of the Godhead and the Incarnation. In the latter case they are formulated as the result of Christian experience. Here again we may notice a further sub-division of method. If Christian experience be recorded by the person who experiences it, it will be in terms different from those used by an observer of his progress. The record of Christian experience by Christians themselves is usually given the name of *Mystical Theology*, though much which is not usually included under the name should rightly be drawn upon as well. The recording and examination of Christian experience from the standpoint of an impartial observer has been developed very fully in recent years,

---

[1] It may be noticed that the tendency of the Roman Church has been consistently in the direction of substituting the *a priori* for the *a posteriori* method in moral theology. Thus while the Christian character and sin are discussed by St. Thomas Aquinas wholly under the (psychological) headings of the cardinal and theological virtues, the vices opposed to them, and the capital sins, in modern Jesuit manuals they are invariably approached from the point of view of the decalogue. An interesting account of this development will be found in C. Gore, *Dominant Ideas and Corrective Principles*, chap. 6.

Many of the defects of Roman Catholic teaching are traceable to this tendency. Thus, by regarding Christian conduct primarily as obedience to law, theologians have been led to formulate a system of casuistry, whose main object is to discover what actions are *legally safe* rather than *morally commendable* ; and by insisting upon the *culpability* of sin, rather than upon its character as separating from the grace of God, the priest in absolution has become more of a judge than of a friend— absolution, in fact, has been separated from spiritual direction.

The tendency in modern times seems to be due to the prevailing juristic interest of the Society of Jesus, which culminated in their doctrine of the Church as *Societas Perfecta* (A. Robertson, *Regnum Dei*, pp. 338–347), and received an enormous stimulus by the withdrawal, first through the Protestant Reformation and then through the French Revolution, of the ' checks ' upon the legalistic tendencies of the Church provided by ' Emperors, Cities, Bishops, and Universities ' (F. von Hügel, *Eternal Life*, pp. 357, 358). Cp. T. C. Hall, *History of Ethics within Organized Christianity*, chaps. 6 ; 8, § 10.

and goes under the name of *Religious Psychology.* The work of Professors E. D. Starbuck, William James, Stanley Hall, and G. A. Coe stands out especially in this connection.

It is clear that, here again, a combination of the results given by the various methods is most desirable ; especially as in this matter—the most delicate and sublime in the whole range of moral theology—error and self-deception are not only most easy but most dangerous. But a threefold cord is not easily broken ; and where deductive theology, mystic experience, and scientific examination concur—as they do with surprising frequency—we can well affirm that a law of spiritual life has been discovered of which the certainty can scarcely be open to doubt.

(d) The work of the priest in fostering spiritual progress.

This has always been treated under the head of *Ascetic Theology*—the theology, that is, of *training* or *educating* the soul ; *Pastoral Theology* is the name under which it more usually goes in England. Its affinities with the *Psychology of Education* should be recognised. Both aim at developing character to its fullest possible extent ; the difference between the two lies in the fact that the priest has the possibility of a more certain conception of the goal to which his work should tend than the teacher can ever have. The method of both is *a posteriori* or empirical ; it formulates the results of experiment and experience.

(e) The hindrances to spiritual progress are mainly two

—temperament and sin. The former is a matter of psychology ; the latter of Christian ethics, guided both by the teaching of Scripture and by Christian experience. The *means* by which the hindrances may be removed are considered in ascetic theology, as well as in the doctrine of the sacraments ; but one special means—that of the *Sacrament of Penance*—has evolved so large a volume of literature that it has become almost a separate branch of study, commonly known by the name of *Penitential Theology*.

(*f*) *The principles to be observed in cases of doubtful morality.*

This peculiarly difficult subject is usually known by the name of *Casuistry*. Greatly though it has been misused and prostituted, it is yet true that a certain degree of casuistry is necessary in the guidance of souls. So many problems arise in which it is impossible at first sight to say, ' This course is right,' or ' That course is wrong,' that the priest is continually required to adjudicate upon difficulties of conduct for individual Christians. He will therefore find himself bound to ask the question, ' Will the course of action proposed lead to a deterioration of character, or involve the neglect of any recognised Christian duty ? ' ; and before giving his answer to consider as far as he can the implications of the action involved. This is casuistry —the science of bringing particular cases under general rules. St. Paul, in dealing with the questions of circumcision, mixed marriages, and meats sacrificed to idols, was doing no more than applying general principles to particular difficulties, for which his converts had been unable to find solutions, in the light of a wider experience and a deeper grasp of spiritual truths than theirs. This much at least every priest must be prepared to do.

Casuistry then is a natural and necessary branch of the pastoral office. The discredit into which it has fallen is due to two causes. First of all, by allowing the authority of the priest to be final in *doubtful* cases,[1] it has imperceptibly given to that authority such sanction as to lead Christians to have recourse to it in cases where their own conscience should have been called upon to give a final decision—in other words, it has blunted the discernment and narrowed the range of the individual conscience. In the second place, the doctrine of *Probabilism*—the doctrine that a ' probable opinion ' (i.e. a course of action in which ' good and wise men see no sin nor danger of sin ') ' may be

[1] The penitent, however, is not *bound* to follow the priest's opinion, provided that the alternative course is supported by *probability*. But in any case the priest in the confessional is, according to the Roman theory, the final judge of the penitent's *disposition*, and as such has practically unlimited authority. See J. Gury, *Compendium Theologiae Moralis*, vol. i. § 78.

followed even by one who knows and holds that the contrary opinion is more probable'[1]—however much it be safeguarded, opens so wide a door to tendencies which lower the standard of morality and deny the possibility of there being an absolute right and wrong in *every* case, if only it could be found, that it constitutes a very real danger to the maintenance of a high ideal of conduct in the Christian community. In the Church of England, however, there is little fear that enhanced attention to the problem of doubtful cases will produce either of these two results; whilst, on the other hand, there is great need of emphasising the fact that every proposed course of action must be tested, wherever possible, by reference to general principles. Here again the prevailing English tendency is to vagueness of thought and lack of principle in action; and a movement of thought in the opposite direction is urgently required to redress the balance.

The position to be taken by casuistry is indeed clear enough. It should be a collection of precedents and considerations—none of them with any absolutely binding force—intended to guide the Christian in his decisions, or the priest in the advice he gives to the undecided. To such a study there can be no objection; indeed nothing can be of greater importance for the present day than to provide the clergy, and all who are to any degree whatever the keepers of their brother's conscience, with a system of this kind. Each age indeed must have its own lines of solution, under the general guidance of the Christian law; just as each age too has its own difficulties waiting to be solved. For the present day what is required is a clear investigation, in the light of modern conditions, of what should be the Christian man's action in regard to the problems of labour and wages; of temperance and total abstinence; of gambling and betting; of literature and the drama (in view of tendencies which to some degree at least are bound to have immoral effects); of the

---

[1] T. Slater, *Manual of Moral Theology*, vol. ii. p. 551. See further *infra*, pp. 194 ff. A full appreciation of the values and limits of casuistry will be found in H. Rashdall, *Theory of Good and Evil*, bk. iii. chap. v. —a discussion by no means biased by any affection for ecclesiasticism.

restriction of the birth-rate, and the other problems which cluster round the Christian conception of marriage ; of the relation of individual to community ; and the like. Every priest could contribute to such a list matters which in his own parochial experience have presented him with problems of the utmost difficulty, and on which he would have welcomed guidance from a systematic study of this kind. The matter lies beyond the immediate purpose of the present pages ; but it is one which the Church should lose no time in taking in hand.

In the chapters which follow it will be impossible to cover the whole ground of moral theology even in the most cursory fashion. We must confine ourselves to those points which are most necessary to the priest in the normal cases which come to his notice for advice or help. Questions of psychology therefore—of the natural endowment of the soul—will be considered only as they arise, and not in any formal discussion. The wider demands of Christian ethics— those which concern social, national and international intercourse—will be set altogether on one side ; as also the question of *particular* duties—the obligations of ecclesiastical law, of contracts, marriage, and the like—and of duties peculiar to different states of life : the clergy, members of religious communities, doctors, judges, witnesses, &c. The reader will find these amply treated in modern theological writings.[1] The doctrines of grace and the sacraments are not discussed ; the principles of casuistry are only touched upon. We shall attempt simply to describe the ideal of Christian character on its internal side (on which, after all, its external manifestations all depend) ; the stages through which the soul approaches that ideal ; the methods by which the priest can foster its progress ; the hindrances of temperament and sin, and the means to be employed for their removal. These questions are no more important than the others which we have chosen to disregard ; but at least they touch upon the majority of those points which present practical difficulties to the priest in his work.

[1] See bibliography, *infra.*

3. *The Postulates of Moral Theology*

It has already been mentioned that moral theology does not approach its task with an absolutely open mind; it starts from certain *assumptions* the validity of which it does not question, as it receives them on the warrant of Christian dogma as a whole. They may be set down somewhat as follows :—

(*a*) *The objective reality of spiritual experience.* It has recently been suggested that the principal theological controversy of the near future will centre round the two contradictory propositions : (1) ' That religion is the communion of man with some other being higher than himself ' ; and (2) that it is the ' communion of man with his own subliminal consciousness, which he does not recognise as his own but hypostatizes as some one exterior to himself.' [1] Whether this controversy be imminent or no—and evidence seems to show that it is—the fact remains that it is no concern of moral theology. If it be true that there is no God except a man's subliminal self, moral theology indeed, with every other shred of Christian doctrine, is an idle myth ; but the task of defending the faith rests with the apologist, not with the student of conduct. For our purposes it is enough that we accept the fundamental Christian propositions that God exists, that He was Incarnate in Jesus Christ, that He gives to men grace and power by the Holy Spirit ; and that in consequence, whilst there may sometimes be a certain degree of self-hallucination in so-called ' religious experience,' the greater part of what is known by that name is *genuine experience of intercourse on the part of man with ' another Being greater than himself.'* [2] And from this follows a second assumption no less vital.

(*b*) This is, *that the co-operation of the Holy Spirit may be confidently expected and unhesitatingly recognised in the work of reconciling souls to God.* The priest will expect to see around him sure evidence of his great Coadjutor's over-

---

[1] Kirsopp Lake, *Earlier Epistles of S. Paul*, pp. 251, 252.
[2] In support of this assumption see, e.g., C. C. J. Webb, *Problems in the Relation of God to Man*, pp. 6 f., 139 ff. ; A. Chandler, *Cult of the Passing Moment*, chap. ii.

ruling assistance. True it is that he will be able to see only the slightest part of the full work of the Spirit; but he is justified in attempting to identify, in the course of his work, the points at which God has definitely and certainly guided or restrained him, or granted success where his own efforts merited nothing but failure. How great a source of consolation and help this practice may be to the shepherd of souls it is difficult to express; but we can at least say that if he will not trust himself to look for and to find sure indications of God's guiding and overruling power, the ultimate result of his efforts will be but small.

The Christian who believes in God, but dare not look around for clear proofs of God's beneficence and power, might as well have no faith at all for all the good his faith will do to himself or his fellows. The priest who goes about his work saying, in effect, ' I have no doubt that God is helping me, but do not ask me to point to any special indications of His help,' may be a sincere and earnest worker, but he is in no sense a full believer. He will lead his flock—if he leads them anywhere at all—to the service of a God unknown and unknowable. If he sees any value in the faith he preaches or the practices he advocates, it will be because they appear to edify, not because he knows them to be true. He will justify the sceptic's sneer that most men do not know or understand God, they use Him;[1] he will be powerless to fight doubts which will infallibly arise some day; he will lay himself open to the charge of intellectual dishonesty and make-believe. Far better for him to abandon the fiction of God and immortality and the gifts of the Spirit, and base his work and preaching upon some plain human incentive to action, such as the betterment of society, the welfare of posterity, or the ideal of self-realisation. So doing he will be both more consistent and more sincere; in the end in all probability he will find that he has done better and more lasting work.

(c) Of the assumptions of moral theology as to the *nature of the soul* we have already spoken. It is assumed that the soul has a natural tendency to seek God, however

---

[1] J. H. Leuba, quoted in W. James, *Varieties of Religious Experience*, p. 506.

much it be clogged and retarded by tendencies of a contrary character ; and that it is *free* to seek God and to find Him, and in finding Him to ensure the perfection of its own nature. Such a *good-will*—or tendency to reject what is lower for what is higher—is demanded as a postulate not merely by Christian ethics, but by any system of ethics whatever except the most frankly hedonistic. ' There is a philosophy of the Spirit which asserts the supremacy of the Spirit and which has established the truth about the nature of man and the nature of the universe, a truth which every man can confirm for himself by his own experiments. The philosophy of the Spirit tells us that the Spirit desires three things and desires them for their own sake and not for any further aim beyond them. It desires to do what is right for the sake of doing what is right ; to know the truth for the sake of knowing the truth ; and it has a third desire which is not so easily stated . . . the desire for beauty. . . . The aim of life is to exercise each of these three faculties for its own sake, and a man who does not so exercise them is not living at all.' [1]

(*d*) Yet moral theology also assumes, on the general basis of Christian doctrine, that man *cannot achieve his ideal* (whether it be expressed in terms of finding God, or perfecting character, or achieving truth, beauty or goodness) *by his own unaided effort*. It accepts, that is to say, the doctrine of *original sin*. And this introduces a consideration of the greatest importance for Christian ethics. Other systems of ethics have provided rules for the guidance of conduct ; Christian ethics, whilst it provides such rules—and whilst they are not unlike those of other systems—also recognises that *the rules are useless unless personality is infused by a higher and divine power*. Therefore among the principal rules of life advocated by Christian ethics are some which have no place in other systems— *rules directed towards obtaining, preserving and developing*

---

[1] A. Clutton-Brock, *The Ultimate Belief*, chap. ii. To bring the passage quoted into complete conformity with Christian doctrine, we ought to add the words, ' because they are seen to be the only true means of reaching the goal of human life—the knowledge of the glory of God,' after the words ' for their own sake.'

that grace without which the normal rules of conduct cannot be observed. It is true no doubt that this grace can be gained by no mere human effort; it is something given wholly from without; but a man can so rule and order his life as to open it out to divine influence, and to give that influence the fullest possible scope when once it has been received. It is in the supreme emphasis laid upon this principle that Christian ethics differs from every other system.

It is sometimes urged against Christianity that it puts personal holiness before the service of God and our neighbour. There is truth in the accusation, and it is a truth which is fundamental to the Christian system. The service of others—the observance, that is to say, of the normal rules of conduct—can only be truly performed by the man who is aspiring to personal holiness—to that disposition of life which will render him most susceptible of the influence of divine grace. And *some* of the rules of personal holiness —rules of prayer, meditation, self-denial, communion, and the like—have no apparent bearing upon the good of others. The Christian need not hesitate to assert that in this matter there is a real difference between his thought and that of any non-Christian system of morals; though he must also unhesitatingly reject that perversion of Christianity which regards the rules of holiness as being *purely* internal, and disregards the fact that the service of others is no less a means through which grace may be received than prayer or communion. He must, in fact, accept the ordinary rules of conduct both as an end—the external manifestation of that life of service which Christian and non-Christian alike recognise as the true ideal of character—and as a means to that end; but he must add to them as a further means to the same end—and as a means no less necessary than the former—rules which to the non-Christian are meaningless: rules of prayer and communion and the like. The power of Christ is necessary to the service of others; and we cannot receive the power of Christ in all its fullness except by observing those rules which most lay our lives open to its influence. To seek God, we may say, is a necessary condition of serving Him;

though to serve Him is also a necessary condition of finding Him.

(*e*) So much is it the case that moral theology regards human effort as unavailing without divine assistance, that it even *tends to deprecate any rules of life or conduct, even the most spiritual, which might divert the soul's attention from Christ to itself.* Many therefore of the most cherished principles of non-Christian ethics are relegated into the background, and even regarded as undesirable, by Christian ethics. A systematic ' self-culture ' is wholly foreign to the Christian teaching, which finds its ideal rather in a love for Christ leading to complete self-forgetfulness. The soul which is occupied exclusively or even mainly with rules of conduct is a soul in danger of losing its hold on spiritual reality. Excellence of character will be attained, not by following rules, but by following Christ. Once the soul has fixed its attention upon that Pattern, the less it thinks of itself and its own conduct the better.

There is a curious instance of this in the ' De Officiis ' of St. Ambrose, the first constructive attempt at a Christian scheme of ethics. His book begins with a series of character-sketches from the Old Testament, and only when interest has been aroused in that way does he go on to his description of the cardinal virtues. Later Christian experience would doubtless have pointed out that the person of Christ forms an infinitely higher example of moral and spiritual achievement than any of the Old Testament saints ; but the importance of St. Ambrose's work lies not so much in its details as in its method. This method of first presenting living examples of goodness and only afterwards examining its parts scientifically, he tells us, he chose deliberately with the purpose of stimulating his reader's enthusiasm by giving priority of place to a ' mirror of virtue,' rather than exciting merely intellectual interest by a ' catalogue of shrewd or clever actions.' [1]

Christian ethics goes further even than St. Ambrose. It sets before the Christian not merely a picture of Christ upon which to meditate, but the *hope of a mystic personal union*

[1] Ambrose, *De Off.* i. 25.

with Him [1] which shall transcend, not merely rules of conduct, but even meditation upon His character, as a means of
grace—and not merely as a means of grace but as an end
of all effort. The character of this personal union we must
later attempt to consider, recognising always, however,
that words are utterly inadequate to explain it, and that to
multiply them will simply intensify the mystery. It will
be seen, however, that the influence of this factor in religion
—the last and greatest assumption of moral theology—is
not merely to deprecate rules, but even to aim at banishing
them from life altogether in favour of a community of
experience with Christ which shall guide conduct in its
most intimate details from moment to moment. The law
is ' a schoolmaster to lead us to Christ '; ' but after that
faith is come we are no longer under a schoolmaster.'
' Christ is the termination of the law for righteousness.' [2]

How great is the gulf which therefore separates Christian
from non-Christian ethics in consequence of this fact may
be dimly illustrated by a passage in which Ruskin compares
his method in art with that of some of his critics. ' Some
men,' he says—speaking of those whose life and thought is
dominated by strict adherence to rule—' may be compared
to careful travellers who neither stumble at stones, nor
slip in sloughs, but have, from the beginning of their journey
to its end, chosen the wrong road ; others to those who,
however slipping and stumbling at the roadside, have yet
got their eyes fixed upon the true gate and goal (stumbling
perhaps even the more because they have), and will not
fail of reaching them.' [3] It is perhaps untrue to the spirit
of Christianity to say that those whose principal care is to
avoid ' stumbling at stones and slipping in sloughs ' are in
every case on the wrong road ; but it is supremely true to
say that, unless a man has his eyes fixed upon the ' true

---

[1] The *visio Dei*, which to the theologian as much as to the mystic
is the ultimate goal of human life. *Summa*, i. : q. 1, a. 4 ; q. 12, aa. 1,
4, &c. ; ii. 2 : q. 44, a. 1 ; cp. Irenaeus, *Haer*. iv. 34, 7 (ed. Harvey ;
or Massuet, iv. 20, 7), ' Gloria Dei vivens homo ; vita autem hominis visio
Dei.'

[2] Gal. iii. 24, 25 ; Rom. x. 4. Cp. St. Thomas Aquinas on the ' New
Law,' *infra*, p. 183.

[3] *Modern Painters*, vol. iii. Intr.

gate and goal,' no amount of care as to his footsteps will carry him through his journey. And if we have to choose between the two—and attention can only with difficulty be directed to two separate objects at once—it is infinitely better to keep the gate and goal in sight and neglect partially, if not entirely, that sedulous attention to the details of conduct which is comparable to the diligent care of the footsteps. God will guide our feet aright, provided always that we walk with Him.

If we attempt to summarise briefly the Christian attitude towards rules and law, it must be by saying that during the *formative* period of the soul's development they are indispensable ; but that in proportion as the soul reaches spiritual maturity—growing, that is to say, in communion with Christ—they may and should be discarded little by little ; provided always that, even in this later period, no element of *antinomianism* is allowed to obtrude itself. The danger of such a lapse can never wholly be discounted ; law therefore in some degree, though only a slight one, will always be necessary to that life of liberty which is the Christian's heritage.[1]

·   ·   ·   ·   ·   ·   ·   ·

In addition to the assumptions already discussed, a moral theology which is to be of use in the Church of England must start from certain postulates of its own, chiefly dealing with the peculiar status of the Anglican clergy. There are those no doubt who wish that the status of our clergy were different from what it is ; but it must be recognised that, as things stand with the Church of England, we cannot adopt without serious modification a moral theology intended for other conditions and other times. The facts which make modification essential are as follows :—

(*a*) The practice of sacramental confession is not regarded as obligatory by the vast majority of English churchmen.

---

[1] The statement occasionally made that ' there can be no such thing as a science of Christian morals,' whilst true as an *ideal* (for the ideal Christian would act spontaneously as the result of his complete communion with Christ, without reference to any code of rules), is not true in the actual circumstances of ordinary life, in which such communion is only partial and interrupted.

Whatever view the priest may take on this controversial question, whatever view he may press upon his parishioners or congregations, he must recognise that to many of them confession as a sacramental obligation is summed up in the words ' open to all, advisable for some, demanded of none.' The consequences of this fact are obvious. Many of those whose souls are committed to his charge will not normally come to him for spiritual direction in the ordinary course of events, as is bound to be the case in the Roman communion. He will, therefore, be forced to go to them ; he will, moreover, if he takes the initiative in offering advice, encouragement, or reproof, be obliged to do so under the disability of being in the dark as to their real spiritual condition, except in so far as his own discernment has enlightened him.

The Anglican priest is here at a very real disadvantage compared with his Roman brother, though it must be asserted that there are on the other side very real compensations. There is, for example, less danger, in the case of such of our laity as are in the habit of making use of the sacrament of penance, of hypocrisy or dissimulation. They come of their own free will, under the stimulus of a genuine spiritual need ; the priest therefore has little cause to doubt their *bona fides*.[1] The Roman priest, on the other hand, —as penitential manuals very clearly show—is under the continual necessity of weighing carefully the sincerity of his penitents.

(*b*) It must be acknowledged also that the Anglican layman is not accustomed to recognise the authority of the clergy as final in matters of faith and conduct.[2] Here

---

[1] Cp. A. Chandler, *English Church and Reunion*, p. 104, footnote : ' I believe thoroughly in Confession, and appreciate its value, for myself and others, and I wish the number of those who practise it were enormously increased. But I have an obstinate and stubborn conviction that freedom is of the essence of all moral and religious action ; and it seems to me especially clear in this matter of confession, that the value of the act depends very largely indeed upon its being freely performed ; compulsion cannot secure the sincerity and contrition which make a good confession, and may easily produce qualities which make a bad one.' See also *supra*, p. xvi. ; *infra*, pp. 161, 255.

[2] This characteristic of the Church of England to-day is well recognised by E. T. Churton, *Use of Penitence*, pp. 128, 129, 175–177.

D

again is a fact which, whether we deplore it or no, whether we acquiesce in it or labour to alter it, cannot be overlooked as things are. The Englishman of to-day regards the admonitions of the clergy as advice, not as definite rulings. If he disregards their warnings or instructions it may indeed result in spiritual harm, but he does not regard the sin he may commit as in any way aggravated by the fact that it was a *priest's* injunctions which he set aside. Right or wrong, this is the attitude of the average Anglican layman ; and it is an attitude to which in many cases the priest must adapt himself if he wishes his advice to be accepted. His words may be listened to with respect if he speaks as a candid friend, whilst they would be rejected with decision if he assumed the character of a spiritual superior.

These two considerations, whilst they do not affect the *principles* of a universal theology of morals, must make considerable difference to the *emphasis* with which those principles are expressed for the special requirements of the Anglican communion of to-day. It is not enough for our purposes to translate unquestioningly the theology of the schoolmen or that of modern Roman Catholic writers. We may learn much from them no doubt ; but—apart from any question as to the truth of each and all of their conclusions —their tone and point of view are wholly unsuited to the requirements of a Church in which the majority of the faithful do not as a matter of fact go to confession, nor recognise the priest as having any authority in questions of faith or morals other than that derived from his training, intuition, or experience.

To serve the widest possible purpose among clergy of the English Church—as we know it to-day, and irrespective of what it has been in the past or may in the future become—moral theology must therefore be entirely rewritten ; not indeed with a view to altering its eternal principles, but with the simple object of providing an instrument adapted in the fullest possible degree to the conditions normally obtaining among English Christians. This must be our justification if we seem to deal too freely or irreverently with categories and methods hallowed by traditional usage, and vindicated by long experience in various

epochs and branches of the Catholic Church. So long as
the fundamental truths of Christianity are not violated,
the right of adapting teaching and usage to the needs of
the moment is the peculiar prerogative of the Church of
England ; and in this matter as in others such adaptation
is not merely legitimate but laudable.

CHAPTER II

THE CHRISTIAN CHARACTER

1. *Preliminaries*

DIFFICULTIES have at times been placed in the way of sketching out an ideal of the Christian character. That the priest needs such an ideal—a pattern to guide him in moulding, so far as is in his power, the souls committed to his charge—can hardly be disputed. Exhortation, advice, rebuke, would all be of little value unless they had some clear aim in view. But it has often been suggested (as, for example, by Locke [1]) that there can be no final, unvarying ideal of character. Moral conceptions are so influenced by social requirements that they must vary from age to age and from continent to continent. In a military nation, they will take one bias from the national need ; in a commercial nation, another ; in a pastoral community, a third.[2] Or, again, it has been said that every man is so endowed temperamentally that certain virtues only are congenial to his nature, whilst others are beyond his capacity ; that no single ideal can be held up for all alike. This latter tendency, in its simplest form, appears at almost every stage of Christian history in the theory of the *higher* and *lower* states of the devout life ; the latter open to all, the former, with its more rigorous exactions, confined to persons of a definitely religious genius. In our own time it is manifested in the opinion, widespread and very powerful, that the pure ideal of Christian morality which laymen do not hesitate to demand of the clergy, must be

---

[1] *Essay Concerning the Human Understanding*, bk. i. chap. 3. See the whole subject discussed in W. E. H. Lecky, *History of European Morals,* vol. i. pp. 91 ff.

[2] Lecky, *op. cit.* vol. i. pp. 136 ff.

relaxed and mitigated for business men, or for the artistic temperament, or—in general—for any leading a secular life.

These objections are no more than a revival of the old materialistic fallacy that environment, or heredity, or both, are the final determinants of character. As against them the Church has always maintained with unflinching emphasis that character, rooted and grounded in Christ, and continually replenished with grace through the Holy Spirit, can and must rise superior to all the limitations imposed upon it from without and within. That God will make allowances for those who, through overwhelming pressure of one or both of these causes, fall short of the ideal, we have every reason to hope ; that man can urge as an excuse for his own shortcomings either the stress of circumstance or the power of temperament is a denial of all the essentials of the Gospel. The proof of this position belongs rather to Christian dogma as a whole ; it is one of those intellectual weapons with which the priest must be already furnished when he goes out to his work of making or remaking character. We cannot deal with it here.

It is enough for us to recapitulate on this point the unanimous declaration of the Church. As against the theory that the Christian ideal of character is a shifting, not a stable thing, we can point to the simple fact that this ideal is enshrined, not in any form of words, but in the person of Christ, Whose nature does not change. Forms of words we shall need in plenty; but only for the purpose of drawing out, and making clearer, the things that may be seen in Him. On this point, too, we can quote the verdict of authorities who, whatever their private convictions may have been, were not writing from the specifically religious standpoint. Professor James, in a happy but too florid phrase, spoke of a ' certain composite photograph of universal saintliness, of which the features can easily be traced.' [1] ' By this time,' says Professor John Adams, ' we have reached a fairly general agreement about the qualities we consider it essential

---

[1] *Varieties of Religious Experience*, p. 271. It is true that he says this character is the ' same in all religions,' thus denying any special value to the Christian revelation.

to find in a fully-developed ego.'[1] Even Lecky, who was quite alive to all that could be said for the relativity of moral standards, admitted in the end that ' the world will never greatly differ about the essential elements of right and wrong.'[2]

Furthermore, as against the theory that the higher stages of Christian morality are closed against men engaged in secular pursuits, or those of Christian experience against all but the so-called ' religious genius,' we have the almost unanimous voice of the greatest theologians and the greatest mystics. Lesser men, indeed, hesitated often enough, and were prepared to accept a double standard of conduct ; but the Church as a whole never committed herself to this fundamentally untrue position.[3] The question, as regards morality, was fought out even in the New Testament. Whether our Lord's words in St. Matthew (v. 48) [4] are to be taken as a prophecy or a command, they at all events imply the possibility of perfection for every disciple. The apostles are rigorous in demanding that the Christian shall live without spot of evil ; without any lowering of standard.[5] It has, moreover, been explicitly stated by some at least of the greatest masters of the religious life, that—although in the abstract the ' contemplative ' life may be higher than the ' active '—yet there is no degree of union with the Father through His Son for which the Christian may not reasonably hope, however he be hampered by circumstance or endowment, provided that his heart be rightly set and his efforts unfailing ; sometimes even it is suggested that a measure of entanglement with the affairs of the world will forward this union,

---

[1] *Evolution of Educational Theory*, p. 300.

[2] *Map of Life*, pp. 55, 56.

[3] E. von Dobschütz (*Christian Life in the Primitive Church*, Eng. trans., pp. 279 ff.) points out that the ' double-standard ' theory of morality crept into the Church as a reply to the rigorous demand of the Gnostics for universal asceticism. It was ' a large concession to dualism, but it saved one of the most precious possessions of Christianity—the evangelical conception of morality.'

[4] ' Be ye therefore perfect, even as your Father which is in heaven is perfect.'

[5] E.g. Rom. xii. 1, 2 ; 2 Cor. vii. 1, xi. 2 ; Col. i. 28, iv. 12 ; Jas. i. 4 ; 1 Pet. i. 15, 16.

if it be rightly used.[1] Bishop Wilson, in the 'Sacra Privata,' goes even further. 'In order to dispose our hearts to devotion,' he says, ' the active life is to be preferred to the contemplative. To be doing good to mankind disposes the soul most powerfully to devotion.' A secular life, in short, is no real barrier to spirituality. God is faithful ; the Holy Spirit is all-powerful ; grace is indefectible ; nothing can separate us from the love of Christ, except our own unwillingness to tread the path of divine love.

It should be possible, then, to draw out an ideal of the Christian life which shall be at once authoritative, final, and uncompromising, and yet within the reach of the humblest and least talented. The task of Christian ethics has been to elaborate and justify such a picture. We can see at once that it must have two sides, the outward and the inward. The priest must know, not only how the true Christian should behave himself in all the varying circumstances of his life, but also what must be the hidden sources and virtues from which this outward behaviour springs. Knowing the first, he will be able more surely to advise in those cases of conscience or difficulty in which the right course is not on the surface apparent ; knowing the second, he will learn by degrees how best to foster that inward communion with God which alone, in the last resort, is strong enough to produce the flower of Christian virtue.

2. *The Outward Signs of the Christian Life— The Cardinal Virtues*

The Christian ideal of character, we have seen, is the person of Christ, as manifested in His earthly life. Nothing

---

[1] Cp. Gregory, *Moralia in Job*, vi. 37 ; Walter Hilton on the ' mixed life ' (of activity and contemplation), *Treatise to a Devout Man of Secular Estate*, chaps. 4–7 ; A. Baker, *Holy Wisdom*, Treat. i., sect. 3, chap. 1. See also *Summa*, i. 2, q. 108, a. 4 ; ii. 2, q. 182, a. 3 : ' Exercitium vitae activae confert ad contemplativam ' ; a. 4 : ' Illi qui sunt magis apti ad activam vitam possunt per exercitium activae ad contemplativam praeparari ; et illi nihilominus qui sunt ad contemplativam apti possunt exercitia vitae activae subire, ut per hoc ad contemplationem paratiores reddantur,' and *cf.* F. von Hügel, *Mystical Element of Religion*, vol. ii. pp. 351–358.

short of that suffices as a guide. And the simplest summary of this pattern of Christian goodness is to say that it exemplifies in the highest form the love and the service of God and our fellow-men.[1] To love God and to serve Him; to love men and to serve them; this is the essence and the whole of Christian duty—the purpose of man's life.

But this pattern requires to be articulated and examined, and its leading *motifs* set out in plain form, in order that its demands may be brought into relation with the circumstances of a more elaborate civilisation than that of Galilee and Judea.

It is, of course, open to the Christian to separate himself from the world and its business and live a life of evangelical simplicity in poverty, celibacy, and even seclusion. There are those, no doubt, for whom such a course is the only one by which they can attain to single-hearted union with God. If de Cressy's estimate of John Inglesant was the right one, the latter was one of these : ' You are like the young man who came to Jesus,' the Benedictine said, ' and whom Jesus loved, for you have great possessions. You have been taught all that men desire to know, and are accomplished in all that makes life delightful. You have the knowledge of the past and know the reality of men's power and wisdom and beauty, which they possess of themselves, and did possess in the old classic times. . . . You wish this life's wisdom, and to walk with Christ as well ; and you are your own witness that it cannot be. The two cannot walk together as you have found. To you especially this is the great test and trial that Christ expects of you to the very full. We of this religious order have given ourselves to learning, as you know ; nay, in former years to that pagan learning which is so attractive to you. . . . But even this you must keep yourself from. *To most men this study is no temptation : to you it is fatal.* I put before you your life with no false colouring, no tampering with the truth. Come with me to Douay ; you shall enter our house according to the strictest rule ; you shall

---

[1] *Summa*, ii. 2, q. 25, a. 1. ' Love of one's neighbour is a necessary part of loving God ' (*ib.* q. 26, a. 3 ; cp. 1 John iv. 20).

engage in no study that is any delight or effort to the intellect ; but you shall teach the smallest children in the schools, and visit the poorest people, and perform the duties of the household—and all for Christ. I promise you on the faith of a gentleman and a priest—I promise you for I have no shade of doubt—that in this path you shall find the satisfaction of the heavenly walk ; you shall walk with Jesus day by day growing ever more and more like to Him ; and your path, without the least fall or deviation, shall lead more and more into the light, until you come unto the perfect day ; and on your deathbed—the deathbed of a saint—the vision of the smile of God shall sustain you, and Jesus Himself shall meet you at the gates of eternal life.' [1]

Characters such as the one here described—men and women with sensibilities abnormally alive to the absorbing interest of truth and beauty, but without the stability of purpose which will enable them to keep such sensibilities under control—can perhaps only develop their spiritual life after a violent and irrevocable act of self-detachment from the world. The world is too strong for them. ' Get thee to a nunnery ' was advice not so much due to any desire on Hamlet's part for Ophelia's happiness ; it was the outcome of some such sense that only complete alienation from a world which fascinated and terrified him at once could save *his own* reason and soul. It expressed a longing for seclusion for himself rather than for her.

Other circumstances, too, and other temperamental conditions may make what is technically called the ' religious life ' the best way in which any given Christian can grow into conformity with his Master's pattern. Christianity recognises to the full the fact of *vocation*.[2] There is only one ideal of the Christian life ; but it will express itself in many different forms according as a man is called, by circumstance or endowment, to the cloister, the library, the workshop or the office. And the cloister, we may say, is the vocation of comparatively few. The majority

---

[1] J. H. Shorthouse, *John Inglesant*, chap. 19. The italics are not in the original.

[2] E.g. Matt. xix. 11 ; Mark iii. 13–15 ; Acts ix. 15, 16 ; 1 Cor. vii. 7, 17–24, 27, xii. 6–21 ; Gal. i. 16, ii. 7 ; Eph. iv. 7, 11, vi. 5–9.

of Christian men and women have to live in the world, though not of it ; occupied with its problems and beset with its temptations. For their guidance we need a translation, into terms of business and home life, of the spirit and example of Him Who had neither business entanglements nor home itself. He Himself laid down the principles upon which this expansion of the essential elements in the Christian life through all the accidents of its varying circumstances must be conducted ; more than that He left to the Church to provide. The apostles, who from the first attempted to regulate home and social intercourse on Christian principles, laid the foundations of Christian ethics ; its amplification has gone on in the Church ever since.

The first business of Christian ethics, then, is to enumerate the main duties of a Christian in normal circumstances. The sketch must not be too vague : for that would leave it out of relation with the situations in which the duties have to be performed. On the other hand, it must not be too detailed, for, as we have seen, the Christian dispensation has always tried to avoid the rigidities of the Jewish law. We need not, however, treat of this branch of our subject at any length ; for the ground has been continually traversed, and any of the recognised text-books on Christian ethics give all that is required. We may, however, notice one or two features about the treatment of the subject which are of importance.

(a) First of all, our attention is drawn by the wealth of material from which selection can be made. From the Bible alone we can choose any one of innumerable different passages or pictures as a groundwork. Greatest of all of them is the person of our Lord as revealed in the Gospels. That pattern can be, and has often been, studied until its main features stand out clearly as a model for all time. So too with His teaching as with His life ; it has been formulated time after time with a view to giving a clear but comprehensive survey of the Christian virtues. In particular, the Beatitudes have been used for this purpose. Their half-dozen clauses enshrine the greatest virtues of the Christian character.

From the apostolic writings can be chosen the hymn of

love (1 Cor. xiii.), or the fruits of the Spirit (Gal. v. 22), or the ' soberness, righteousness, and godliness '[1] of Tit. ii. 12, or St. James' brief summary (Jas. i. 27)—' to visit the fatherless and widows in their affliction and to keep himself unspotted from the world.'

The Old Testament too, interpreted in the light of the New, is no less illuminating. The decalogue, read in the spirit of the Sermon on the Mount, with its negative enactments emphasised on the positive side, has been used in this way throughout the Church's history.[2] The gifts of the Spirit (Isa. xi. 2, 3) have passed into Christian usage in the Confirmation Service ; the various pictures of the righteous man (Ps. i., xv., xxiv., &c.) or the wise man (Prov. iii., &c.) can all be used as true outlines of an ideal to which the New Testament supplies colour and detail. There is no set form or scheme with which theologians have approached their task ; every student of Christian ethics is at liberty to travel by the path which suits him best.

(b) Yet it is to be noticed—and this is the second point to which we should give attention—that Western theology, at all events, under the successive guidance of Ambrose, Augustine, Gregory, and Aquinas, has on the whole chosen to base its picture of the Christian ideal not upon any one of these Scriptural foundations, but upon a pagan classification of virtue. Through the medium of Cicero's ' De Officiis ' St. Ambrose first of all, and then his successors, drew from Plato and Aristotle that Greek classification which has always gone by the name of the *Cardinal Virtues*[3]—Prudence, Justice, Temperance, and Fortitude. But Christian theology did not adopt them in any slavish spirit of imitation. It reinterpreted them and filled them with a Christian content, so much so that in the end it reversed those parts

---

[1] This is the basis of Jeremy Taylor's scheme in *Holy Living*, where ' soberness ' is taken as covering our duty to ourselves ; ' righteousness,' our duty to our neighbour ; ' godliness,' our duty to God.

[2] But see C. Gore, *Dominant Ideas, &c.*, chap. 6, and *supra*, p. 10.

[3] Also called the *natural* or *moral* virtues : *natural*, as distinct from *theological* (see p. 41) ; *moral*, as distinct from *intellectual*. This last distinction dates from the confusion of the Greek word ἀρετή, meaning at once *virtue* in the ordinary sense, and *excellence* or *perfection*. See T. B. Strong, *Christian Ethics*, Lect. iii. note 1. The cardinal virtues are mentioned together in the Wisdom literature—e.g. *Wisd*. viii. 7.

of their meaning which had a pagan, as distinct from a Christian, outlook.

'The virtues are recognisable indeed,' says Dr. Strong, in summarising the end of this process of adaptation as it appears in the 'Summa Theologica,' 'there can be no question but that they are the true lineal descendants of those of Aristotle. Fortitude is still the cool steady behaviour of a man in the presence of danger, the tenacious preservation of that which is dearer to him than his life. But its range is widened by the inclusion of dangers to soul as well as body; it is the bravery of one who dwells in a spiritual world. Temperance is still the control of the bodily passions; but it is also more positively than negatively the right placing of our affections. Justice is still the negative of all self-seeking, of all angry conflict with the interests of others; but the source of it all and the ground of its possibility lies in giving God the love and adoration which are His due. Prudence is still the practical moral sense which chooses the right course of concrete action; but it is the prudence of men who are pilgrims towards a country where the object of their love is to be found. The four are recognisable, then, as I have said, but they have suffered serious change.'[1]

We need scarcely remind ourselves that these virtues are called 'cardinal' because all other Christian duties 'hinge' on, or may be referred to, one or other of them. Two-thirds of the second division of Part II. of the 'Summa Theologica' is devoted to a discussion of the virtues dependent upon the four,[2] and their meaning is further developed by discussion of the vices contrary to each. More modern examples of the same method are to be found in Dr. Ottley's Essay in 'Lux Mundi' or in his 'Christian Ideas and Ideals,' and in Professor Sorley's 'The Moral Life.' Putting together these various accounts we may therefore summarise the Christian duties something after the following fashion:

Prudence: the habit of referring all questions, whether

[1] T. B. Strong, *Christian Ethics*, p. 141. Cp. *Summa*, ii. 2, qq. 47–170, and Augustine, *De Moribus Eccl. Cath.* 15, 25, where all four are defined in terms of loving God.

[2] For the exact relation which St. Thomas thought to exist between the cardinal virtues and the minor moral virtues, see W. H. V. Reade, *Moral System of Dante's Inferno*, pp. 148–152.

of ideals or of courses of action, to the criterion of God's will for us. From it derive such virtues as docility, conscientiousness, impartiality, and tact.

Justice : the giving to everyone (including to God and to oneself) his due. Under this head are comprised truthfulness, benevolence, forgiveness, compassion, and the duties of religion [1]—reverence, devotion, obedience, and gratitude to God.   1106106

Temperance : self-control 'for the highest possible development of our nature both for personal and for social ends ' ; [2] including purity, humility, patience, meekness, and even thrift.

Fortitude : the spirit which not only resists and endures, but even triumphs over, the trials and temptations of life ; ' glorifying in its afflictions.' To it we may refer not only such high virtues as moral courage and righteous indignation, but the more every-day yet equally Christian duties of industry and thoroughness.

That such a catalogue is at best of a highly artificial and almost unreal kind can hardly be denied. Yet it has a value of its own for the guardian of souls. It gives him a scheme on which he can build much of his exhortation and his preaching, as well as a rude criterion by which to test the spiritual welfare of his flock. We should all agree, surely, that the clergy would benefit both themselves and their people by greater study of the principal Christian virtues and their demands. English morality, as has already been argued, suffers to-day not from over-rigidity but from vagueness—from an inability to decide what is right and what is wrong ; [3] one cause at least of this lies in the fact that we have ceased to give clear thought and expression to the leading principles of Christian action. The cardinal virtues and their dependent virtues cannot be regarded as anything more than such leading principles ; but so much at least they are, and the priest who is armed with a knowledge of them and their parts goes to his work with

---

[1] Thus St. Thomas makes penance a ' part ' of justice, as being the acknowledgment of a debt incurred to God by sin. *Summa*, iii. q. 85, a. 3.

[2] W. R. Sorley, *The Moral Life*, p. 36.

[3] See the passage quoted from Stevenson, *Lay Morals*, on p. 100.

a surer touch than one who has no more than a vague idea of ' goodness.'

3. *Psychological Basis of the Cardinal Virtues* [1]

It is important to consider the underlying causes which gave the cardinal virtues so prominent a place in Christian thought ; for we should naturally have expected theologians to prefer one or other of the schemes of which the Bible offers so many. It is true, of course, that the pagan classification was part of the normal educational system of the Empire and so provided a natural basis of thought, but this does not account for its survival after the reorganisation of education on a Christian foundation. We can however discern two considerations at work, whether recognised or unrecognised by the successive theologians of the Church.

(*a*) The first is a philosophical one, and so need not detain us. If Christianity is, in the terms of a later thought, the ' effective republication of natural religion,' it was important to show that in the matter of morals too the new religion fulfilled the highest aspirations of the past. Some, at least, of the early Christian thinkers looked favourably on pagan speculations, and saw in all philosophy the work of the Holy Spirit guiding men towards the truth. It would therefore be natural for them to hold out a hand to the pagan moralist, and assure him that he had been rightly guided by the unknown God in his vision of a purer life ; to convince him even, if that were possible, that his ideal could only be realised in and through the gospel.

We need not stop for more than a glance at the importance of this point of view for present-day apologetics. Nothing needs emphasising so constantly as the fact that Christianity recognises to the full the ideals and virtues commonly accepted by the social consciousness—honesty, domesticity, manliness, integrity, and the like ; that the Church need have no hesitation in joining in any and every movement for commending them more earnestly to men's

[1] For fuller consideration of the questions treated in the remainder of this chapter, see particularly F. von Hügel, *Mystical Element of Religion*, part i. chap. 2.

consciences; and that her sacraments offer, through the divine grace they convey, the fullest and highest means of putting such ideals into practice. It is doubtless true, as Dr. Paget admitted, that ' what is deepest in the Christian character can only be seen by Christian eyes.'[1] The Christian ideal enshrines an element of otherworldliness and a degree of self-denial which can only commend itself to the converted ; and in consequence there must be from time to time an apparent divergence between the morality of ' revealed ' and that of ' natural ' religion. But this is simply due to the fact that in commending the ideals of natural ethics the Christian spirit has also transformed them ; the new and apparently unnatural virtues it emphasises are really no more than the old ones, seen at last in their true light and made conformable to the mind of Christ.

(b) This, however, belongs rather to the sphere of apologetics than to that of ethics. For our purpose it is more important to notice a second cause which has contributed to the survival of the cardinal virtues as a true basis for the description of Christian character. Plato, though he accepted them from the current thought of his day, championed their fundamental character on the ground that they were in accord with what was known of the composition of the soul. To him the soul consisted of three elements,[2] the intellective, the appetitive, and the ' spirited '—the last being that factor which promoted initiative, activity, and the special characteristics of the free man as distinct from the slave. To these corresponded three of the four cardinal virtues—prudence to the intellective ' part ' of the soul, temperance to the appetitive, fortitude to the ' spirited ' ; justice, the fourth virtue, being the sum of the other three on their social, as distinct from their personal, side.[3] In other words, the cardinal virtues were justified as *being based upon observed psychological phenomena.*

This psychological character attributed to the cardinal

---

[1] *Studies in the Christian Character*, p. viii.
[2] See G. S. Brett, *History of Psychology, Ancient and Patristic*, pp. 68, 69.   [3] Plato, *Rep.* bk. iv. 435-445.

virtues never left them, though it changed with a changing psychology. In one way or another the four virtues are always found referred to the three main elements in consciousness—the intellect, the appetites, and the ' active ' principle, or will.[1] Modern psychology has done much to define the various terms employed to designate these three elements and to analyse afresh the manner in which they co-operate. It deprecates the application to them of any such name as ' faculties,' implying the possibility of their separate and independent existences ; for it recognises that consciousness is an indivisible unit whose ' parts ' are no more than logical abstractions. At the same time it reaffirms the psychology of less scientific days by recognising the same three ' regions ' or factors as operative

[1] To St. Thomas, who adopted the Aristotelian rather than the Platonic view, the soul consisted of five ' powers,' of which two only, the intellective and the appetitive, are characteristic of the ' rational ' soul—the soul, as we should say, capable of conscious action and so of morality—the human soul (*Summa*, i. q. 78). In both these ' powers ' he recognised a lower and higher part : in the intellective, the lower stage of sensory perception, and the higher of discursive reason ; in the appetitive, a lower stage of sensory desire, and a higher one of rational desire (*Summa*, i. q. 80). Sensory perception, however, lies at the back both of discursive reasoning (for every train of reasoning can ultimately be traced back to a stimulus in sensation) and of sensory desire, nor is it susceptible of control by the mind ; it is therefore, for practical purposes, eliminated by St. Thomas from his moral scheme.

We are left, then, with an analysis of the soul into three elements, not so very unlike those of Plato : the intellectual, the lower affective (the element of sensory desire or, as we should say, of the animal passions), and the higher affective. This latter, representing the combination of reason and desire—the realm of spiritual emotions in short—should be the determining factor in every action for which a man may be held responsible (*Summa*, i. 2, q. 9, a. 1), though the *impulse* to action may originate either in an intellectual or an appetitive source (*ibid*. a. 2 ; cp. q. 10, aa. 1, 3). To this ' intellectual-appetitive ' element in consciousness St. Thomas seems to give the name of ' reason ' (*ratio*), though his use of this latter term, as also of ' will ' (*voluntas*), is ambiguous (see *infra*, p. 39, footnote 2).

The lower appetite he divides, following his Greek models, into two further elements, the ' spirited ' (*irascibilis*) and the ' concupiscible ' (*concupiscibilis*). We have thus, in effect, four ' parts ' of the rational soul : the intellective, the irascible, the concupiscible (these last being the two sub-divisions of the lower appetite), and the rational-appetitive, the ultimate ground of action in the moral consciousness. To each of these four respectively he makes one of the four cardinal virtues correspond—to the first, prudence ; to the second, fortitude ; to the third, temperance ; to the fourth, justice (*Summa*, i. 2, q. 61, a. 2).

in every conscious action[1] : the cognitive, the appetitive, and the conative—intellect, desire, and will or purpose.[2] There is no conscious activity of life into which these three factors do not enter—to co-operate in the soul which is at perfect harmony with itself, to contest and conflict in the soul which has not as yet found a balance between them.

Such balance or stability may be achieved in two ways. Either one of the conflicting elements may become so powerful as to dominate the other two, as in those rare cases where everything else is subordinated to the pursuit of knowledge,

---

[1] And even by recognising the special affinity between the appetitive and conative elements, which ' we may regard as identical without risk of serious error.'—W. McDougall, *Psychology* (Home University Library), pp. 111, 112.

[2] The term *will* is ambiguous. It may mean either (a) the *efferent motor force*—the automatic agency by which any suggestion emerging into consciousness produces some action, inhibition, or change of tissue ; or (b) a factor akin to St. Thomas's ' rational desire '—a *formed purpose* which acts both as a check upon the suggestions of consciousness and as the final motive in reasoned action. It is in this latter sense we use it when we speak of a man as being *strong-willed* : we mean that he has a purpose in life, and that that purpose is strong enough to dominate other motives to action. For any psychology which admits the possibility of *free-will* this is the obvious and only meaning of the word. A will which acts automatically in response to intellectual or appetitive stimulus cannot possibly be *free*. It would be better, therefore, if the word *purpose* (which is less ambiguous than either *reason* or *will*) were used for the conative factor in consciousness. The whole question is discussed, from the metaphysical and physiological standpoints respectively, in T. H. Green, *Prolegomena to Ethics*, bk. ii. chap. i. ; W. McDougall, *Physiological Psychology*, pp. 163 ff. ; *Social Psychology*, pp. 236–240.

St. Thomas's use of the word *voluntas* is characterised (as he himself admits—i. 2, q. 19, a. 2, ad. 2) by the same ambiguity. He employs it to mean, (a) strictly, the power (peculiar to human beings—i. 2, q. 6, a. 2) *of tending towards a recognised ultimate end* (i. 2, q. 1, aa. 2, 3, 4 ; q. 6, a. 1 ; q. 8, aa. 1, 2)—the maintaining of a *purpose*, in short. In this strict sense, *will* and *rational desire* are synonymous (*ibid*. q. 77, a. 1, *in corp.* ; cp. q. 78, a. 1, *in corp.*). In this sense the will is supreme, and ' commands ' all the ' powers ' of the soul, including the reason and sensory appetite (*ibid*. q. 9, aa. 1, 2). (b) In a derivative sense, *voluntas* is the *power of action directed to this or that object* (i.e. the efferent motor force), and so is ' moved ' automatically both by the practical reason (q. 9, a. 1) and by sensory appetite (q. 9, a. 2)—cp. i. q. 93 ; ii. 2, q. 47, a. 8.

The ambiguity is further elucidated by two parallel distinctions (a) between the *inward* or formal acts of the will, and the *outward* or material (i. 2, q. 18, a. 6) ; (b) between *intention* or ultimate purpose (q. 19, a. 7) and *choice* (of particular means)—(i. 2, q. 13, aa. 3, 4, 5 ; cp. ii. 2, q. 47, a. 1, ad. 2).

E

or in the commoner ones where passion of one kind or another, or the sheer love of activity (which is the constant expression of the conative or purposive element undeterred by moral or rational considerations), achieves complete control. Or else the three elements may be harmonised—' the divided self,' in Professor James' phrase, ' unified '—in such a way that, in the end, they will never be found to drag the soul in different directions.

It is the Christian position that, of these two possibilities, only the second will give the soul that freedom and power which enables it to conform to the pattern of Christ : and that this possibility can only be realised under the influence of the Holy Spirit through the gospel of Christ.[1] It is true that at times, or in certain sections of Christian thought, it has been held desirable to suppress completely either the intellect or the passions in order to achieve the fullest degree of Christian grace. But these contentions, strongly though they have been held from time to time, are foreign to the main trend of Christian opinion, which demands, both as a privilege and as a duty, that the individual shall develop all of his powers to the utmost. And for this to be possible intellect, desire and will must all be directed to the same object and goal— the love of God and our neighbour. The intellect must be convinced that this and this alone is the supreme object of existence ; the desire for God and for His Kingdom must be so strong that all other desires fade into insignificance beside it ; the will must be strengthened to the utmost so that every nerve may be strained towards this single end.[2]

---

[1] Thus *Summa*, i. 2, q. 73, a. 1, ad. 3 : ' Amor Dei est congregativus, in quantum affectum hominis a multis ducit in unum ; et ideo virtutes quae ex amore Dei causantur connexionem habent. Sed amor sui disgregat affectum hominis in diversa.'

[2] Strictly speaking, the highest form of Christian character demands not merely that intellect, emotion and will shall all be *rightly directed*, but also that they shall be *highly developed*. Here the two meanings of virtue (' excellence ' and ' moral righteousness ') meet one another. The ideal Christian would be a man not merely of good will, but of strong will too ; not merely of right desires, but of *strong* right desires ; not merely of a well-guided mind, but of a well-guided and *active* mind. In most cases, however (except in the phlegmatic type of character), the emotional element in human nature is strong enough, and the priest is there-

It is here that we see the real importance of the cardinal virtues. It is necessary to assert that intellect, desire, and purpose must all be rightly and strongly exercised to the one end of the love and service of God and man. Each then must be *virtuous*, and from their virtues all others will depend. And it would be hard to find better definitions of the virtues of intellect, desire and will respectively than those of the four we have mentioned. Prudence we called ' the habit of referring all questions to the criterion of God's will for us ' : this is the virtue or true exercise of the intellect. Fortitude and temperance are respectively the spirit of triumphant resistance to all that hinders that will, and the due control of all desires which, although under right direction they can be brought into its service, may also lead to its neglect—virtues each of them of the appetitive element in the soul. And justice is the formed purpose of giving both to God and man that meed of love and service which Christ demands of us—the virtue or true exercise of the will.

4. *The Internal Characteristics of the Christian Life —the Theological Virtues*

Seen in this light the cardinal virtues become for us a summary enumeration not so much of a Christian man's duties to his neighbours, as of the true interior dispositions from which the proper fulfilment of those duties will spring. At the same time we must recognise that there is a practical distinction between the external virtues and the internal dispositions in which they have their source. And therefore moral theology reserves to the former the names of the four cardinal virtues which it drew from Greek philosophy ; and for the latter selects with a true instinct the list of terms employed by St. Paul in 1 Corinthians xiii.—faith, hope and love.[1] These three—the *Theological*

---

fore not concerned to strengthen it ; but often it *is* his concern to attempt to strengthen the mind, and *almost always* the will. This explains the close connection that has always existed between religion and education.

[1] So, too, in Rom. v. 1–5 ; 1 Thess. i. 2, 3 ; Col. i. 3–5 ; Heb. x. 22–24 (R.V.) ; 1 Pet. i. 21, 22.

Virtues [1]—are, in Bishop Jeremy Taylor's words, ' the internal actions of religion, in which the soul only is employed, and ministers to God in the special actions of faith, hope and charity.' [2] ' Morality,' says Dr. Strong, ' is more than the due performance or avoidance of certain acts ; it expresses the final constitution of the man ; it is the most profound exposition of his inmost character. It is this inward side of things which the theological virtues most accurately represent.' [3]

As with the cardinal, so with the theological virtues, we find that they can easily be referred to a psychological basis. They emphasise, that is, by pointing each to one of the three elements of intellect, desire and will, what we have seen to be the fundamental assertion of moral theology —that each several power that a man possesses must be dedicated to the one supreme ideal of love and service.

Faith, St. Thomas says, is of the intellect ; hope of the will ' as moving the intention ' ; love of the will ' as transformed into its end ' ; [4]—or, as we may paraphrase it, hope is the soul in desire or aspiration ; love, the soul in the process of achievement. And faith and hope are subsidiary to love, just as intellect and desire should be subordinated to (but not obliterated by) purpose, for love is the fulfilling of the law, the greatest of the three, [5] the bond of perfectness. More simply Jeremy Taylor says : ' Faith gives our understanding to God ; hope gives up all the passions and affections to heaven and heavenly things, and charity gives the will to the service of God.' [6]

---

[1] So called because—
(a) they alone lead to our ' supernatural ' end—the vision of God ;
(b) they are given by God alone, and by revelation ;
(c) they are concerned with the end of life, whilst the moral virtues have to do with its incidents.
              Summa, i. 2, q. 62, aa. 1, 2 ; q. 61, a. 1.
St. Thomas had, however no very clear conception as to the relation between the cardinal and theological virtues ; there is an obvious suture at the point where pagan philosophy and Christian thought meet in his system.   See W. H. V. Reade, *Moral System of Dante's Inferno*, pp. 163–165, 170.   [2] *Holy Living*, chap. iv. init.
  [3] *Christian Ethics*, p. 114.   [4] *Summa*, i. 2, q. 62, a. 2.
  [5] *Summa*, i. 2, q. 62, a. 4 ; cp. ii. 2, q. 184, a. 1.
  [6] *Holy Living, loc. cit*.   It is to be observed that Ottley (*Lux Mundi*, pp. 360 ff.) regards *hope* as the virtue which consecrates the will, and *love* that which consecrates the passions.   In a matter of this kind,

In thus representing the Christian ideal as the perfection, by supernatural assistance, of every natural endowment, rather than as obedience to a formulated code of laws,[1] the Church has undoubtedly been true to the apostolic conception that liberty, not law, is the essence of the gospel. Law indeed, as we shall have occasion to observe in various connections, has its place in the Christian life ; but the keynote of that life is the freedom of love, not the bondage of duty. And wherever the Church has fallen from this conception and been content to preach obedience to a code, the result, whilst perhaps bringing in its train a momentary purification of morals, has been to lower the whole Christian standard both in theory and in practice, and has tended to destroy the sense of individual responsibility which is the essence of Christian conduct.

We cannot, however, dismiss the theological virtues without fuller consideration. Faith, hope and love are the three most pregnant words of Christian ethics, and their implications are so inexhaustible that it is hard to define the content of each. Indeed they continually merge into each other ; so that St. Paul can sometimes speak as though the words might be used interchangeably.[2] Yet because they represent the three essentials of the

where we are dealing with words which have no authoritative definition, and where all the words employed have so many points of contact with each other that one meaning is continually tending to pass over into another, it would be foreign to the true spirit of theology to contest the point. The difference is principally one of definition. But it may be suggested that the interpretation given in *Holy Living* is better than Dr. Ottley's—first, as suiting better the definition of hope and fear (see p. 45) ; and second, as emphasising the fact that Christian love is in essence a matter of purpose rather than of passion ; love, not liking ; ἀγάπη not ἔρως. Hooker, we may add, says of faith that its ' principal object is that eternal verity which hath discovered the treasures of hidden wisdom in Christ ' ; of hope, that its ' highest object is that everlasting goodness which in Christ doth quicken the dead ' ; of charity, that its ' final object is that incomprehensible beauty which shineth in the countenance of Christ the Son of the living God ' (*Ecclesiastical Polity*, bk. i. chap. xi.).

[1] Thus A. D. Sertillanges, *S. Thomas d'Aquin*, vol. ii. p. 298, sums up St. Thomas's teaching in the words, ' La morale n'est pas un ordre venu du dehors, même du ciel ; c'est la voix de la raison reconnue comme une voix divine.'

[2] See *supra*, p. 5.

Christian life we cannot pass on without attempting to explore their meaning ; and to find out—not how they can be implanted, for that is the work of the Holy Spirit alone—but how they can be fostered and nourished. And because of the perplexing halo which adorns yet confuses their outlines in the apostolic writings, it will be easier perhaps to turn to the simpler yet even deeper phrases of our Lord, and see if there can be found some clue to the meanings we require.

Macarius preserves what may have been a traditional saying of the Lord's in which the three virtues actually occur together : ' Give heed to faith and hope, from which is born that love to God and man which leads to eternal life.' [1]   But whether or no this be the source of the apostolic triad, we can recognise in our Lord's demands upon His disciples three elements not altogether dissimilar from the theological virtues. That he demanded *faith* of those who wished to know His power is recorded by the evangelists [2] : St. John above all emphasises the necessity of this virtue for all who would win eternal life.[3]   A second condition of entrance to the kingdom of heaven is *repentance*,[4] and we shall not be wrong in saying that repentance is an act, and penitence a disposition, specially concerned with the passions and desires. To repent means to feel sorrow for, and repugnance towards, whatever grieves God ; but the ground from which these emotions spring must be, as we shall see in the next chapter, *the desire to be as God would have us be.* So repentance in the full sense means to direct the desires aright ; to love what God loves as well as hating what God hates. This virtue or gift (for repentance, like faith and love, can only come as a gift of the Holy Spirit) we exercise first of all with regard to our own sins and failures in the past ; but it has its fruit in the present and the future : repentance is incomplete without amendment of life.

It is possible, therefore, to assert, in general terms, that

---

[1] For a discussion of this passage see Strong, *Christian Ethics*, p. 113
[2] E.g. Mark i. 15, xi. 22 ; Matt. xxi. 22, &c.
[3] E.g. John iii. 16 *et passim*.
[4] E.g. Matt. ix. 13, xi. 20 ; Mark i. 15.   Cp. Acts ii. 38, iii. 19, xvii. 30.

repentance and hope mean very much the same thing. Both of them bear primarily upon the appetitive or affective region of life—upon the passions and desires. Hope is defined by St. Thomas as being akin to desire, but surpassing it both in the difficulty and excellence of that at which it aims, and in the eagerness and passion with which it strives.[1] For that at which hope aims with the full force of a divinely-given fervour is the fullness of the promises of God : it is a superhuman desire for the beatific vision, and, no less, for such gifts and graces as may help us to attain it.[2] The word, then, implies something much more than a placid expectation ; it implies a keenness and passion exceeding that of any desire for ordinary things. That this is the case—that hope concerns primarily our desires and aversions—may be seen from the added fact that it is continually mentioned in conjunction with fear—not human fear, but the supernatural fear of God.[3] ' He who hopes without fear grows careless, just as he who fears without hope is downcast and sinks into dejection like a stone.' [4]

Fear, indeed, is the necessary counterpart of hope—its negative aspect ; and the two together come near to that repentance which should be not merely an initial act but a permanent disposition of the Christian life. For if hope is the surpassing desire of the gifts and graces which God

---

[1] *Summa*, i. 2, q. 25, a. 1 : ' Spes supra desiderium addit quemdam conatum et quamdam elevationem animi ad consequendum bonum arduum.' This definition, it is true, applies primarily to hope as a *passio*. It is clear, however, from the relation which St. Thomas regards as existing between this *passio* and the theological virtue of hope, that the definition in this respect is applicable also to the latter. See ii. 2, q. 17, aa. 1, 5.

[2] *Ibid.* i. 2, q. 69, a. 2 ; ii. 2, q. 17, a. 2. Augustine, *Enchiridion*, 114, says that the ' objects of hope ' are to be learnt from the several clauses of the Lord's Prayer.

[3] *Filial* fear, as distinct from *servile* and *worldly* fear. *Summa*, ii. 2, q. 19, a. 2 ; i. 2, q. 67, a. 4. The distinction is clearer in French than in English : ' Il y a beaucoup de gens dont il ne faut pas dire qu'ils craignent Dieu, mais qu'ils en ont peur ' (J. A. Spender, *Comments of Bagshot*).

[4] [Augustine], *Sermo X ad Fratres in Eremo*. Cp. J. Welton, *Psychology of Education*, p. 79 : ' As fear is an original part of our nature, it is impossible, even if it were desirable, to eradicate it. The educational task is to attach it to those things, and to those only, which are worthy of being feared.' Cp. J. A. Hadfield in *The Spirit*, pp. 99–101.

gives as a means to eternal life, fear is the mother of humility
and repugnance to all the impulses which clog our spiritual
progress : it ' consists in the consideration of our own
nothingness, insufficiency, weakness, faults, shortcomings
and inborn propensities, which incline us to evil; all
which motives inspire the soul with distrust of self and keep
us in humility and lowly-mindness. . . . Without it the
soul resembles a ship with sails fully set but without
ballast ; the lighter it travels, the greater the risk it runs of
stranding and of wreck. ' [1]

We can trace in our Lord's demands one other factor,
corresponding with the devotion of the will to the service
of God.   Faith and repentance may easily become static,
placid things ; and therefore Christ calls upon His disciples
to lead a life of active service, to take up a cross and
follow.[2] Time after time He calls for a surrender of the
will to His commands, for an active imitation of His example,
instead of a merely passive acquiescence in His promises
and claims.   Once again we may follow Jeremy Taylor, and
give to this characteristic the name of *Zeal*, which he
regards as the apotheosis of love. ' The least love that
is,' his definition runs, ' must be obedient, pure, simple, and
communicative. But the greater state of love is the zeal
of love, which runs out into excrescences and suckers like
a fruitful and pleasant tree.' [3]

Whether, therefore, we consider the threefold requirements of our Lord, or the theological virtues, we can conclude that the inward dispositions, without which progress
in the Christian life is impossible, involve the dedication,
or purification, or right orientation, of intellect, desire and
will. The first of these may be called faith, the second
penitence or hope, the third the zeal of love. These inward
dispositions are the gift of the Holy Spirit, though even
in his natural state man is not altogether without them.
For, as we saw in the last chapter, it is impossible not to

---

[1] J. B. Scaramelli, *Directorium Asceticum*, Treat. iv. §§ 92, 126.
[2] See, for example, Matt. vii. 16, 24, ix. 9, x. 38, xxv. 35; Mark
x. 21 ; Luke ix. 23, xiv. 27.
[3] *Holy Living*, chap. iv. sect. 3.

recognise in every man, however little touched by religion, a tendency to progress towards a higher condition. Call it, if you will, the desire for truth, beauty and goodness ; call it the conscience of the natural man : it is there, and there are few natures so debased as not to retain some trace of it which will respond to the right appeal. Man, that is to say, is endowed not merely with intellect, emotion, and will, but with a tendency to exert the three in the direction of refined ideals.

Materialistic philosophy has made many attempts to find an origin for this tendency—referring it, for example, to the instinct for maintaining the race, or to the social sentiment. None of these attempts are very satisfactory : they explain the unknown by a further unknown : their importance lies in the fact that they tacitly admit the tendency we have spoken of—the tendency towards the refinement or right direction of the intellect, feelings and will.[1]

The three following chapters will be devoted to a fuller consideration of the nature of these three fundamental dis-

---

[1] It is probably in this tendency that we may find the origin of *conscience*. It is generally admitted that to define conscience as a separate *moral sense*, or *religious sense*, or *instinct*, is a mistake. It implies that there is a certain conflict of aims between moral and religious effort on the one hand, and æsthetic and scientific aspiration on the other. In practice there often will be ; but in strict theological truth we must maintain that God is the *summum bonum*—that He includes in Himself all other aims and aspirations of the soul. On the other hand, to regard conscience purely as a function of the intellect is to ignore the all-important fact that it contains an *emotional* element of attraction to what is good and repulsion from what is evil. This is only partially safeguarded by defining it, as is commonly done, as a function of the *practical* reason : a definition which, while admitting the elements of emotion and will in conscience, makes them subsidiary to the intellectual element. Reflection must convince us that the complexity of conscience is made up of all three factors equally. Hence conscience is best regarded as the general tendency towards self-refinement, towards the choice of the higher in place of the lower, which is to be seen, though perhaps faintly only, in every effort of mind, emotion and will. And that progressive purification and strengthening of this trinity of elements in which we have seen true spiritual life to consist may perhaps most simply be defined as the *education of conscience.*

See further R. L. Ottley, *Christian Ideas, &c.*, pp. 56 ff. ; H. Rashdall, *Theory of Good and Evil*, i. 146 ff. ; Hastings' *Encyclopædia of Religion and Ethics*, s.v. ' Conscience ' ; and *infra*, Chap. VIII.

positions, and the means by which they may be fostered.[1] But in the meantime we may examine briefly and in general terms the nature of spiritual progress, and learn from it, if they can be learnt, the laws in conformity with which the Spirit of God normally works in the hearts of men, and leads them on from strength to strength.

5. *The Laws of Spiritual Progress*

In the preceding paragraphs we have examined, first of all, the ideal of Christian character in its outward aspect, and found that it consists in the unremitting exercise, in the service of God and man, of all the powers of the soul, and primarily of the three fundamental ones of mind, desire and will.   This result is formulated for us, in technical language, by the scheme of the four cardinal virtues.   We have seen, further, that these powers cannot be exercised in their fullest and freest manifestations until they are completely dedicated, strengthened and maintained by spiritual grace in the inward life of the soul.   No less than this is demanded of the Christian by his Master, no less is promised to him through the gift of the Holy Spirit ; and the technical formulation of these necessary dispositions is to be found in the theological virtues, or in the three parallel requirements of our Lord's teaching—faith, penitence and zeal.

But we are not to suppose that these dispositions, or their effective manifestation in the Christian virtues, spring suddenly to life in the disciple in the full strength of maturity. Rather we are to think of them as present in germinal form in every man born into the world—for no such man is altogether void of the light and life of the Spirit [2]—but gradually strengthened and developed in two several ways :

---

[1] The student of Christian ethics should examine for himself how these same three necessary dispositions are laid before the Christian in the Acts and Epistles ; as also at the various turning points or crises of the Christian life—at baptism, confirmation, the preparation for communion, ordination, and in the sacrament of penance. He should notice, too, the arguments by which St. Thomas links with the cardinal and theological virtues the virtues of the Beatitudes (*Summa.* i. 2, q. 69), and the gifts (*ibid.* q. 68) and the fruits (*ibid.* q. 70) of the Spirit.

[2] John i. 9.

first of all, by the continued renewing of grace through both sacramental and extra-sacramental channels ; second, by the constant effort of their possessor, and the wise and discerning guidance of those to whom the spiritual care of his soul has been entrusted.

It is significant how constantly the Bible uses the analogy of the tree and its fruits, the grain of mustard seed, the vine,[1] to disclose the truth of this slow maturing of the spiritual life. It is significant, too, how our Lord was willing to perform miracles in answer to a faith far feebler than that which will subdue kingdoms, work righteousness, obtain promises, and stop the mouths of lions. A simple confidence in His ability and willingness to help was all He asked at the outset.[2] So, too, He indicated that repentance, sufficient at least to win divine compassion, need not have attained the full force of supernatural contrition. The prodigal son was more conscious of his need than of his sin ; the penitent thief can have had no more than a glimpse of the true ideal of life that he had recklessly discarded ; yet each was welcomed to the Father's house. The disciples were men of weak faith,[3] and only imperfect detachment from worldly things ;[4] but such faith and penitence as they had was sufficient to warrant the Master in teaching, guiding and inspiring them, in the confidence that His power was enough to give them the increase they required.

We may expect the spiritual life, therefore, to grow from small beginnings. It is a life of *conversion* [5]—not in normal cases of a sudden change from worldliness to godliness,

---

[1] See, e.g., Ps. i. 3 ff. ; Isa. v. 1 ff. ; Jer. xvii. 8 ; Matt. vii. 16–20, xiii. 31 ; Mark iv. 26 ; John xv. 2–6 ; 1 Cor. iii. 6 ff.

[2] Matt. viii. 10 ; Mark v. 34, ix. 23, x. 52 ; Luke xvii. 6.

[3] Mark iv. 40.

[4] Matt. xix. 27 ; Mark ix. 34, x. 35.

[5] Conversion as a *turning away* may have reference either to ideals, or to methods, or to both. In the first case, a man may have to abandon a worldly ideal for a spiritual one. In the second case, though his ideal be truly spiritual, he may be pursuing it by methods which, if he is to succeed, must be replaced by others (e.g. he must learn that his goal can be reached only by self-surrender, not by self-exertion). In the third case, he requires a change both in ideals and in methods. Much of the confusion with which the word is surrounded is due to this triple connotation. G. A. Coe (*Psychology of Religion*, p. 152) distinguishes *six* senses in which the word is used.

but of a slow turning and progress from the lower ideal towards the higher. In this spiritual journey those who have travelled it have noticed three definite stages, each leading on to one above it. Expressed, as all spiritual life must be, in terms of love, they are these. The first, the stage in which the soul, though still loving the world, at least may be said to love it no more than it loves God : the stage at which the love of God and the love of the world struggle for mastery. In the second phase the love of God has conquered, and bears fruit with growing ease and readiness, but is still hampered by trivial faults and accidents which have yet to be removed. In the third stage (never to be attained at more than isolated moments in the present life), no obstacles separate the soul's love from God its goal ; love and its object are completely united ; they share a single will, a single purpose and a single joy.[1]

This was expressed in more technical terms in the doctrine of the *threefold way*, which became the central tenet of Christian mysticism. Three ' ways ' in succession lie before the soul : that of *purification*, in which it is purged of all the grosser passions ; that of *illumination*, in which it is irradiated by the light of divine truth, and is enabled in its growing strength to break even the smallest habits of sin which still separate it from God ; and that of *union*, in which it becomes identified wholly and completely with the will of God.[2]

Here again we shall not be wrong in seeing in these three stages the transformation of desire, intelligence and will respectively into the image of Christ. It is only, of course, in the strictest logic that the three processes can be regarded as necessarily following each other in the above order. In reality they are simultaneous processes going on throughout life. Yet at one stage of spiritual development one of them will usually be most prominent, at another,

---

[1] *Summa*, ii. 2, q. 24, a. 9 ; and cp. q. 184, a. 3.
[2] See, for example, *Summa*, ii. 2, q. 24, a. 9 ; q. 183, a. 4 ; Scaramelli, *op. cit.* Treat. i. § 31 ; A. Baker, *Holy Wisdom*, Treat. iii. sect. 2, chap. 1 ; W. R. Inge, *Christian Mysticism*, pp. 10–13 ; E. Underhill, *Mysticism*, p. 112 ; A. Saudreau, *Degrees of the Spiritual Life, passim*, &c.

another. It is clear, for example, that so long as the soul is bound down by any passion strong enough to contest the claims of God, spiritual progress is a practical impossibility ; [1] and that a clear understanding of the end and manner of the spiritual life must precede any enlightened or whole-hearted dedication of the will.

There is a sense therefore, and a very real sense, in which the subjugation of the passions must be achieved before any illumination of the mind can avail, and in which both are preliminaries necessary to the maturing and stabilising of a formed Christian purpose. It is this logical sequence, with its vital practical consequences, which is enshrined in the doctrine of the threefold way.

At the same time, it would be absurd to suggest that any one of the three processes can at any time be forwarded apart from the other two. Human personality both on its natural and spiritual side is far too closely knit for such to be the case. Nor did the mystics hesitate to admit this. For they held that whilst the three paths were, in strict logic, successive, they were to a great extent in Christian experience concurrent. Even the soul still struggling with passion in the purgative way received constant rays of illumination and occasional moments of mystic union with God—foretastes of the privileges to come, as well as means of strength and encouragement for the conflict of the present. [2]

All experience of practical pastoral work, whether at home or in the mission field, points to the same conclusion. The first need felt by the mission priest, after men have

[1] Passion must be eradicated from the soul as a preliminary even to a clear intellectual vision. ' Sin, in the Christian view, disorders the intellect as much as the body or the will' (J. R. Illingworth, *Christian Character*, chap. v.).

[2] Scaramelli, *op. cit.* Treat. i. § 29. Cp. A. Baker, *Holy Wisdom*, Treat. iii. sect. 2, chap. i. : 'Notwithstanding what hath been said of the distinction of these three ways of a contemplative life, we are to observe that they are not so absolutely distinguished, but that sometimes there may be a mixture of them ; for it may happen that a soul, being as yet in the most imperfect purgative way, may in some fits be so abundantly supplied with grace, as that during the exercise of meditation she may oft be enabled to produce immediate acts of the will, yea, and perhaps aspirations too, so joining together exercises both purgative, illuminative, and unitive in one recollection.'

been attracted to the gospel, is that of instilling into his catechumens the elements of a moral code—of breaking them from the grosser or more dangerous sins. The second requirement is definite and full instruction in the truths of the gospel. Once the passions and the mind have thus been disciplined, and have received at all events a bias towards their true orientation, there is hope that the convert's whole personality will in time be absorbed by the single end ; until these preliminaries have been achieved progress can scarcely be expected.

Modern psychology, and especially the investigations of Professor Starbuck and Professor Stanley Hall, has amply confirmed these data of Christian experience as to the laws of the normal development of the spiritual life. More than that, it has in two particulars added to our knowledge.

(a) In the first place, Professor Starbuck has shown that there is no essential difference between what are usually known as ' sudden conversions ' and the more gradual development of the normal soul. To the person who experiences such a sudden conversion it may well appear to be no part of a continuous process, but, on the contrary, a complete break with the past history of his soul, yet ' there is not a single instance of the spontaneous awakening type in which there have not been some antecedents in thought or action which may be regarded as causes leading to the awakening.' [1]

After exhaustive discussion of some hundreds of cases of each kind, Professor Starbuck concludes that the change of character which occurs in spontaneous conversions is identical in all essential points with the transformation of character that gradually takes place in normal religious development. There is a difference of emphasis, no doubt : the sense of sin is usually more strongly marked, the satisfaction of the intellect less fully required,[2] in the cases of spontaneous awakening than in those of the other class ; there is a possibility, too, that the suddenly converted soul may be more altruistic but less self-controlled than the

[1] E. D. Starbuck, *Psychology of Religion*, chap. xxviii. ; and cp. W. James, *Varieties, &c.*, p. 238.
[2] Starbuck, *op. cit.* p. 364.

slowly maturing one. But in the main the results in either case—'the distinctive things which set the new life off against the old'—are the same.[1] Conversion, in short, in the suggestive phrase of another writer,[2] is a phenomenon resembling 'a falling in love'; and whether it takes the form of a sudden or slow awakening, the change of character it effects is substantially the same.

It is of interest to observe the terms in which Professor Starbuck, writing, of course, as an impartial observer without any theological bias, expresses the change that comes over the human consciousness by the awakening and maturing in it of a spiritual life. He formulates it in the terms of a fourfold transition, which may be seen no less in the cases of apparently spontaneous conversion than in those of gradual growth—a transition from self-interest to the love of God and the service of others; a transition from receptivity to activity; a transition from credulity to insight; a transition from self-assertion to self-control.[3] It is perfectly clear, upon this point, that psychology and theology have joined hands; there is little more than a verbal difference between the character in which this transitional process issues and the cardinal virtues of the schoolmen.

(b) The second contribution of modern psychology to the understanding of the laws of spiritual progress is no less important, for it emphasises the truth that the Holy Spirit normally employs natural processes and means in the consummation of spiritual results. This, of course, is not a conclusion drawn by the psychologist himself; but it is a legitimate deduction of theology from the facts presented to it by psychological investigation. Those facts are, briefly, as follows. It may be shown that what we have called the laws, or sequences, of spiritual progress are identical with the laws and sequences of the ordinary growth of the full human consciousness; so that we may fairly say that the soul awakens to each successive stage

---

[1] Starbuck, *op. cit.* pp. 369–372.   [2] Mr. Kenneth Saunders.
[3] *Op. cit.* pp. 392–394. Cp. James' statement of the primary characteristics of the 'composite photograph of universal saintliness' (*Varieties, &c.*, pp. 272–274).

in its approach to God, in the same manner, if not always at the same time, as it awakens to succeeding stages in the development and widening of its ordinary human experience.

The boy or girl emerging from childhood into adolescence is plunged into a period of what has been called ' storm and stress '—of emotional and intellectual upheaval.[1] New emotions, possibilities and ideas press in upon the soul from every side, producing in it a state of chaos. In the earlier years of adolescence the emotional crisis is the greater, in the later years the intellectual. The period is one of great possibilities and of equal dangers ; the problem lies in the difficulty first of all of ordering and controlling the newly acquired emotional life, and then of reaching a satisfactory solution of the new questions of the mind. The statistical inquiries of psychologists show clearly that it is just at this period, as a rule, that the soul awakes to the supreme importance of religion. Childhood, it is true, has a religion of its own, but it is an impersonal religion, in so far as it is mainly taken on trust. The religion of adolescence, on the other hand, comes into immediate conflict with other factors awakening at the same time—the urgent claims of newly discovered sympathies, pleasures and emotions, the sincere questionings of a mind embarked upon the search for truth ;—it has to be tested, proved, and made a personal possession. Maturity brings with it a stage of reconstruction and calm, in which is developed a stability of character based upon the control of the emotions and the development of formed and confident habits of thought.[2] By this means is made possible the final devotion of the entire personality, in harmony at length with itself, to a single purpose in life.

If then we trace scientifically the religious history of a normal individual from the dawn of adolescence onward, we find in it first the clash of religion with passion in a more or less acute form ; then the questioning of faith by

---

[1] This generalisation, of course, cannot be applied in its entirety to certain rare souls (the ' once-born ') who reach maturity without any period of inward stress ; though it may be doubted how far any of this class really exist. See further *infra*, p. 60.

[2] Starbuck, *op. cit.* p. 277.

the awakened intelligence in search of a sound foundation ; lastly (if passion has been dominated and doubt satisfied, even to a limited degree only), the development of a gradually maturing and unifying will to service. The successive stages of the threefold path appear again, under new names indeed, but unchanged in character and degree ; and are seen to be the outcome of an interaction between religious aspirations and the normal growth of conscious life and experience. And once again, we are warned, by psychologist as well as theologian, that while in strict logic we may regard these phases as successive, in life as we know it they are inseparable and concomitant ; although at one period one of them has chief prominence, at others each of the other two.[1] The Christian life, in fact, viewed either as by the theologian, or as by the mystic, or as by the psychologist, is simply the progressive purification of thought, desire and will into faith, penitence and zeal, showing fruit in the virtues of prudence, fortitude, temperance and justice, and the qualities that depend from them.

[1] Starbuck, *op. cit.* pp. 417, 418.

F

CHAPTER III

1. The ' Once-born ' and ' Healthy-minded '

'THE work of the religious teacher,' writes Professor
Starbuck, whose evidence is important as being that of a
scientist rather than a theologian, ' consists in creating
such an environment that each of the instincts which enter
into the fabric of religion shall be called out by the proper
stimuli ; that they be lifted into the higher psychic centres ;
that each shall have its due emphasis during its nascent
period of development; that they be richly interwoven
into the texture of the normal psychic reactions, and thereby
become spiritualized.' [1]

Discarding the repellent Americanisms of this paragraph
we must recognise its complete inherent truth. The
principal ' instincts which enter into the fabric of religion '
we saw to be the fundamental natural endowments of
intellect, emotion and will. In life they are inseparable ;
each plays its part in every conscious action. But for the
purpose of *understanding* life they may be separated in
thought, provided always that the student recognises such
a separation as being wholly unreal and for the purpose
of a deeper comprehension only. To ' lift them into the
higher psychic centres ' means to concentrate all desires
and emotions in the one supreme desire of hope ; to illuminate the problems of the mind by the truth that faith
alone can teach ; to subordinate all purposes of life to the
one supreme purpose of love—or to demand of the soul
penitence, as the purifying of desire ; faith as the regulation
of thought ; and Christian zeal as the direction of purpose
to the service of God and man.

[1] *Op. cit.* p. 416.

First of all, because as we have seen it comes first in time in the beginnings of mission or pastoral work, we must consider the regulation of emotion and desire. 'Repentance' is the name which, in accordance with our Lord's teaching, we have given to the act or succession of acts by which desires are purified; by which the soul expresses a distaste for all that offends God and a desire for all that is of His giving. 'Penitence,' 'contrition,' or (if it be preferred) 'hope' with its twin sister 'fear,' are names for the habit of mind by which such distastes and desires are maintained as permanent elements in character.[1]

That such a regulation of the emotions is essential to the Christian life can hardly be denied ; a man must be the master, not the slave, of his passions. But the question is not as easy as that ; the problem with many earnest minds is rather, Can such a disposition be best acquired—in many cases can it be acquired at all—by definite acts or moments of sorrow for past sin ? Is repentance, in the sense of an attempt to arouse right emotions, either a desirable or a necessary factor in the lives of many Christians ? Is the desired result not better achieved by leaving the past out of sight; by leaving the dead to bury their own dead ; by concentrating thought not upon sin but upon goodness ?

The problem has been presented in three separate ways, each of which emphasises a slightly different aspect of the case. (a) It is urged that there is a large class of Christians —the *once-born* or *healthy-minded*—whose spiritual growth is so natural, regular and unchecked from childhood onwards that sin is something of which they have no real experience, and repentance therefore an unmeaning act. They are ' just men who need no repentance.' (b) It is urged that there are others who, though they have experience, and perhaps bitter experience of sin, are of a character to which emotion of any kind is foreign. They are able perhaps to *turn* from sin, but they cannot feel any concomitant *sorrow* for it ; and to urge such sorrow upon them, to appeal to emotion at all in such cases, is again to take an unnatural course. (c) A third class, again, appears—a

---

[1] ' Penitence ' and ' hope ' are bracketed together as ' causes ' of confession, *Summa*, Suppl. q. 7, a. 3.

class with real experience of sin but also with high emotional characteristics. Here emotionalism is not unnatural, but if anything *too* natural—the soul is so accustomed to a welter of sentiment that *no* emotion has more than a passing effect upon it. Nor does the evil stop there. An emotion indulged in but not responded to—a feeling of love or pity or sorrow which is enjoyed but not acted upon— is actually detrimental to character ; it confirms a senti- mental habit in which the desires—instead of leading to action—approximate more and more to the character of useless but cherished luxuries, and lead the soul away from its purpose in life.[1] Such a nature will sound the whole gamut of feeling without ever striking a note to which character genuinely responds ; it will even sin for the mere purpose of tasting again the joys of penitence—that grace may abound.

We must recognise the existence of these three types of character—the first, those whose natural spiritual growth is apparently unimpeded by serious sin ; the second, those with whom emotion of any kind is rare ; the third, those with whom it is all too common—with whom it becomes a shallow sentimentalism, without practical effect upon character.

To secure repentance and contrition from the first would seem, at first sight, unnecessary ; from the second, im- possible ; from the third, undesirable. In the once-born type, spiritual growth seems to go forward without need of exhortation, warning or reproof ; in the second, sin can be abandoned by an act of will without any stirring of feeling ; in the third, some means must indeed be adopted to secure a life of purpose rather than one of feeling, but at first sight it would appear that any appeal to the feelings themselves must be sedulously avoided.

The only way of reaching a solution of the various problems here involved lies in an examination of the place of emotion in character, and in particular of its relation to the will. Before we proceed to this, however, something must be said of the three types of character under considera- tion, and especially of the first.

[1] Cp. W. James, *Principles of Psychology*, vol. i. p. 125.

(a) The *once-born* or *healthy-minded* have been given perhaps an undeserved prominence by the writings of Professor William James; but the source of the classification in modern thought is to be found in Francis Newman's 'The Soul: Its Sorrows and its Aspirations.'[1] 'God has two families of children upon earth, the " once-born " and the " twice-born. " ' The former ' see God not as a strict Judge, not as a glorious Potentate; but as the animating Spirit of a beautiful and harmonious world: Beneficent and Kind, Merciful as well as Pure. The same characters generally have no metaphysical tendencies: they do not look back into themselves. Hence they are not distressed by their own imperfections: yet it would be absurd to call them self-righteous; for they hardly think of themselves at all. . . . Of human sin they know perhaps little in their own hearts, and not very much in the world; and human suffering does but melt them to kindness. Thus when they approach God, no inward disturbance ensues, and without being as yet spiritual, they have a certain complacency and perhaps romantic sense of excitement in their simple worship.'

Professor James regards this type of character as the product, to a large extent, of a new emphasis in theology. ' The advance of liberalism, so called, in Christianity, during the past fifty years, may fairly be called a victory of healthy-mindedness within the Church over the morbidness with which the old hell-fire theology was more harmoniously related. We have now whole congregations whose preachers, far from magnifying our sense of sin, seem devoted to making little of it. They ignore or even deny eternal punishment, and insist on the dignity rather than on the depravity of man. They look at the continual pre-occupation of the old-fashioned Christian with his soul as something sickly and sentimental and reprehensible rather than admirable; and a sanguine and "muscular" attitude, which to our forefathers would have seemed purely heathen, has become in their eyes an ideal element of Christian character.'[2]

---

[1] Third Edition, 1852, pp. 89–91. Quoted by James, *Varieties of Religious Experience*, p. 80. [2] *Op. cit.* p. 90.

At a later stage Professor James recurs to this subject in the following words : ' Within the Christian body, for which repentance of sins has from the beginning been the critical religious act, healthy-mindedness has always come forward with its milder interpretation. Repentance, according to such healthy-minded Christians, means getting away from the sin, not writhing and groaning over its commission. The Catholic practice of confession and absolution is in one of its aspects little more than a systematic method of keeping healthy-mindedness on top. By it a man's accounts with evil are periodically squared and audited so that he may start the clean page with no old debts inscribed. Any Catholic will tell us how clean and fresh he feels after the purging operation.' [1]

It has been necessary to quote these passages at length in order to bring out a point which is commonly neglected. It is clear from a comparison of them that Newman's ' once-born ' and James' ' healthy-minded ' man are two entirely different types. The first stands for a character which has had no conscious experience of sin ; the second for one which has sinned, but ' gets away from the sin ' without, in ordinary phrase, ' making a fuss about it.' We may dismiss the ' once-born ' type, therefore, as representing merely religious immaturity ; it is, in Newman's own words, ' not yet spiritual.' The soul's ascent has not yet begun ; it has yet to learn the lessons of life. The mere fact that repentance is so far foreign to its nature is no evidence that it must always be so. If the type really exists—if ' once-born ' is anything more than an unfortunate euphemism for unthinking superficiality—it exists only in the childhood of the soul ; its outlook is narrow and inexperienced ; we cannot learn from it what the requirements of a maturer spiritual life must be.

(b) We come then to our second class, to which, rather than to the ' once-born,' James' ' healthy-minded ' type really corresponds—the man who, in St. Gregory's phrase, ' forsakes his sin without repenting of it.' [2] In its rarer form, this is to be found in connection with a type of character void of emotion of every kind.

---

[1] *Op. cit.* p. 128.   [2] *De Past. Cur* iii. admon. 31.

Charlotte Brontë's Madam Beck is such a person :
'devoid of sympathy' though possessing a 'sufficiency
of rational benevolence'—'not even the agony in
Gethesmane, nor the death on Calvary, could have wrung
from her eyes one tear.' [1] With Mr. Jaggers, such characters
seem to say, 'I'll have no feelings here.' But extreme
cases of this kind are unusual. More commonly we find the
'healthy-minded' type allied to a phenomenon widely spoken
of at the present day as 'the decline in the sense of sin.'

It is commonly asserted, with reference to this phenomenon, that the modern world has 'lost the sense of sin.'
The usual implication of the statement is, that the Church
can no longer secure conversion and spiritual life by stressing
the danger and degradation of a life of sin, but should appeal
rather 'to service, to adventure,' [2] in addressing the younger
generation. It is alleged that the 'failure of the Church' is
due to her inability to adapt herself to this change of attitude
upon the part of human nature. But it is probably more
true to say that the change of attitude itself (if it has not
been exaggerated) is due to a change of emphasis in Christian
theology. *The sense of sin is deficient because the Church
has ceased to emphasise its importance.* It cannot be appealed
to, because we have ceased to foster it. This at least is
the implication of the statement quoted from William James
on a preceding page. 'Healthy-mindedness' exists because
the clergy have preferred to 'insist upon the dignity rather
than the depravity of man' ; and not *vice versa*.[3]

[1] Quoted, W. R. Sorley, *The Moral Life*, p. 119.

[2] *National Mission Report on the Evangelistic Work of the Church*, p. 13.

[3] It is, however, to be questioned whether this alleged 'decline in
the sense of sin' is really a *decline*, and not rather a *re-direction*. See
C. J. Shebbeare, *Religion in an Age of Doubt*, p. 40. ' " The ' higher
man ' of to-day," says Sir Oliver Lodge, " is not worrying himself about
his sins at all." These words no doubt contain an element of truth.
. . . Yet if future ages are led to conclude from such contemporary
testimonies that we are a peculiarly light-hearted generation, it is not
clear that they will be wholly right. . . . Is Sir Oliver Lodge himself,
indeed, a conspicuously light-hearted phenomenon ? Surely no generation has been so sensitive as ours is to the faults of its social system.
If we are less occupied than our fathers in explicit confession of personal
misdeeds, still we are much in the habit of confessing, like Daniel, " the
sins of our people," admitting at the same time our own share in the
common responsibility.' Cp. in the same sense, G. A. Coe, *Psychology of
Religion*, p. 226.

It is easy to see why recent theology should, on the whole, have taken this turn, and in doing so have produced an apparently new type of character. It is a reaction against the mere emotionalism into which the evangelical revival in so many cases deteriorated. It represents an attempt to give the will an equal share in spiritual things with the emotions ; just as the evangelical revival, following upon eighteenth-century theism, gave the emotions an equal share with the intellect. In other words, the ' healthy-minded ' character, the ' sanguine and muscular ' attitude of which Professor James speaks, is merely a reaction from emotionalism to a religion of action. As such it is spoken of in the two famous passages often quoted in its defence. One is from the Quietist Molinos : ' Would he not be a fool who going out to tilt with others and falling in the middle of the course should lie weeping on the ground, afflicting himself with reasonings about his fall ? " Man " (they would say), " lose no time ; get up quickly and take up the contest again ; for he that rises again quickly and continues his race is as though he had never fallen." ' The other is that of a more modern writer, Professor Höffding : ' Religion is not simply to be regarded as the ambulance which follows the army and picks up the wounded ; it must also be a pillar of fire leading on to victory.' [1]

There is nothing, then, in the doctrine of ' healthy-mindedness ' which invalidates the need for repentance in the Christian life. It may indeed ignore or minimise that need ; but in essence it is simply a protest against *ineffective* repentance. As such, we shall see that it emphasises what has always been a fundamental point in Christian theology. What concerns us at the moment is this : ' healthy-mindedness ' is primarily a doctrine rather than a type of character. The doctrine, indeed, has *produced* a type of character, but it is not a new type : it is in its extreme form that of the man who ' forsakes his sins without sorrowing for them,' which was known to St. Gregory. Whether such a type can do without repentance has still to be considered.

(c) Of the third type of character which has led the doctrine of repentance to be impugned—the type whose

[1] Quoted, K. Saunders, *Adventures of the Christian Soul*, pp. 66, 102.

repentance is no more than a passing luxury of emotion—we need hardly speak. It takes many forms, from shallow sentimentalism to morbid despair; but every form is the same in this, that it does not lead to spiritual development. ' Such a condition may be due to physical weakness or mental disease, and may end in religious mania; or it may be the upgrowth of a false humility, which is but a specious form of pride. Men and women will sometimes speak effusively of their sins, whilst they would resent the suggestion of a friend or of a parish priest who took them at their word and urged amendment of life.' [1]

That such a type of character is untrue to the Christian conception of penitence is obvious; and the fact that it has from time to time been produced by the preaching of penitence, while it shows that the preaching may have been ill-directed or unbalanced, is no evidence that penitence is superfluous to the Christian life.

We find, then, from our examination of these three types of character—the ' once-born,' the ' healthy-minded,' and the sentimentalist—that, whilst people do exist who are without penitence or who misuse it, there is nothing in them to warrant that it can ever wisely be dispensed with. We may therefore turn to examine its character; and we can best approach it by considering the place which emotion or feeling in general should take in religion.

2. The Place of Feeling in Religion

Penitence, in the sense in which we are using the word, is not merely sorrow for the past; it is the organisation of the whole emotional element in religion—the purification of feeling, so that nothing but what is good is desired, and nothing but what is evil is abhorred. It is in this wide aspect of its meaning—the aspect in which it corresponds to hope with its sister fear—that we are now to consider it.

[1] H. B. Swete, *Forgiveness of Sins*, p. 155. The passage refers particularly to the ' morbid sense of sin,' which is the ' result of excessive and unbalanced self-introspection, and refuses to believe the divine love or to accept the divine gift '; but its application is general to all sentimentalism.

(a) First of all, it is evident that *feeling is not the most important feature in repentance or in any other aspiration of the spiritual life.* Action—spiritual achievement or progress —enhanced love and service of God and our neighbour— takes precedence of everything else. And therefore no one need be troubled if he cannot discern in himself the heights and depths of passion which he knows the saints to have had. He should ask for such passionate love of God and sorrow for sin, for they are gifts of the greatest value ; he should hope to realise them in his own experience ; but he is not to force them into an unnatural growth, nor despair if he cannot feel them. The Supplement to the ' Summa Theologica ' marks this clearly in the matter of penitence by a distinction between ' essential ' and ' emotional ' sorrow for sin.[1] Of these the former ' resides in the will, and is that by which we disavow the evil we have done, and repent of it by an act that is not sensibly felt ; the latter has its seat in the emotional part of the soul, and is only an overflow of the act of the will.'

Commenting on this, Scaramelli says : ' Everything belonging to the essence of contrition proceeds from the will. It is not a feeling of the sensitive part of our nature. And sorrow of the will, not mere emotion of the feelings, is required for confession. The feeling of sorrow is a sympathetic correspondence [of the emotions] with the regret or disavowal of the will, and it does not depend upon us to feel it or not, since it affects the sensitive appetite ; which, as the Angelic Doctor observes, at times obeys and as frequently disobeys the superior part of the soul. Thus it may frequently happen that the will is sincerely repentant without making any impression on the emotional part of the soul ; so that one who is really penitent may not appear to himself to have any contrition at all. If then the director finds that his penitent asks God for the necessary sorrow, and uses all his endeavour to stir it up, at least in his will, and is further resolved to sin no more, he may relieve that penitent's mind from all scruple, and remove all anxiety, by assuring him that he has the necessary sorrow, even

[1] *Summa,* Suppl. q. 1. a. 2 ; q. 3, a. 1 (from *Sent.* iv. dist. 17, q. 2, a. 1, q. 3).

though he feel it not, and though his heart be harder than flint.'[1]

(b) And just as feeling is not the most important outcome of repentance, or of any other religious impulse, so we may add that *if it is the only outcome, the result is bound to be disastrous.* This surely is St. Paul's meaning when he distinguishes between the sorrow of the world which bringeth death and godly sorrow leading to repentance and life.[2] The 'Summa' recognises, in addition to the crude emotionalism which is simply the 'overflow' of the will, two other forms of sorrow for sin, corresponding roughly to St. Paul's—*attrition* and *contrition.*[3] Contrition arises from *filial fear :* from that true love of God as a Father which cannot fail to move the will to amendment of life : which is indeed identical with the 'zeal of love '—the devotion of the will, and with it the whole personality, to God's service. Attrition, whilst not wholly independent of love for God, is mainly an outcome of *servile fear* [4]—the fear, that is, of evil consequences to oneself from sin either in this world or the next.

It is clear that attrition, in this sense, while it may produce a cessation of particular sins, will effect little if any change for the better in character.[5] It is often no

---

[1] *Directorium,* Treat. i. § 341 ; cp. *ibid.* Treat. i. § 187 ; G. Herbert, *Country Parson,* chap. 33 ; W. W. Webb, *Cure of Souls,* p. 30 n. ; V. Lehodey, *Ways of Mental Prayer,* p. 100.

[2] 2 Cor. vii. 9–11. Cp. Ecclus. iv. 21 on the two kinds of shame.

[3] *Summa,* Suppl. q. 1, aa. 2, 3. Cp. *Sent.* iv. d. 17, q. 2, a. 1 ; and *infra,* p. 249, note 3 ; W. W. Webb, *op. cit.* p. 24 ; F. G. Belton, *Manual for Confessors,* pp. 23–31. The distinction was recognised as early as Clement of Alexandria : τοῦ μετανοοῦντος δὲ τρόποι δύο · ὁ μὲν κοινότερος, φόβος ἐπὶ τοῖς πραχθεῖσιν, ὁ δὲ ἰδιαίτερος, ἡ δυσωπία ἡ πρὸς ἑαυτὴν τῆς ψυχῆς ἐκ συνειδήσεως (*Strom.* iv. 6).

[4] Servile fear is *timor poenae*—fear of punishment ; filial fear, *timor culpae*—fear of incurring the guilt of offending the Father. St. Thomas recognises also *timor mundanus,* ' when a man turns *from* God because of evils which he fears,' and *timor initialis,* a state intermediate between servile and filial fear. *Summa,* ii. 2, q. 19, a. 1.

[5] Such, at least, was the opinion of Bishops Bull and Jeremy Taylor. See E. T. Churton, *Use of Penitence,* p. 144. On the other hand, cp. *infra,* Chap. VII. p. 148. See also Augustine *in i Joann.* iv. 18, ' Si nullus timor, non est quâ intret caritas ' ; and cp. J. A. Bengel, *Gnomon,* on the same passage, where the part played by fear, servile and filial, in progress is expressed as follows : ' Varius hominum status : sine timore et amore ;

more than the substitution of one form of selfishness for another. Remorse, fear of consequences, respect for convention and public opinion, a sense of folly committed—these are the emotions of attrition ; and it can scarcely be said that any one of them is better than the sinful purpose which perhaps they may inhibit. Indeed, if they are successful in inhibiting it, the soul may be in a worse condition than before. It may pride itself upon having abandoned sin, whilst in reality it has merely exchanged a gross for a subtle form of self-love.

(c) But although the emotion of sorrow for sin is not the most important feature in repentance, and may, if wrongly motived, even be a barrier to progress, we must not on that account conclude that emotion is altogether superfluous. So far from this being the case, we may fairly maintain that *the act of turning from sin can in no way be so well motived and fortified as by sorrow for sin committed and desire for grace and forgiveness.* The sense of sin is essential to penitence in its highest form, even though in the earlier stages it sometimes appears to be wholly absent. The fullness of the Christian life can never be attained unless the desires, as well as the will, are wholly directed towards God and away from sin ; and though penitence, as we have seen, is idle without a redirection of will as well, yet we shall not be wrong in maintaining our original definition of it as the purification of desire, and in asserting that purified desires are of the essence of the Christian life.

Evidence to this effect accrues from all sides, and from widely different points of view. Psychology, metaphysics, Christian experience all concur in the same conclusion. We have quoted Professor James as the chief supporter of the doctrine of ' healthy-mindedness,' yet even he is forced to conclude that as a philosophy of life it is inferior to a point of view which emphasises the sense of sin ; and such a point of view, we may surely add, is only possible

cum timore sine amore ; cum timore et amore ; sine timore cum amore.'
For the seventeenth-century controversies about attrition, see 1. von Döllinger and F. H. Reusch, *Geschichte der Moralstreitigkeiten,* vol. i. pp. 70–94.

to one who has *felt* the burden of sin. His words are worth quoting, both for their truth and for their picturesqueness:

'Unexpectedly from the bottom of every fountain of pleasure, as the old poet said, something bitter rises up; a touch of nausea, a falling dead of the delight, a whiff of melancholy, things that sound a knell. . . . Even if we find a man so packed with healthy-mindedness as never to have experienced in his own person any of these sobering intervals, still if he is a reflecting being, he must generalise and class his own lot with that of others; and doing so, he must see that his escape is just a lucky chance and no essential difference. . . . What kind of frame of things is it of which the best you can say is, "Thank God, it has let me off clear this time!" Is not its blessedness a fragile fiction? . . . Take the happiest man, the one most envied by the world, and in nine cases out of ten his inmost consciousness is one of failure. . . .

'We are bound to say that morbid-mindedness ranges over the wider scale of experience, and that its survey is the one that overlaps. The method of averting one's attention from evil, and living simply in the light of good, is splendid so long as it will work. . . . But there is no doubt that healthy-mindedness is inadequate as a philosophic doctrine, because the evil facts which it refuses positively to account for are a genuine portion of reality; and they may after all be the best key to life's significance, and possibly the only openers of our eyes to the deepest levels of truth. . . .

'The completest religions would therefore seem to be those in which the pessimistic elements are best developed. Buddhism, of course, and Christianity are the best known to us of these. They are essentially religions of deliverance; the man must die to an unreal life before he can be born into their real life.' [1]

More soberly, and with an abundance of statistical tables, Starbuck traces the psychological value of emotions in religion, and particularly with reference to repentance. Without entering into the details, which occupy many pages

[1] *Op. cit.* pp. 136, 163, 165.

of his 'Psychology of Religion,' we may summarise his conclusions as follows :—

(i) The emotional element, and especially the sense of sin, is far more dominant in cases of spontaneous conversion than in cases of normal growth ; *even where the person converted has previously led an upright life* (p. 69).

(ii) By comparing the final condition of those who have experienced spontaneous conversion with those who have grown steadily to religious maturity, it appears that the former show less tendency to relapse,[1] greater activity and initiative, a deeper sense of union with God, and more sympathy and altruism than the latter (pp. 357-372) ; though it is true that they also show less intellectual interest, and less effort at self-regulation.

Statistics procured, as Starbuck's were, by the *questionnaire* method, are, of course, peculiarly liable to error, as has often been pointed out.[2]   But speaking wholly apart from the statistics, the writer gives us reason to believe that his experience justifies our conclusion.   'A few persons,' he says, ' seem to have an uneventful [religious] development, because they do not leave the religion of childhood ; perhaps never wake up to an immediate realisation of religion. They raise the question whether it would not have been conducive to growth even to have suffered a little on the rack of storm and stress.'[3]

Naturally enough Dr. Starbuck, as a psychologist, draws only the minimum conclusion from the facts he quotes. Far more outspoken is the dictum of Christian experience. Scaramelli, for example, warns his readers against thinking

---

[1] This may at first seem extraordinary to those whose experience of ' missions ' has led them to suspect the permanence of many apparent ' conversions.'   When, however, it is considered that among those who reach religious maturity by normal development must be included the many thousands of boys and girls who present themselves for confirmation with every apparent intention of perseverance, and then fail almost entirely to justify their promises, the conclusion is not by any means unwarranted.

[2] J. Welton, *Psychology of Education*, p. 48 ; G. A. Coe, *Psychology of Religion*, pp. 44-47.   The only limitation Starbuck appears to admit to his method is that its results are not necessarily true of ' savages, statesmen or Catholics '—psychology, like poverty, making strange bedfellows (*op. cit.* p. 13).

[3] *Op. cit.* p. 310.

that *any* beginner in the Christian life can possibly have any great spiritual strength, however highly he appear to be endowed with virtue. Such strength ' can only be acquired amidst temptations, afflictions and contradictions, and after repeated victories over ourselves. True virtue cannot possibly be found in beginners, who cannot have stood the test of many and serious conflicts.' [1] It is true that he is not here explicitly speaking of the need for repentance ; but he *is* urging that the first stage of the spiritual life must be given, however little it appear to be necessary, to long and patient discipline of the emotions, in which as we have seen repentance, or the conscious expression of hatred towards sin, is a fundamental element. We may paraphrase his meaning thus for our purposes : there is no sin of which careful introspection will not show the earnest Christian some trace in himself ; and until he knows, at least in some degree, the strength of each several sin, he is not wholly armed against it. Careful self-examination will reveal the nature of the sin, even in embryo ; repentance—the adoption of an attitude hostile to the sin—will give strength to resist it if ever it rises in force against the soul.[2]

Repentance, then, in the wide sense in which we use the word, is necessary for the soul. First, because without the sense of sin we cannot frame a true philosophy of life ; faith will be void of many of its noblest elements ; large parts of the creed will be unmeaning. We cannot approach an understanding of the Cross unless we share, to some slight extent at least, the hatred of sin and the passion for purity which led the Saviour to it. Second, because it

---

[1] *Op. cit.* Treat. i. § 37.
[2] Compare the following on Hosea x. 11 : ' Cattle being unmuzzled by law at threshing time, loved this best of all their year's work. Yet to reach it they must first go through the harder and unrewarded trials of ploughing and harrowing. Like a heifer, then, which loved harvest only, Israel would spring at the rewards of penitence, the peaceable fruits of righteousness, without going through the discipline and chastisement which alone yields them. Repentance is no mere turning, or even re-turning. It is a deep and ethical process—the breaking-up of fallow ground, the labour and long expectation of the sower, the seeking and waiting for Jehovah till Himself send the rain ' (G. A. Smith, *Book of the Twelve Prophets*, chap. xxii.).

is the main source of sympathy with others, of perseverance and of communion with God. Lastly, because it alone gives us the experience and strength which will enable us to resist the onset of sin. Many other virtues spring from it, no doubt ; perhaps the whole may be summed up in a sentence of Dr. Ottley's quoted by Dr. Burn [1] : ' Penitence is often the unsuspected source of joyousness, simplicity, evenness of mind, a child-like spirit, and thoughtful tenderness for others.'

3. *Penitence in its Full Character*

Repentance, let us repeat, is the act of rousing the right emotions about sin and godliness ; penitence is the disposition which sustains those emotions when aroused. But this statement is incomplete unless we add, as the definition of contrition taught us, as well as the connection of hope with fear, that *the right emotions about sin can only be roused and sustained by the right emotions about God.*

The former indeed are necessary to the Christian life, but they can only grow upon the stem of the latter. And therefore in this respect, as in every other, spiritual progress can only be achieved by those whose hearts and minds are set upon God.

We must, however, reserve the question of *how* true penitence is to be roused and fostered, both in the normal soul and in the ' once-born,' ' healthy-minded,' and sentimental types, for later chapters. At present we have to analyse the conception of penitence and arrive at a conclusion as to its full and perfect character.

Writers on the psychology of religion are accustomed to devote many pages to descriptions of the emotions accompanying repentance. Often, too, the material for this description is drawn from the autobiographical records of men and women who have experienced spontaneous conversion in its most violent and painful forms. Such a treatment of the subject, while no doubt legitimate, is nevertheless misleading. It suggests—what we have seen to be wholly untrue—that emotions of this

---

[1] Introduction to Andrewes' *Preces Privatae*

description are the most important feature in conversion ; it suggests also that true repentance cannot have taken place unless the emotions in question have been experienced in their most violent form. Often enough the records to which reference is made must be regarded as the quite abnormal outpourings of morbid and neurotic souls ; the tendency of religious psychology is to represent them as normal and natural.

We shall not be wrong if we discard all such evidence as suspect, and turn to the saner atmosphere of the Bible for our material. There indeed we find an abundant analysis of the emotions which go to make up the sense of sin. This is particularly the case with the Old Testament. In the New Testament sorrow for the past is merged in joyous expectation of the future ; even in our Lord's teaching repentance, as has often been noticed, ' falls into the background before the wider conceptions of faith and the new life.' But the penitential Psalms, and such deeply moving passages as the ninth chapters of Ezra and Daniel, the seventh chapter of Job, and much of Jeremiah and Ezekiel, will give all we need. And we shall recognise, further, that the Bible is never content with emotionalism. It demands also certain objective actions of repentance designed to lay the foundations of the new life. Without these mere feeling is of no avail.

Putting together the evidence from these sources, we may summarise briefly the emotions which together characterise the sense of sin. *Shame and confusion* are there (Gen. iii. 7, 8 ; Ezra ix. 6 ; Jer. xxxi. 19) ; *hatred of oneself* (Job xl. 4, xlii. 6 ; Ezek. vi. 9, xx. 43 ; Ps. li. 2), sometimes expressed as a sense of *personal uncleanness*; *remorse for the waste and folly of the past* (Job xxxiii. 27), often spoken of as a lamenting, weeping or groaning (Ps. vi., xxxi. 10, xxxviii. 8, 9) ; a feeling *of burden, weariness and bondage* (Ps. vi. 6, xxxviii. 8) ; *loneliness*—for sin indeed cuts us off no less from man than from God (Ps. cii. 6, 7 ; Jer. xxiii. 39 ; Dan. ix. 18) ; *self-abasement* (2 Chron. xxxii. 26, xxxiii. 12) ; *guilt and fear* (Gen. iii. 10 ; Ps. vi. 1 ; xxxviii. 1) ; and last, and running through the fibre of it all, an *intense desire for help and deliverance*.

G

All these, we need not doubt, the Christian should hope to realise in his own experience, preparing himself for their advent by self-examination and reflection upon his alienation from God. The 'Private Devotions' of Lancelot Andrewes are an example for all time of how a Christian soul disposes himself to allow the Holy Spirit to produce in him fruits meet for repentance. Often enough the sense of sin first manifests itself in a sense of impediment, of effort frustrated, of wasted life, of inability to face the trials of circumstance. This in itself is not repentance ; it is simply the soil in which repentance most commonly grows.[1] Repentance begins when a man realises *that in part at least the impediment, though apparently external, is really within himself* ; that his own disregard of the law of God has caused the check and incompatibility with his surroundings. The priest is continually consulted by anxious Christians who are conscious of such a feeling of frustration and unhappiness ; and the first lesson he has to teach them is that they must find in themselves the cause of their lack of ease.

Other lessons that the penitent beginner must learn we have already considered. One is that, whilst the emotions of penitence are of real value, they will not produce *effective* contrition unless they are based upon the love of God. Mere self-pity is not repentance, nor yet a conviction that one has wasted one's opportunities or been guilty of egregious folly. ' Except in relation to God (and to other people) the sense of sin is only selfish regret and morbid remorse. It is only a mood of the " morning after." '[2]

Why is it, we may ask, that only love for God will produce effective contrition ? The answer surely lies in the character of God as revealed in the New Testament. The purpose of contrition, of repentance, is to be the gateway to a new life ; and a new life is only possible in the light of hope. Mere regret for the past can never produce a change of character, if unaccompanied by a guarantee of a better future. Such a guarantee, foreshadowed in

---

[1] Thus *Summa*, Suppl. q. 2, a. 1 : ' Regret for lost strength is not in essence contrition, but rather its source ; it is from this that contrition springs.'

[2] Rev. N. Talbot in *The Modern Churchman*, vol. viii. p. 237.

the Old Testament, is given in the New : God has commended His love to us, in that while we were yet sinners
Christ died for us. In this we know ourselves loved with
a love that is able to overcome all impediments in ourselves ; and shame for the past and hope for the future
spring to life together. With the heroine of 'The Egoist'
we can exclaim, ' To know oneself loved, that is shame ! '—
and not shame alone, but hope of amendment too.[1]

This third lesson, that repentance is idle unless it is
the gateway of the new life, is enforced with overwhelming
emphasis both in the Old Testament and the New. ' Cease
to do evil, learn to do well '[2] is the burden of all that the
Bible teaches about repentance ; it is a turning, or rather
a re-turning from sin to God ; a process of convalescence,
as William Law would have us think.[3] Three preliminary
acts are required in this process ; acts both to initiate
us into the new life, and to fix our resolution by converting
it at once into something concrete. We may regard them
as the necessary outward concomitants of penitence. They
are respectively *confession of sin, reparation* and *amendment.*

The penitent sinner must *confess* his sins, to God at all
events, often enough to man as well. This confession to
man as well as to God is explicitly required or openly performed in many cases (Lev. v. 5 ; Num. v. 7 ; Josh. vii. 19 ;
I Sam. xiv. 43, xv. 24 ; 2 Sam. xii. 13 ; Matt. iii. 6 ; Acts
xix. 18 ; James v. 16)—even if we do not accept the
conclusion of Westcott (Commentary on I John i. 9) that
ὁμολογεῖν τὰς ἁμαρτίας means not merely to acknowledge
sin, but to ' acknowledge it openly in the face of men.'

Penitential theology recognises no doubt certain sins
for which confession even to a priest is not desirable ;[4]

---

[1] Cp. I John iv. 19, and Aug., *De Cat. Rud.* iv.: ' There is no mightier
invitation to love than to anticipate in loving.'

[2] Isa. i. 16, 17.

[3] *Serious Call,* chap. 18.

[4] Sins, namely, the confession of which might almost certainly bring
serious moral harm to the penitent or his confessor. Even so, Roman
Catholic theologians hold that the penitent is only excused from confessing them if (*a*) it is impossible to find another confessor ; (*b*) the
confession cannot be put off ; and (*c*) all other sins or circumstances are
confessed. See Schieler-Heuser, *Theory and Practice of the Confessional*
pp. 199, 203–205 ; W. W. Williams, *Moral Theology of the Sacrament
of Penance,* pp. 44 *sqq.*

and it has always been a part of Christian doctrine that
venial sin can be expiated by the ordinary means of religion
without the assistance which confession to a priest
undoubtedly gives.[1]   But in general it cannot be doubted
that definite confession of sin committed, before man as
well as before God, is a means to spiritual progress sanctioned
and encouraged both by the Bible and the Church, though
much neglected in the Church of England to-day.[2]

The penitent must also perform such *reparation* for his sin
to those he has injured as is possible in the circumstances[3]
(Exod. xxii. 1; 1 Sam. xii. 3; 2 Sam. xii. 6; Luke xix. 8).
To omit this is an almost certain sign of unreal penitence.
Reparation also must include *apology*, wherever the latter
can be made without spiritual harm to the person injured.
The third external condition of repentance is of course *a
definitely expressed purpose of amendment of life* (Jer. vii. 3;
Dan. iv. 27; 1 Pet. iv. 8)—a resolution to forsake sin and
to adhere to the service of God.   'Afterwards he repented
and went' is the shortest and yet the best summary of the
essence of penitence that man could wish for.

It remains only to see how these indications of the
character of repentance were taken up in the penitential
theology of the Church.   As the external requirements
of true repentance the same three conditions were insisted
on—confession, reparation[4] and amendment.   The subjective requirements were summarised under four headings :
repentance must be *internal* (of the heart, that is to say,
not of the lips or feelings) ; *supernatural* (motived by love
to God) ; *supreme* (willing to do *anything whatever* in order
to escape from sin and live a godly life) ; and *universal*
(covering all branches of thought, life and conduct ; and not
merely one or two).[5]   With such a summary it is impossible

---

[1] See references *infra*, Chap. XI. p. 252.

[2] For further considerations as to the place of sacramental confession
in the Church of England, see *supra*, pp. xvi, 23; *infra*, pp. 161, 255.

[3] For a discussion of cases in which a penitent is excused from making
reparation see T. Slater, *Moral Theology*, vol. i. pp. 437–451.

[4] Including *satisfaction*, which in one aspect is a form of reparation
towards God.   See *infra*, p. 207.

[5] Slater, *op. cit.* vol. ii. p. 156 ; Schieler-Heuser, *op. cit.* pp. 98 ff.
Cp. *Summa*, Suppl. q. 1, a. 1 (from *Sent.* iv. d. 17, q. 2, a. 1 *et seq.*) on the
derivation and meaning of ' contritio.'

to disagree ; its implications will be more fully discussed
on a later page.[1]

4. *The Duration of Penitence*

Complaints are sometimes made by good Christians as
to the frequency and vehemence of acts of confession in
the services of the Church. They find it unreal to repeat
the general confession at Evensong after saying it at Matins ;
they cannot elicit any emotion responsive to the words
' miserable sinners ' in the Litany. This raises a very
real question. Certain emotions and resolutions connected
with sin must be stirred up at the beginning of the Christian
life ; is it however necessary that, once a soul has turned
to God, it should *continue* to feel those same emotions
and resolutions all its life ? Must the quest for penitence
be lifelong, or may it cease with the first act of renuncia-
tion which begins the Christian pilgrimage ?

On this point history reveals a complete change of
attitude on the part of the Church. Her earlier teaching
demanded of the baptized Christian so high a degree of
purity that the possibility of a renewal of penitence being
required seemed almost inconceivable. ' Baptismal penitence and remission ought to be the only penitence and
absolution of the new life.' [2] Trifling impediments or
set-backs in the spiritual pilgrimage there would be, no
doubt ; but they could be swept aside or made good
by the vehemence and impetus of the Christian's daily
prayer. Later it was found that mortal sin *did* occur
after baptismal grace had been conferred. Christian
charity and hope forbade the Church to believe that such
sin could cut a soul off eternally from God ; and therefore
confession and penance were allowed as a ' second plank ' [3]
by which the sinner might rescue himself from utter ship-
wreck. Even so, he might only sin mortally *once* after
baptism ; a second sin cut him off from the communion

---

[1] *Infra*, Chap. V. pp. 114 ff.
[2] H. B. Swete, *Forgiveness of Sins*, p. 144.
[3] Tertullian, *De Poenit.* 7.

though not (except by his own act) from the discipline
and care of the Church, until his deathbed.[1]

Later ages saw this early rigorism even more drastically
relaxed. The process and its results are beautifully described
by Canon Lacey in his 'Conscience of Sin.'[2] 'Consciousness
of habitual sin was not to be denied. But the darkness
was illuminated by a new light. If sin was habitual, it was
found that penance might also be habitual. Not many
things that we owe to the Middle Ages are worth preserving,
but this is one of them ; and we owe it chiefly to the
preaching of the Friars. It is not surprising that the sons
of St. Francis, who renewed in his own person all the sweet-
ness of the gospel, should have found a new method of
applying to the moral weakness of mankind the healing
power of the gospel. The penitential discipline of the
Church, remaining the same in principle, became a new
thing in practice. Absolution was free to all comers, even
for the worst of sinners. Such procedure would have seemed
intolerable to the saints of an earlier age ; the Apostles,
I should say, never dreamt of anything like it ; but the
roots of it are in the teaching of our Lord Himself.[3]

'The Christian life is become a life of penance. Not
sinners only but saints are penitents ; and advance in
holiness does but deepen penitence. The holiest men and
women make the fullest and most tearful confessions. We
seem to be far removed from that fresh vigour and cheer-
fulness of the beginnings of the gospel. And yet it is not
really so. The Christian community [indeed] has lost
confidence ; sin is taken as a matter of course. . . . But
for the individual penitent there is still the old freshness of

---

[1] J. Tixeront, *Histoire des Dogmes*, vol. iii. p. 390. It is possible,
however, that the rigours of this system were mitigated by a *private*
absolution, which (a) forestalled the public readmission to communion
in cases where a long penance was imposed ; and (b) gave some relief to
conscience in cases of grave sin *after* the 'second plank' had been used.
See E. T. Churton, *Use of Penitence*, pp. 62, 80, 81, 84 ; P. Batiffol, *Études
d'Histoire et de Théologie Positive*, p. 209. The possibility is strongly
contested by many authorities.

[2] P. 96. The whole process is fully described by Tixeront and Batiffol,
opp. citt.

[3] We may instance, for example, the command to forgive 'unto
seventy times seven.'

renewal, the same joyous hope. With a difference : there is still the splendour of conversion ; but now it is Christians who are converted. And conversion is not one great crisis of a life, as it was for St. Paul or St. Augustine. It is a frequent renewal.'

For many different reasons we have seen that this must be so. Contrition is not servile, but filial fear. It does not cease, like that of a slave, when the penalty has been paid ; it continues, like the sorrow of a son for an offence against his father, even when that offence has been forgiven.[1] Sin, too, though repentance for it may win even greater grace than was in the soul before, leaves an indelible impression ; ' the man never gets back to his first innocence ' ;[2] here is matter for regret. Or, again, we may return to our definition of penitence as the regulation of desire, and realise that such regulation cannot take place in a moment, but must continue for a life-time, growing wider and deeper as desire itself is widened and deepened by experience. Indeed, it must be impossible, as Scaramelli shows, for a child in the earlier stages of the spiritual life to know the full force of penitence : it is just because of this impossibility that the ' healthy-minded ' doctrine of the superfluity of repentance has so specious an appeal. The prodigal, the penitent thief, St. Peter at his call, had each some degree of contrition ; but it was small compared with that which characterises the mature Christian life of the saints. ' When sorrow ends, penitence dies.'[3]

There is an even deeper reason why continued penitence should be an invariable element in the Christian life. The solidarity of mankind extends to sin ; every member of a community shares both in the virtues and the guilt of the rest. If one suffer, all suffer with him ; if one sin, all sin with him. This, as was pointed out by Dr. Moberly, is

---

[1] *Summa*, Suppl. q. 4, a. 1 (from *Sent.* iv. dist. 17, q. 2, a. 4) ; cp. Jeremy Taylor, *Duct. Dub.* bk. i. chap. 1, rule 2 : ' True peace of conscience is always joined with a holy fear.' Yet love will gradually cast out fear : thus Augustine, *Serm.* 348 (ed. Ben.) : ' Tanto minor sit timor, quanto patria quo tendimus propior ; major enim timor debet esse peregrinantium, minor propinquantium, nullus pervenientium.'

[2] *Summa*, Suppl. *loc. cit.*

[3] [Aug.] *de ver. et fals. poen.* chap. xiii.

one of the central truths of the Atonement ; by identifying Himself with us our Lord ' became sin for us ' and expiated our sins by His life of perfect sacrifice. He is the perfect Penitent.[1] For this reason, then, above all others, Christians should endeavour to stir up penitence in themselves all through their lives. If a man is honestly able to say that he has little in his own heart for which to be sorry, and that God, since his last failure and restoration, has blessed him beyond measure with virtue and spiritual strength— and there ought at least to be times when every Christian can say this of himself—there remains yet for him a higher task of penitence. Let him try to identify himself in heart with the sinful world around him ; to feel the burden of its sin as though it were his own ; and so by prayer, contrition and constant pleading of the sacrifice of Christ, attempt to make that burden lighter for those who have not yet learnt the way of penitence for themselves.[2] In strict logic, perhaps, this ' sorrow for the sins of others ' cannot be called ' contrition ' ;[3] but may not this be because it is contrition raised to so high a degree of mystic worth that it has overflowed into something ineffable which human logic is altogether unable to embrace ?

5. *The Signs of Growing Penitence*

We conclude, then, that the instinct of the Church is right in prescribing the quest of penitence for us at all stages of Christian experience. By what means the priest may help men to acquire and deepen it is a question we reserve for later treatment. Here it will be enough to consider the signs by which its presence and growth may be recognised.

A decline in sinfulness is the first sign of true penitence, as it is also the greatest. With it will go an increasing

---

[1] The explanation of this paradox lies in the fact that perfect penitence must consist in looking at sin as God looks at it ; it can, therefore, only be experienced by One Who shares the divine nature in its fullness—Who is, in fact, Himself sinless.

[2] Cp. Neh. i. 6 ; Daniel ix. 3–20. For instances in the lives of the saints see A. Chandler, *Cult of the Passing Moment*, pp. 106–113.

[3] *Summa*, Suppl. q. 2, a. 5.

humility, shown both in willingness to accept reproof and advice, and a decline in the tendency to find excuses for sin, as also a constant hopefulness for God's pardon and assistance to ultimate victory. With regard to others, the growth of penitence must produce a greater sympathy for their sufferings under temptation, greater tenderness when they fall, a greater readiness to forgive them for injuries done. ' It is oneself one cannot forgive when one denies forgiveness to others ' [1]—the connection between penitence and the forgiveness of others has rarely been more incisively expressed than in this sentence. And a last sign of true penitence is that it will manifest a growing anxiety for the spiritual welfare of others : it is the great missionary motive. A man who has learnt to abhor sin in himself, and who has suffered the bitter pains of remorse and humiliation, will scarcely be willing to leave others to a like torture without some attempt at help.[2]

So too the signs of *defective* penitence are clear. Among them are unwillingness to make reparation or to keep oneself out of temptation ; despair of the possibility of amendment (for he who has learnt the true character of sin will never rest till he has eradicated it) ; the expectation of immediate release from temptation or from punishment consequent upon sin—for the man who repents simply to achieve worldly or spiritual peace is only making a bargain with God. A morbid interest in little sins is a sign that a motive of intellectual or even emotional interest has been touched rather than genuine contrition. Lastly, we may say that an unbalanced character, a character alternating between hope and despair, between exaltation and depression, is a sign of defective penitence ; for the gift of penitence should be a stabilising force, directing the soul to calm, unswerving hope in God, and steady progress towards perfection.

[1] R. L. Stevenson, *Prince Otto*.
[2] Cp. St. Paul's list of the offspring of true penitence, 2 Cor. vii. 11.

CHAPTER IV

FAITH

1. *The Problems of Faith*

WE are to consider in this chapter the problem of the consecration of the mind to the service of God. To this consecration—following the definition of Jeremy Taylor—we give the name of *faith*, considered as a theological virtue. In so using this great Christian word we are admittedly forcing it into an unnatural isolation, and severing it from the wonderful associated ideas of loyalty and self-committal to our Lord with which Christian piety has always surrounded it. But in a psychological and ethical inquiry such a limitation of meaning is almost essential; for unless we define faith with primary reference to its intellectual character, it becomes almost indistinguishable from hope and love. We have a certain warrant for assigning this very limited meaning to the word in the use of πίστις and πιστεύειν in the New Testament; [1] but our main ground is

---

[1] In the strictly limited sense of ' to believe,' ' to hold as true,' the verb πιστεύειν is used some half-dozen times in the New Testament (e.g. Matt. xxiv. 23; John vi. 69, viii. 24; Acts viii. 37, ix. 26; Rom. vi. 8; James ii. 19)—not a large proportion of the two hundred or so instances in which it occurs. Both Simon Magus and the devils are spoken of as ' believing '—cases in which the word can have no meaning except a purely intellectual one. The occasional use of ' the faith ' as a phrase expressing the compendium of Christian belief (e.g. Jude 3, 20) is in accordance with this use. In about forty cases the verb (used with the dative) is ambiguous, meaning either to ' believe in a person ' or to believe that what he says is true. In sixty cases (with prepositions) the meaning is almost entirely expressed by the phrase to ' have confidence in ' God or Christ or the promises, the intellectual factor being almost entirely neglected. In the remainder of the instances of its use (about fifty per cent.) it is employed absolutely—' to believe ' simply; in these we may fairly say that, if the intellectual element is not absent, it is certainly not primary. For full discussions see Sanday and Headlam, *Romans*, pp. 31–34; T. B. Strong, *Christian Ethics*, pp. 190 ff.; W. R. Inge, *Faith and its Psychology*, pp. 8 ff.

that of expediency in definition. A compendious term is required to cover the intellectual element in religion ; and by common and traditional consent ' faith ' is the one of the three theological virtues selected to perform the duty—though at this point consent may be said to stop abruptly. For the moment we attempt to define faith, even in this limited sense, the widest divergencies of opinion become manifest.

The reader will indeed by this time have recognised how extraordinarily difficult it is to define closely any of the elements that enter into the spiritual life. Will, desire, reason ; penitence, faith, zeal—these are words whose meanings continually merge into one another ; and the cause of this merging of meanings is that the *things* themselves (if we can call them things at all) are none of them self-contained ; they do not exist as separate entities. There is no phase of consciousness into which the affective, the conative, and the intellective dispositions do not enter ; and it is impossible to draw a line at any point and say, for example, ' Here reason ends and will begins.' So too with penitence ; it has implications both of an intellectual and of a purposive character, and no one can say at what stage the *essential fact* of penitence can be distinguished from these implications.

But no word with which moral theology has to deal is subject to this disability to the same extent as faith. The general meaning of the word ' penitence ' is clear ; we had merely to decide at what point to limit that meaning so that the meaning of other fundamental words should not be unduly encroached upon. It would be possible to describe the whole of the spiritual life in terms of penitence or hope ; equally possible to describe it all in terms of love or of faith ; we are merely deterred from taking this course by the fact that Christian experience seems to recognise the equal importance of all three elements, though of course giving the final pre-eminence to love as the ultimate characteristic of the converted life. But with the idea of faith the problem is not merely to limit its meaning so as to allow full scope to words of equal importance ; but to decide between conflicting meanings. The implications of the word are so vast that it takes, upon different lips, meanings of exactly opposite content. This is due to two causes : one, the existence in the English language of a large number of words of kindred meaning, none susceptible of very clear definition ; the second, the vast reach of the spiritual experiences centring round the idea of faith.

(a) The English language is specially rich in words denoting various kinds and degrees of intellectual conviction, whose exact definition has never been clearly agreed upon. Such words are ' faith,' ' belief,' ' opinion,' ' knowledge,' ' understanding,' ' judgment '—we might even add ' credulity ' and ' superstition.' That each contains a delicate tinge of meaning peculiarly its own we may fully recognise ; the difficulty lies in securing agreement as to the exact shade of meaning to be assigned to it. The confusion is increased by the fact that for the two nouns *faith* and *belief* there is only one corresponding verb, *to believe*.

(b) The second difficulty is one which concerns theology more closely. The spiritual implications of faith are vast— vaster even than those of penitence ; and lead to such different conclusions as to its essential character that problem after problem is presented to the inquirer. It must be understood therefore, at the outset, that the word is here used solely to denote the offering of the intellectual element in life to the service of God.

The problems which concern the position to be assigned to faith (in the above sense) in the Christian character are as follows :—

(a) It will hardly be denied that a love of truth, and an ardent search for truth, must characterise every earnest Christian.[1] But the Church has always regarded truth in the light of a present possession as well as in that of a future prize. And here at once comes a conflict of opinion between Christian and conventional thought on the subject. For while it is commonly held that belief is without influence upon conduct, the Church has always maintained that the attempt to live the full Christian life must, as one at least of its essential conditions, involve the acceptance of certain

---

[1] *Summa*, ii. 2. q. 4, a. 2, ad 3 : ' Veritas prima quae est fidei objectum, est finis omnium desideriorum et actionum nostrorum.'

doctrines about the nature and self-manifestation of God as true. Such acceptance, in individual cases, may indeed at any given moment be implicit, inarticulate, even unrealised. But even so the Church would claim that the intellectual implications of every true Christian life, *if they were fully thought out*, would be found to involve convictions of this order ; and that as those convictions become more and more intelligible and consciously apprehended, so in proportion the life is enabled to develop more and more fully in the path of Christian perfection—its capacity for spiritual progress is increased. But this contention has to be established against a vast body of opinion which holds that belief in general—and Christian belief in particular—has no regulative value for conduct.

(*b*) If we find on examination that intellectual convictions of a Christian order are an essential condition of the mature Christian character, we have yet further questions to consider. Of these the first is that of the means by which these convictions are reached. Is it by a process of argument, akin to that which obtains, let us say, in scientific demonstration ; or by some other process ? Is ' faith,' in fact, allied with, or independent of, ' reason ' ? On this point the widest diversity of opinion has been held in the Church, but the question did not grow acute until with the expansion of the new learning it became widely suspected that the conclusions of ' faith ' and ' reason ' were seriously at variance. Till then it had been possible to hold either that faith was based upon reason ; or that, though its conclusions were doubtless in accord with those which reason would reach *if it could*, they were in general of a higher degree of certainty, and concerned with more ultimate things, than the evidential conclusions of natural investigation and argument.[1] Once, however, reason, in the guise

---

[1] *Summa*, i. q. 1, aa. 1, 2. St. Thomas' position seems to be, that there are two orders of truth—a lower, which can be apprehended by reason, and a higher, which is the subject-matter of faith. He admits, as an abstract possibility, that the latter order is essentially *reasonable* ; but tends to deny that it is to be apprehended as true by the operations of any one normal human intelligence. He never, in fact, wholly emancipated himself from the dualism of reason and revelation. See, e.g., *Contra Gentiles*, i. 3.

of science, had thrown the gauntlet down, first of all on matters which were really indifferent to theology (though in actual fact she claimed to settle them)—as, for example, the relative movement of celestial bodies, or the process of cosmogony ; but later, on questions essential to religion— questions of miracle, or divine guidance and the like—the problem became vital.

(c) In these circumstances theology tended more and more to abandon any attempt to harmonise faith and reason, and began to look for the sanction of faith in authority—the authority of a book, or of the Church, or of personal experience. This, however, led to two further problems : Which of these contesting authorities is the final one ? and, What must now be the place of reason, of evidential inquiry, in the Christian life, if authority and reason clash ? Is reason a gift of God, or a temptation of the devil ?

Theoretical questions such as these lie behind practical problems of immense importance. We may formulate the latter somewhat as follows :—

(a) Is the priest to emphasise belief or conduct most in his teaching ? Shall he put dogma before morals, or morals before dogma ?

(b) Is he to stimulate or to deprecate free inquiry as to the evidences of religion on the part of his people ?

(c) How is he to reconcile (if they conflict) the different kinds of authority—the Church, the Bible, and personal experience—with each other, as well as with the conclusions of individual thought ?

(d) What course of action is he to urge upon those who are genuinely troubled with intellectual doubts ?

These questions are familiar to every parish priest ; and there are no greater divergencies of opinion in the Church to-day than upon the answers to be given to them. Theoretical inquiry at this point, at least, is essential to moral theology ; there is no rule-of-thumb solution of the problems under discussion ; we must consider some of the philosophical difficulties which lie behind.

2. *The Intellectual Factor in Religion*

It can scarcely be denied, as we have seen, that the spiritual life must have an intellectual side ; that the activities of the mind must be brought into conformity with the purposes of God. God is a God of truth ; the offering of the intellect to God means, therefore, that it must be directed by truth. As soon, then, as the spiritual life of each Christian reaches the conscious stage, he will begin to ask himself the questions, ' What do I believe about God—about Christ—about the sacraments ? '—or, more positively, ' Do I accept such and such propositions presented to me by the Church as true ? ' Only too often there ensues a period of doubt, anxiety, and questioning of the most painful intensity ; indeed, with many Christians doubt is a recurring experience throughout their spiritual life. But little by little emerges a state of mind in which the soul is able to say, ' This is what I believe ' ; and when that state of mind is achieved the Christian has at length a *Credo* ; faith has realised some part at least of her intellectual heritage.

It is a fundamental postulate of moral theology that such a state of mind is an essential element in the spiritual life ;[1] and that this life is most likely to advance upon the line of Christian perfection, if, without violating its intellectual honesty, it can arrive at this attitude of conviction towards the primary doctrines of Christianity. But such a process will often be very gradual ; and it must never on any account be forced. Nor is it claimed that without such explicit acceptance of Christian doctrines the spiritual life is impossible even to a considerable degree ; what is claimed is that a growing apprehension of their truth and value must, at some stage or other of the Christian life, take place if that life is to be lived in all its fullness.

The proof of this assertion, as of so many more, lies with apologetics, and so is beyond the scope of the present

---

[1] *Summa*, ii. 2, q. 1, a. 4 : ' Fides importat assensum intellectus ad id quod creditur . . . per quamdam electionem . . . cum certitudine absque formidine.'

discussion. It is, however, important to recognise that
the Church has always insisted upon *works* as the necessary outcome of true faith. No more than penitence may
faith be ineffective. ' Faith without works ' was spoken of
by the schoolmen as *fides informis*—faith not manifesting
itself in the *form* of love (to distinguish it from *fides formata*
—faith so manifested) ;[1] but it would have been better if
it had been denied the name altogether. For faith,
from the first, meant not merely the acceptance of certain
propositions as true, but the acceptance of them in such a
way as to inspire a corresponding course of life, a *moral
temper* (as it is often called) of a definitely Christian cast.
It is one evidence of the weight which Christianity has always
attached to moral results, that to a large extent this moral
equivalent of faith has entirely displaced the intellectual
element in popular definitions of the word. So we find faith
defined as ' The power by which a man gives himself up to
anything '—to commerce and pleasure as well as to religion
(William Law) ; ' a receptive attitude of soul ' (Starbuck) ;
' an entire self-commitment of the soul to Jesus the Son of
God,' and so forth. John Ruskin, indeed, asserted (with
doubtful etymology) that action rather than belief was
the original connotation of the word in Latin. ' In so
far as it alone assuredly did, and it alone *could* do, what
it meant to do, and was therefore the root and essence of
all human deed, it was called by the Latins the ' doing,'
or *fides*, which has passed into the French *foi* and the
English *faith.*'[2]

Yet in spite of the insistence which the Church has always
laid, and rightly, upon the *effective* character of true Christian
faith, and the essentially faulty nature of faith that is
not effective, we are continually met by the common
assertion, ' It doesn't matter what a man believes so
long as his life is all right.' To those who hold this opinion
the very attempt to teach Christian doctrine, except on the
side of bare morality, appears a barren waste of time ;
and any effort to secure or maintain purity of doctrine by

---

[1] *Summa*, ii. 2, q. 4, aa. 3, 4, 5.
[2] *Modern Painters*, part viii. chap. 1. St. Augustine had already used
the same etymology for ' fides.'—*Ep.* 82 (ed. Ben.).

argument is regarded as even worse. This matter is therefore a very important one for the priest ; for it means that
a great part of his work, in the eyes of the world, is misdirected and valueless. And as it is essential that, if there
is any value in Christian truth at all, the priest should
never falter in his own conviction of the fact, even though
he be unable to convince others of its importance, it is worth
while to investigate the causes of this common neglect of
belief as a dominant factor in life.

(a) The first cause, no doubt, is the obvious truth that
the conduct of many professing Christians is apparently
uninfluenced by the high beliefs they hold. When D'Arcy
confessed that he had been a selfish being all his life, ' in
practice though not in principle,'[1] he was merely owning
to an anomaly of which far more flagrant instances, unhappily, may daily be observed. We may indeed go further,
and with Dr. Paget find in this miserable truth the root
of the objection not merely to doctrine as such, but to all
religion. ' While critics and apologists with their latest
weapons (or with the latest improvements of their old
ones) are charging and clashing amidst clouds of dust—
with the world still thinking that here at last is the real
crisis—the practical question between belief and unbelief
is actually being settled for the vast majority of men by
the silent and protracted conflict between the consistent and
inconsistent lives of those who alike profess themselves
Christians.'[2]

(b) A second cause of the contempt for the intellectual
element in religion must undoubtedly be the apparent
remoteness of a great part of Christian doctrine from the
affairs of everyday life. It is a regrettable fact that the
majority of the questions in dispute between different
communions—in so far, at least, as they come to the knowledge of the public—have no apparent bearing whatever on
matters of conduct. ' What does it matter,' says the
ordinary man, ' whether this or that point of theological
nicety be true or false ? Will it help me to keep a higher
standard of life ? '—and if, on casual inspection, he finds

---

[1] Jane Austen, *Pride and Prejudice*, chap. 58.
[2] *Studies in the Christian Character*, p. xxiv.

H

it will not, he dismisses it at once as merely another instance of tedious and unprofitable mental gymnastics on the part of the clerics. And as he finds one piece of doctrine or another to be remote from his daily interests, he tends more and more to condemn all doctrine as having the same futility at bottom, and to regard all religions and forms of thought as identical, ' because they are all going to the same place.'

It is to be noted in both of these popular objections to the intrusion of anything more than an intellectual minimum into religion, that the question at issue is not that of the *truth*, but that of the *value*, of the Christian doctrines. This distinction is a real and important one. Ultimately, no doubt, all truth is of infinite value ; but for practical purposes there are certain truths, in science and philosophy as well as in religion, which to the ordinary man seem of theoretical importance only. They cannot be shown to bear upon his life. We may hazard the opinion that there is, in the common mind, no rooted or widespread belief that the doctrines of Christianity are untrue. What is alleged against them is that, even if true, they are valueless.

(c) This gives us a hint of a third reason, deeper even than the two we have considered, for the popular disregard of the intellectual side of religion. It is that men can only with the greatest difficulty be brought to *test* the value of the Christian beliefs. For, as has often been pointed out,[1] to test the value of the Christian creed a man must adopt the form of life which the creed demands. Value can only be proved or disproved by experiment ; and the Christian experiment involves, as a preliminary, entrance upon the full Christian life. Few of the critics of Christianity care to make the experiment on these conditions ; the value of dogma is in effect condemned untested, because the test demands too much of the investigator. But without the test, dogma will always appear valueless.

This last, then, is the real reason why dogma is adversely criticised—its critics are loth to accept the conditions upon which alone it can be fairly tested. But the other two reasons—which may be called, in comparison, the *alleged* reasons for its condemnation—are insidious, and

[1] Cp., e.g., H. S. Holland, *Logic and Life*, p. 20.

require examination and refutation. In answer to both it may fairly be pointed out as a universal fact of life that beliefs, opinions, creeds, dogmas—however they may be called—*never fail* to influence conduct. Their influence upon it may be unnoticed—so much so as to give rise, with some justification, to the charge of inconsistency; it may be wholly inadequate in comparison with the ideal, but it is there. Instances of it occur so constantly in everyday life that it is idle to begin to quote them. Without going to the length of the Socratic assertion that virtue is knowledge— without identifying the wise man with the righteous man —we need not hesitate to affirm a hidden but very real connection between truth and morality. True convictions will *tend* (we cannot say more) to produce morality; untrue convictions will gradually lead to the toleration and justification of immorality. The issue of these influences may never be seen in their fullness in any individual life; but taken over a length of time, and in a whole society, their results will be discernible as described.

The proof of this position belongs rather to philosophy as a whole than to ethics; though evidences of it may, as we have said, be seen every day. That it is a keynote of Christian ethics we need scarcely re-assert. In the vocabulary of the New Testament, indeed, the words πίστις and πιστεύειν emphasise only faintly the importance of the intellectual element in religion. When, however, we turn from the letter of the Canon to its spirit, the matter appears in a very different light. Our Lord's promise that the truth shall make us free; St. Paul's insistence that neither an apostle nor an angel from heaven is to be listened to if he preach 'any other gospel' than that 'which ye have received'; his injunction to Timothy, repeated time and again with all the emphasis that variation can give, to 'hold fast the form of sound words'; St. James's praise of the 'wisdom which is from above'; the Seer's curse upon any who should add to or take away from the words of the book of his prophecy—all these and many other passages testify to the supreme importance of pure belief for Christian conduct.[1]

---

[1] John viii. 32; Gal. i. 8, 9; 1 Tim. i. 19; 2 Tim. i. 13, ii. 2, iii. 14; James iii. 17; Rev. xxii. 18, 19.

'It does not matter what a man believes' would have been, to the apostolic writers, a doctrine no less absurd than intolerable.

We may pause at this point to draw one or two practical conclusions which bear upon the priest's ministry, though perhaps more in his capacity as messenger to a community than as shepherd of individual souls. Yet they are important because, if he acts upon them in the course of his general preaching and exhortation, they will provide an atmosphere in which his advice to individuals will be more readily received.

(*a*) He must never fail to impress upon professing Christians the supreme importance of testifying to the value of their beliefs by increased purity and unselfishness of life. 'By their fruits ye shall know them' is, rightly, the ordinary criterion which the world applies; and though in true Christian practice there will be some things at least which the normal observer cannot understand or appreciate, there will yet be enough, and more than enough, that appeals to his innate moral consciousness to convince him of the efficacy for right action of Christian doctrine. It is when such practice is deficient, intermittent, or distorted from its true character that the casual observer is justified in concluding that doctrine is without effect upon conduct. No amount of argument will convince a man of the fallacy in this conclusion; only the example of professing Christians will be sufficient evidence.

(*b*) The priest must use every endeavour to show the relevance of each point of Christian doctrine for conduct, and the disastrous effects which must result from its being ignored. Here is required of him a grave and disciplined effort of mind to which many of us, we must in fairness confess, are unaccustomed. He must *see for himself* why such and such a doctrine is of importance for the Christian. With the primary articles of the creed this is not so difficult a task; with the secondary ones—and it is particularly the secondary ones which come into public notice, for it is to them that so much of the cleavage which separates the different Christian bodies is due—the difficulty is greatly enhanced. But the priest must be prepared to show that every secondary, or derived, point of doctrine he regards it necessary to uphold is, if not actually itself of influence upon conduct, a bulwark or outwork of one of the primary ones—that to surrender it is to endanger the whole of Christian truth, and with it the whole of Christian morality. This requires of the clergy a keen and intelligent grasp of the inseparable unity of Christian doctrine and a full understanding of all its moral implications. Nothing short of this will suffice.

(c) He must urge the same study upon all of his congregation whose powers of reasoning are sufficiently developed to undertake it. Scaramelli wisely says : ' It is a remark commonly enough made, that a large proportion of Christians transgress the law of God, and lead licentious lives, because faith has become extinct in their souls. . . . But in reality I do not think that this is the cause of all the evil ; for as far as the substance goes there is faith ; and if we sound the heart of a Catholic, no matter how loose his life may be, we shall find there is not one article of our faith, though ever so abstruse and difficult, which he does not firmly hold. The whole ruin of souls then, which we deplore in the Church, proceeds not from want of faith, but *from want of thought upon the truths taught by faith.* . . . How does it avail us that the truths of our faith have in themselves a sovereign efficacy to remove from us every vice, to keep us far from every mortal sin, if the Christian believing in these truths, does not fix his mind upon them, never gives them any real attention, never brings them into contact with his will by seriously pondering upon them ? ' [1]

This is all the more important, because the doubts which commonly gather round Christian doctrine in the later stages of adolescence are almost invariably due to a want of reflection upon, or even to a complete misunderstanding of, its character. Doctrine has often been acquired merely as a mnemonic feat, like the multiplication table, without any corresponding effort of understanding or assimilation into the fabric of character ; and with the first breath of free thought the whole structure collapses. This is perhaps

---

[1] *Direct. Ascet.*, Treat. i. § 154.

one of the commonest causes not merely of defection from the Church, but of moral failure, and it cannot be too earnestly guarded against.

(d) Wherever the priest meets with anyone who seriously professes goodwill towards Christianity, but has an honest doubt as to the truth of what it teaches, he should urge him to test the truth of the doctrines by practical experiment. Let him assume their truth as a working hypothesis, make the necessary changes in his manner of life, and, after a period sufficient for evidence to accumulate, ask himself whether he has now reasons enough to warrant his accepting them.   It is, of course, absurd for a man in a moment of stress to say, in effect, ' Well, I will see what prayer can do '—and so to turn, for a moment, to long-neglected prayers.   That is not in any sense an acceptance, even as a working hypothesis, of the *true* doctrine of prayer, or of anything but a pagan travesty of it ; nor does it allow sufficient time for an experiment.   What would be needed, as a test of the truth of prayer, would be the embracing and maintaining, over a period of reasonable duration, of the full life of prayer with all its demands.   Of the success of such a test there is every reason to be assured.

3. *Faith and Reason*

It is, therefore, a fundamental demand of Christian ethics that the moral life must have a sure foundation, not merely in right desire (or penitence), but in right belief (or faith—at all events in the narrowest sense of the word). And with faith as with penitence, it is further demanded that the Christian should neglect no effort to make it *operative*, to give it the outward *form* of loving service ; for faith without works is dead. We have next to consider *on what evidence* the priest should urge, and the Christian should accept, the truth of Christian doctrine. Are we to say, ' Receive this on the authority of the Church ' ? or, ' Examine it and see how it accords with the ordinary rules of evidence ' ? or, ' Wait until God, in answer to your prayers, commends it to you by the virtue of some supernatural grace ' ? These questions, which **are** of vast practical importance, merge in what is at first sight one of theory only—the relation between faith and reason.

By faith, using the word still in its limited sense, we mean the acceptance of the truths of Christian doctrine, whatsoever the psychological process by which such acceptance is reached. By reason, we mean the acceptance of any truth whatsoever, either by a process of argument (from premises to conclusion), or as the result of an intuitive apprehension of its self-evidence, or from a perception of its necessary coherence with the whole of truth as otherwise known to us—that is, by one of the processes commonly known as rational. The question, then, may be stated as follows : Is faith to be allied with reason—is dogma, in other words, never to be accepted by the mind except on strictly rational grounds ; or is the possibility of a conflict between faith and reason to be admitted, and, when such a conflict apparently occurs, may dogma be received as true by a process which goes beyond reason or even defies it—a process, in short, of unreasoning, or at least unreasoned, faith ?

There is no point in Christian or Christianised thought on which such widely divergent views would appear at first sight to have been held as on this. They range from the extreme rationalism of eighteenth-century theism, to the extreme obscurantism of Tertullian's ' credibile quia ineptum, certum quia impossibile,' [1] Anselm's ' credo ut intelligam,' [2] Kant's distinction between the practical and the speculative reason, the Ritschlian theory of value-judgments, and the various schools of authoritarian and mystical thought. This diversity of opinion is fully and clearly treated in many books, for example in Dean Inge's ' Faith and its Psychology.' It is enough for us here to indicate what on the whole has been the general attitude of the Church.

(a) It has generally been held that *faith and reason must*

[1] *De Carn. Christ.* 5. Though it may be doubted whether Tertullian really meant to depreciate the position of reason quite so strongly as this passage suggests.

[2] *Proslogium*, i. The epigram was already current in the time of Augustine. See his *Sermo*, 43 (ed. Ben.) : ' Intellige ut credas, verbum meum ; crede ut intelligas, verbum Dei.'

accord as far as they cover the same ground. Christian theology owed too much to pagan philosophy to condemn the processes of rational thought as ungodly or perverse. Isolated thinkers, indeed, assumed this attitude from time to time ; but the Church as a whole never wavered for long from the conviction that the human reason is a God-given power, and on that account, though it may go astray,[1] it must, if enlisted in the earnest search for truth, accord with the dictates of faith. Thus, Clement of Alexandria could say, ' Faith is a compendious knowledge of essentials, whilst knowledge is a sure and firm demonstration of the things received through faith, carrying us on to unshaken conviction ' ;[2] or the pseudo-Clementine ' Recognitions ' : ' It is not safe to commit those things to faith without reason, since truth cannot be without reason. . . . The more anxious a man is in demanding a reason, the more secure will he be in keeping his faith ' ;[3] or St. Augustine, ' Faith seeks and reason finds ' ;[4] or St. Thomas, ' We do not demonstrate [by reason] the matters of faith, but *we prove that they are not impossible.*'[5]

(*b*) Yet it is equally held by the considered judgment of the Church that *faith transcends reason in some of its most important particulars.* Evidence and argument, so far as they will go, must be adduced for the matter of faith ; but it is at all events unlikely that to any one Christian at any given time they will wholly establish the truth of what is offered to him as the intellectual implications of the full spiritual life. Some minds are too dull to achieve the labour necessary for the testing of religious truth ; all are liable to error ; few have time enough, none perhaps so great a capacity as to perceive, in a single comprehensive survey, the intelligibility of all that the Church proclaims as true.[6] It would be idle for the Christian to wait for full proof of all that is offered to his belief ; he might never achieve it in this lifetime ; he might make mistakes by the way ; the highest truths, though *provable*, may well lie

---

[1] *Summa*, i, q. 1, a. 1.   [2] Clem. Alex., *Strom.* vii. 10.
[3] *Recognitions*, ii. 69.   [4] *De Trin.* xv. 2.
[5] *Summa*, ii. 2, q. 1, a. 5.
[6] *Summa*, i. q. 1, a. 1 ; cp. ii. 2, q. 4, a. 8 ; q. 8, a. 2.

beyond the reach of proof even to the most perfect human intelligence. The Christian needs the salutary power of Christian truth *at once* ; he dare not wait, or we, at least, dare not for his own sake allow him to wait ; we must urge his acceptance of it by faith, in default of, it may be in despite of, the lagging and fallible methods of reason.[1]

This without doubt is the position which inspires the New Testament. When faith is defined as ' the substance of things hoped for and the evidence of things not seen ' (whatever the exact meaning of the words may be) ; when it is opposed to ' sight,' or ' discernment,' or ' assent ' (' confession ') ;[2] it must be regarded as something so far in advance of reason as even to appear at certain stages of thought almost opposed to it. The apparent opposition may be no more than that between the clear sight of youth and the dim vision of senility ; or between the faultless periods of an orator and the first stammerings of a child ; but it is enough to enable us to say that the two are ' quite different,' though the difference is one of degree only and not of kind. It is this vast gulf of difference between faith and reason, as it must inevitably appear to the majority of Christian people, which, with only a slight additional exaggeration, has caused the anti-intellectual tendencies already noticed of authoritarianism and mysticism. But these tendencies, in their extreme form, are unjustified. Reason may be timid, halting, and fallible in comparison with faith ; but it is on the same road and pressing to the same goal, and should be regarded not as an enemy but as an ally.

This, then, is the traditional attitude of the Church.[3]

[1] Cp. Augustine, *Ep.* 102 (ed. Ben.) : ' Sunt [quaestiones] innumerabiles quae non sunt finiendae ante fidem, ne finiatur vita sine fide.'

[2] Heb. xi. 1 ; John xx. 29 ; 2 Cor. v. 7 ; 1 Pet. i. 8 ; Rom. iv. 9, xiv. 1, 23 ; James i. 6 ; Rom. x. 9, 10. ' To discern intellectually ' (διακρίνειν) in these passages, by contrast with ' to believe,' comes to mean, first, ' the critical self-debating habit of the typical sceptic' (Hastings' *Dictionary of the Bible*, s.v. ' Doubt '), and so ' to doubt '—the very antithesis of ' faith.'

[3] Cp. H. Rashdall, *Universities of Europe in the Middle Ages*, vol. i. p. 367 : ' It is hardly too much to say that the lines laid down by St. Thomas as to the attitude of Reason towards Revelation are, amid all change of belief as to the actual content of Revelation, the lines in which, as much in the Protestant as in the mediæval or modern Roman churches, the main current of religious thought has moved ever since.'

Reason can and ought to be employed to examine, establish and confirm the intellectual position taken up by faith. But the Christian is not required, at any given moment, to be able to justify the full content of his faith on purely rational considerations; though the possibility of being able to do so is an ideal to which he may legitimately aspire. It is on some such premises as these that St. Thomas bases his conclusion that, whilst the principles of religion are to be believed on ' authority,' *the guarantee of this ' authority ' lies in the fact that some at least of its tenets are demonstrable as true by logical means, whilst the remainder are not demonstrably false.*[1]

This last phrase, however, brings to our notice a fact which must be considered further: the fact, namely, that the traditional position we have examined *dates on the whole from a period when there was little intellectual objection to the implications of the Christian creed.* And we have to decide whether the position still holds good at the present day, in which rationalist or scientific objections have reached a far greater degree of cogency.

Rationalism, as an opponent of Christianity, has indeed perhaps passed its zenith; but it is none the less a formidable danger to the Christian. In the eighteenth and nineteenth centuries it developed an attack upon the fundamentals of religion of which echoes may still be heard. Providence, free-will, miracles were all declared to be not merely unproven hypotheses of dogma, but actually at variance with those laws of the Universe which science had discovered and proved to be true. Faith and science, revelation and reason were said to be irreconcilably at variance; the man of science could not believe the truth of Christianity; the Christian must close his eyes to the discoveries of science and the syllogisms of logical argument.

It is beside the point for us to consider the growth of this phase of thought. We must, however, notice its influence upon Christian opinion. The attempt to oppose logic with logic—to support, for example, the cosmogony of the Old Testament against the evidence of geology—was quickly abandoned. Two main lines of defence of

[1] *Summa*, i. q. 1, a. 8; ii. 2, q. 1, a. 5.

traditional orthodoxy were gradually developed. The
first simply revived the obscurantist features which had
always, as we have seen, had some footing in theology;
and found in the authority of the Church or of personal
religious experience a basis for those beliefs which strict
logic impugned. To the latter of these two factors may be
ascribed the modern revival of interest in mystical literature
and methods of religion. It must be admitted, and that
cordially, that much good resulted from this line of defence,
and that it has made genuine contributions to the life of
the Church of the present generation. But as an argument
against rationalism it is fundamentally unsound, for it is
based upon the hypothesis that the free use of the human
reason is dangerous or even morally wrong for the Christian.
And that involves the tacit assumption that reason is not
in essence a gift of God at all.

Nor indeed can it be said that either authoritarianism
or mysticism are very satisfactory guides in the modern
world. St. Thomas, as we saw, based the authority of
the Church in matters of faith upon the fact that, as far
as reason went, it supported that authority; modern
apologetic of the kind we are considering appeals to
authority just on those points to which strict reason is
apparently most bitterly opposed. It can therefore quote
no justification for its appeal to authority at all; the
acceptance of belief on these grounds becomes a matter of
personal fancy alone; and there is, beside, no ground—other
than the rational one—upon which choice can fairly be made
between the conflicting authorities that, unhappily, claim the
allegiance of Christendom. ' Personal experience ' is no less
unsatisfactory a guide. Mystic states are valid only for the
mystic. They provide no fragment of a reason why their
authority should be accepted by any but himself; nor
indeed is it clear what truths, if any, their authority
guarantees even to him.[1]

The other line of defence adopted by Christian thought

---

[1] W. James, *Varieties of Religious Experience*, pp. 423-427. For a
general criticism of the opposition between reason and revelation implied
in the above types of argument, see C. C. J. Webb, *Problems in the Relation
of God to Man*, part i.; T. A. Lacey, *Nature, Miracle and Sin*, Appendix i

has proved more profitable. Taking a hint from the schoolmen—who in the midst of their intellectualism had always a doubt as to the adequacy and final validity of the laws of evidence—it began to inquire into the meaning of ' logical proof.' Newman's ' Grammar of Assent ' and Balfour's ' Defence of Philosophic Doubt ' are landmarks in this inquiry. Briefly, the result at which it arrived, and which may be said now to have been almost universally accepted, is something of this kind. There is no such thing as strictly logical proof. At the moment of accepting any intellectual conviction there comes into play a non-intellectual factor which leaps beyond the converging streams of evidence and accepts as a working hypothesis a truth to which they all point, but which none of them severally nor all of them together can finally establish. To this factor, which approximates closely to the nature of faith, Newman gave the name of the *illative sense*. So-called mathematical or exact proof is only possible in intellectual abstractions, in cases, that is, of self-evident propositions, of definitions so drawn that they contain their own proof within themselves.[1]

The reader need only consider why it is that he believes *anything*, not merely of a religious, but of a scientific or everyday character. First of all, probably, because it has been suggested to him by someone whose authority in this particular matter he recognises.[2] Secondly, because a great many other people believe it ; thirdly, because within his own experience it has proved true. It is clear that none of these reasons prove the truth of his belief, either separately or in conjunction. Authority, consensus, personal experience may all be at fault, even when pointing in the same direction. There remains one other element ; when a certain amount of converging *probable* proof (to use Butler's phrase) has been accumulated, the mind leaps to its conclusion, accepting it as a working basis for further experiment

---

[1] See J. H. Newman, *Grammar of Assent*, pp. 343–345 ; A. J. Balfour, *Defence of Philosophic Doubt*, p. 317. One of the earliest expositions of this argument is to be found in St. Augustine's treatise, *De fide rerum quae non videntur*.

[2] Thus Augustine, *De Mor. Eccl. Cath.* 3 : ' Naturae quidem ordo ita se habet, ut cum aliquid discimus, rationem praecedat auctoritas.'

as well as for life as a whole. That is the method which obtains both in science and in everyday life.[1] And the process by which the Christian accepts religious truth is exactly the same. ' Acceptance of religious dogma is not,' therefore, ' essentially in contrast, but rather is parallel with that of scientific principles.'[2] Both rely to a large extent on authority ; in both the proof of the position taken up is not final at the outset, indeed is never final, but deepens with experience. In both, again, there is contained an *act of faith*, the act by which the conclusion is accepted as a working hypothesis on a basis of accumulated and corroborative evidence, none of which can be said to amount to proof.

It must be admitted that this position, which may be called, in no depreciatory sense, either ' philosophic agnosticism ' or ' pragmatism,' is not wholly satisfactory. This generation like every other generation asks for a sign—for intellectual certainty ; and if what has been said is true, no such sign can be given to it. There can be no final evidential proof of any proposition, either in religion or in science ; only the accumulation of probable proofs, leading to an ever-widening apprehension of its intelligibility and truth. The fact is, however, that the philosophy of pragmatism is still immature. Two things remain for it to do before it can consider its work finished : to convince the popular mind that the distinction between the ' demonstrable ' truths of science and the ' undemonstrable ' truths of religion is wholly unreal; and to elaborate the criteria upon which the ' illative sense ' is justified, in any given case, in making its venture of faith. When these two tasks have been accomplished, it will be more possible to

---

[1] ' It is by the strength, variety, or multiplicity of premises which are only probable, not by invincible syllogisms—by objections overcome, by adverse theories neutralised, by difficulties gradually clearing up, by exceptions proving the rule, by unlooked-for correlations found with received truths, by suspense and delay in the process issuing in triumphant reactions—by all these ways, and many others, it is that the practised and experienced mind is able to make a sure divination that a conclusion is inevitable, of which his lines of reasoning do not actually put him in possession.'—Newman, *op. cit.* p. 321.

[2] Moberly in *Lux Mundi*, p. 160.

state the rationale of faith in terms which give it its true value and dignity.[1]

If, however, the individual Christian can be convinced that an act—a venture—of ' faith ' is involved every bit as much in accepting any ordinary belief of everyday life as in accepting religious beliefs, his intellectual burden will be greatly lightened. He will no longer be distressed because he cannot *prove* the truth of what he believes about God; for he knows that he can prove it—if he is put to the test— every bit as much as he can prove any of the scientific or matter-of-fact propositions he holds to be true. He can produce, that is to say, the probable evidence which led him to his conclusion, and no man can do more than that in religion, logic, or science. At the core of every belief lies a movement non-intellectual in character; a self-deter- mination of the whole personality towards the conclusion to be accepted ; an act of faith.

' Faith's evidential material,' then—like the evidence of every form of science—' is all corroborative and accumu- lative ; it draws it out from an external world which can never wholly justify or account for the internal reality, yet which can so group itself that from a hundred different lines

---

[1] The unsatisfactory state of the problem to-day has been described by Mr. G. K. Chesterton (*Victorian Age in Literature*, pp. 204–5): ' The most final and forcible fact is that this war [between reason and revelation] ended like the battle of Sherrifmuir, as the poet says : " They both did fight, and both did beat, and both did run away." They have left to their descendants a treaty that has become a dull torture. Men may believe in immortality, but none of the men know why. Men may not believe in miracles, and none of the men know why. The Christian Church has been just strong enough to check the conquest of her chief citadel—the rationalist movement had been just strong enough to conquer some of her outposts, as it seems for ever. Neither was strong enough to expel the other ; and Victorian England was in a state which some call liberty and some call lockjaw.' Cp. E. Boutroux, *Science and Religion in Contemporary Philosophy* (Eng. tr.), p. 275: ' Neither science nor religion feels herself fully in possession of the autonomy which both alike demand.'

The disastrous effect of this intellectual *impasse* upon morals was noticed by Robert Louis Stevenson as long ago as the 'seventies : ' By the scope of our present teaching nothing is thought very right and nothing very wrong, except a few actions which have the disadvantage of being disrespectable when found out ; the more serious part of men incline to think all things *rather wrong* ; the more jovial to suppose them *right enough for practical purposes* ' (*Lay Morals*).

it offers indirect and parenthetic and convergent witness of that which is, itself, beyond the reach of external proof.' [1] It would be a good thing that each individual Christian should—to the limit of his intellectual capacity—draw together the probable proofs of his faith, using the reason and sense of evidence and argument which God has given him to the full. He will find no lack of sources for his evidence. History, philosophy, the experience of the saints, his own moral and spiritual development; these and many others go to provide that mass of corroborative proof upon which his faith—little though he may guess it—really rests. ' Discourse and argument, the line of tradition and a never-failing experience, the Spirit of God and the truth of miracles, the word of prophecy and the blood of martyrs, the excellency of the doctrine and the necessity of man, the riches of the promises and the wisdom of the revelations, the reasonableness and sublimity, the concordance and the usefulness, of the articles, and their compliance with all the needs of men and the government of commonwealths, are like the strings and branches of the roots, by which faith stands secure and immovable in the spirit and understanding of a man.' [2]

And if it be urged against the believer that science has proved the falsity of much in which he believes, he can reply with certainty that science has done and can do nothing of the kind. At best it can merely have produced probable evidence against his religious convictions—evidence the precise value of which is still in dispute. But even so, many earnest souls will be disturbed and weighed down by the burden of logical argument against the miraculous and supernatural in Christianity: probable only though this argument may be. The locks of Doubting Castle still

---

[1] H. Scott Holland in *Lux Mundi*, p. 3.
[2] *Holy Dying*, chap. 4, sect. 3. Cp. *Duct. Dub.* bk. i. chap. 4, rule 2 : ' Probable arguments are like little stars, everyone of which will be useless as to our conduct and enlightening; but when tied together by order and vicinity, by the finger of God and the hand of an angel, they make a constellation, and are not only powerful in their influence, but like a bright angel to guide and to enlighten our way. And although the light is not so great as the light of sun or moon, yet mariners sail by their conduct; and though with trepidation and some danger, yet very regularly they enter the haven.'

go ' damnable hard,' and the key called *Promise* is not as effective in the hands of modern pilgrims as it used to be. There is only one course which will give them ease. They must be urged, while holding the balance between the two views of life—the rationalist and the spiritual[1]— still in suspense, to commit themselves, by such an act of faith as we have described, to a practical, experimental acceptance of the one which offers most hope for their moral progress. As to which of the two this is, no one who realises the beauty of the Christian ideal can remain for long in doubt. *It is impossible to build a full spiritual life on a rationalistic foundation.* Only a ' background of the infinite '—of God as love, of Christ as Redeemer, of the Holy Spirit as guide and support—is sufficient for moral growth, either in the individual or in society. Bishop Blougram, holding the intellectual balance in just this way between the two, accepted the Christian view as a working hypothesis because of the material advantages and worldly comfort he obtained by doing so.[2] The earnest Christian inquirer in the same dilemma may be urged to do the same thing—to accept Christianity as a working hypothesis ; but for a very different reason : for the moral progress which he can reasonably expect to be his once he fairly and fully embraces the Christian way of life.

Faith, then, is the power by which, in committing himself fully to the Christian way of life, a man gradually comes to a clearer apprehension of its intellectual implications, laying hold upon them with an ever-growing certainty as to their truth and importance for his life.[3] Throughout the process reason is called into play ; collecting, classifying and weighing the evidence for each point of truth as it emerges, and looking for corroboration of truth already grasped in the new experience to which it continually opens

---

[1] By the ' rationalist ' view of life is here meant, not a temper which doubts the validity of the evidence for such and such a miracle ; but one which denies the possibility of the universe being in any way the creation and continual concern of a free, omnipotent and moral Personality.

[2] Robert Browning, *Bishop Blougram's Apology*.

[3] This is not to deny that faith is a gift of the Holy Spirit. See *infra*, p. 133.

the door. Reason, therefore, we may say, both prepares
the way for faith, and confirms it when it has taken root
in the soul. And there is one other way in which reason
is the handmaid of faith. It helps a man to marshal his
evidence and to make his intellectual position explicit ;
and so equips him for one of the first of his duties
as a Christian—the duty, that is, of giving a reasonable account of the faith that is within him, and so of
becoming, in however limited a degree, an evangelist to
others.

The conclusions we have reached as to faith and reason
are indeed less optimistic than those of St. Thomas ; but
they are in principle the same. The mistake made by the
schoolmen lay in regarding faith as a perfect *habitus* [1]
—an unchanging state of mind—rather than as the slow
process of growth our inquiry has shown it to be. Once
grant this latter fact, with all that it implies as to the
difficulty of belief and the checks and hesitations which
faith no less than reason is in consequence bound to experience, and we may accept the Thomist position in other
respects. Faith still emerges as an order of knowledge
not opposed to reason, but concerned with ' more ultimate
things ' ; reason as the guarantee, though not the ultimate
sanction, of faith.

We conclude, then, that the priest need never hesitate
to encourage reasoning and inquiry on the matters of faith
in those who are committed to his charge ; whenever, in
fact, their intellectual equipment is adequate to the task,
he should urge it upon them as a Christian duty. But he
must at the same time inculcate intellectual humility by
pointing to the manifest errors into which so-called exact
demonstration has led some of its adherents ; and lay due
stress upon the fallibility of human reason. Above all he
must resist the temptation to suggest that a mere submission
of the reason to the authority of the Church, or a blind
acceptance of her teaching even when combined with the
fullest obedience to her rules of life or the greatest activity
in her service, is in any way adequate to the Christian ideal
of faith. For the former of these two suggestions would

---

[1] *Summa*, i. 2, q. 55, a. 1 ; ii 2, q. 4, a. 1.

I

depreciate the true place of the intellectual factor in religion ; whilst the second would deny it any place therein at all.

4. *The Signs of Growing Faith*

We postpone to a later chapter a consideration of the methods by which faith can best be aroused, fostered and maintained in the Christian ; and pass on to the question, What are the visible fruits of a faith that is growing steadily and strongly ? The signs of growing faith may be set down in something like the following terms :—

(*a*) An equable temper in all vicissitudes of human affairs, marked by an unswerving optimism as to the supremacy, at all times, of the providence of God. (*b*) A quality which, if it were not founded upon God but upon self, we should call self-confidence or self-reliance. (*c*) A decline in impulsiveness, leading to prudence [1] (careful consideration of means and consequences) before action, and patience and perseverance in action. (*d*) A certain simplicity [2] and directness which discards, as often as not, all that would commonly be regarded as tact or finesse, and goes straight to the point. (*e*) A spirit of contentment and even of joy in believing (Phil. i. 25). (*f*) An ardour for an ever-increasing knowledge of the truth.

On the other hand, we may set down, as signs of defective faith, spiritual cowardice (an unwillingness to be known as a Christian by an unsympathetic world) ; impatience, discontent and dejection ; ineffectiveness and inconsistency. Where these are to be found, the priest will have good reason to believe that faith is deficient and fitful, and should consider possible remedial methods.

[1] ' Prudence lies in knowledge of the truth.'—Ambrose, *De Off.* i. 25.
[2] ' Non intelligendi vivacitas, sed credendi simplicitas.'—Aug., *Contra Ep. Man.* iv. The whole section is valuable as illustrating St. Augustine's doctrine of faith and reason.

CHAPTER V

ZEAL

1. *Zeal and the Sense of Forgiveness*

A DISTINCTION between lethargic and active religion is clearly marked in everyday experience. It may be expressed in the statement that the former takes such opportunities of Christian service as come in its way, whilst the latter goes out of its way to make opportunities of service. The former is not by any means deficient in penitence or in faith, but it lacks the vehement initiative and resolution to which they should give birth, and which manifests itself in a sincere dedication of the human will with all its purposes to the service of God and man.

This dedication of the will—the principle of action, effort and conquest—to the service of God, is that to which we have already given the name of *zeal*.[1] It has its origin in the natural will of man, but is stirred to more than human power by the grace of God. It is called into being by penitence and faith. It manifests itself, in the soul, as an overwhelming love of God and man. And its external character is that of justice—the giving to all and sundry what the Christian law lays down as their due : to God devotion, reverence and obedience ; to man benevolence, sympathy and charity.

The full Christian ideal enshrines an element of *forcefulness*, of divine discontent, of a violence which would take

---

[1] In the *Summa*, *zelus* is a ' passio,' arising out of ' intensity of love,' and capable of manifesting itself either in a laudable or a culpable form. Where its activity is laudable, it consists in ' a movement against anything that is injurious to the loved one,' ' et per hunc modum aliquis dicitur zelare pro Deo quando ea quae sunt contra honorem vel voluntatem Dei repellere secundum posse conatur ' (i. 2, q. 28, a. 4).

the kingdom of heaven by storm.[1] This forcefulness must not be confused with the desire for adventure, excitement, efficiency or self-assertion which is natural to many men ; it is something much deeper—and often much quieter too—than the restless activity which marks so many human affairs. It partakes of the humility of penitence and the imperturbable patience of faith ; its essence lies not in any self-assertion, but in the self-surrender of the will to God. For this reason its fruits are very different from those of natural activity. It is zeal indeed ; but it is the zeal *of love*.

The distinctive character which marks out the zeal of Christian love from all other forms of activity is derived from the fact that in its truest form it is aroused by penitence and faith through the medium of their inevitable outcome, the *sense of forgiveness*. The man who is truly repentant of the past and eagerly hopeful of grace, and who at the same time has an unshaken faith in God's mercy, cannot but reach the necessary conclusions which come from the combination of the two—that his sins are forgiven, that he is enfranchised in a new life, that he is endowed with power from on high to meet the new demands upon his personality of which by degrees he is becoming conscious.

We have seen that penitence may have its origin in any one of a number of sentiments—the feeling of loneliness, for example, or that of a wasted life, or that of the cruelty of circumstances ; any of these may bring a man to his knees. But only one sentiment can give him that fine flower of supernatural contrition which promises the full fruits of penitence : and that sentiment is one of love for God.

It is the same with Christian zeal. It *may* indeed be

---

[1] Cp. 1 Cor. ix. 24–26 ; Phil. iii. 13, 14 ; Heb. xii. 1. It is just at this point that the doctrine dear to Aristotle, and from him received by St. Thomas (*Summa*, i. 2, q. 64, a. 1, &c.), that virtue consists in a ' happy mean ' between excess and defect, is seen to be inadequate to the Christian demand. It is bound to be interpreted in a qualitative as well as a quantitative sense ; and the *quality* of all true Christian action must be zeal, not moderation. Charles Simeon's paradox is nearer the facts : ' The truth is not in the middle, and not in one extreme, but in both extremes ' (H. C. G. Moule, *Life of Charles Simeon*, p. 97).

roused by sympathy for the oppressed, or by the sense of romance in religion, the appeal to risk all for the sake of a great cause, or by many other motives more or less admirable. But only the sense of forgiveness will sustain it through every check, discouragement and temptation it may meet with ; only that sense will produce its fullest and finest manifestations.

To establish this fact, and at the same time to learn more of the essential character of zeal, we must examine the sense of forgiveness and analyse it into its constituent elements. Here again it is true that psychologists have not failed to gather evidence from the wide field of Christian experience ; but, as before, we shall do better to avoid these slightly artificial products of a self-conscious age and draw our material from the more spontaneous records of the Bible. To those records, therefore, we turn, to discover what can be learnt—not about the *fact* of forgiveness ; that is a matter for dogmatic theology—but about the effect which the *consciousness of being forgiven has upon character*.[1]

Deeply as the sense of sin is ingrained in Old Testament thought, there is to be found there no corresponding certainty of forgiveness—a fact that accounts for the pessimism which never failed from time to time to leap into prominence in Jewish religion ; and accounts, as well, for the passionate Messianic expectation which alone kept faith alive. The Levitical code expressly confined itself to sins of inadvertence and breaches of the ceremonial law; for the sin ' with the high hand '—the sin which really burdened the conscience and broke the spirit—the law knew no forgiveness.[2] Hence the bitterness of despair which characterises so much of Jewish penitential literature. The prophets, it is true, did not a little to lighten the burden ; they promised forgiveness to all on condition of repentance and confession.[3] But prophecy could never take the place of the law given by the hand of angels ; it had not—as a later dispensation had —a new and inviolable covenant to offer, though it saw

---

[1] See H. B. Swete, *Forgiveness of Sins*, part i. chaps. 2 and 4 ; part iii. chap. 4.

[2] Num. xv. 30 ; Deut. xvii. 12, &c.

[3] Isa. i. 18 ; Jer. xxxi. 34 ; Ezek. xviii. 27 ; Hosea xiv. 4 ; Micah vi. 8,

the hope of one in the future.[1] Therefore the forgiveness
it promised could not be held to have its certainty rooted
in any unswerving decision of Yahweh's will. He might, of
His own arbitrary act, be ready to forgive in this case or
in that—His forgiveness might indeed be offered to all who
would fulfil the conditions demanded—but He was pledged
by no covenant to such a readiness. The offer could be
withdrawn, the decision revoked, by an act as arbitrary,
but at the same time as just, as the original promise of
forgiveness.

Even the prophets themselves — the messengers of
divine forgiveness—guarded their message with the warning
that God could withhold His forgiveness at His own good
pleasure. The sinner must not presume upon it. ' Though
your sins be as scarlet they shall be as white as snow ;
though they be red like crimson they shall be as wool. If
ye be willing and obedient, ye shall eat the good of the
land ; *but* if ye refuse and rebel, ye shall be devoured with
the sword : for the mouth of the Lord hath spoken it.'[2]
Forgiveness indeed is offered, but for a limited period only ;
refuse the offer, and you cannot expect it to be made again.
An earlier prophet had uttered the same warning : ' I will
heal their backsliding, I will love them freely : for mine
anger is turned away from him. I will be as the dew unto
Israel : he shall grow as the lily and cast forth his roots
as Lebanon. . . . Who is wise, and he shall understand
these things ? prudent, and he shall know them ? for the
ways of the Lord are right, and the just shall walk in them :
but the transgressors shall fall therein.'[3]

It would be fruitless, then, to look for any full description
of the joys of being forgiven in the Old Testament. Forgiveness was too fugitive and arbitrary a thing to produce
wide results of gratitude, relief, or inspiration. In the
whole of the Psalter there are only two psalms (xxxii. and
ciii.) which take as their exclusive theme the joys of

---

[1] Jer. xxxi. 31. [2] Isa. i. 18–20.
[3] Hosea xiv. 4–9. Cp. Swete, *Forgiveness of Sins*, p. 29 : ' Offers of
mercy [in the Old Testament] are usually guarded by stringent conditions, or modified by solemn warnings. Fear is urged as a motive
rather than love ; appeal is made to the dread of wrath more often than
to the constraining power of the Divine compassion.'

forgiveness—a significant fact when contrasted with the place the same emotion has in Christian hymnology. We must look to the New Testament for any evidence of that *certainty* of forgiveness which alone can transform character into a new thing.

The apostolic writers—and St. Paul in particular— seem almost to have exhausted their vocabulary in the attempt to describe forgiveness and the sentiments it evoked. The time-honoured phrase of ' remission '— ἄφεσις ἁμαρτιῶν—proved altogether too narrow for them ; and so it gradually disappears[1] before a host of words and phrases all designed, often by vivid metaphor, to express the greatness of the new experience. These words fall into two main divisions—those which express *release* from some form of mental or moral tyranny ; and those which express the idea of a divine *gift*, an enhancement of life and power.

Thus the Christian finds in forgiveness his *freedom*, his *ransom*, his *purchase* ' in the market place,'[2] from the power of sin. More specifically, he experiences release from each of the powers of whose oppression he was conscious in his state of sin. He is *justified*—that is, released from the sense of guilt. He finds *peace*[3]— release from misery and remorse. He is *reconciled* and *adopted*[4]—released, that is, from the loneliness and isolation into which his sin had plunged him. Finally, he experiences release from spiritual danger and the fear of ultimate disaster—he is *saved*.[5]

In phrases such as these the earliest Christians expressed

---

[1] It is only twice used by St. Paul—Eph. i. 7 ; Col. i. 14. The corresponding verb, ἀφίημι, occurs once, in a quotation from the Old Testament, Rom. iv. 7. Notice, also, that to express the ' forgiveness ' of God manifest in the Old Testament, St. Paul prefers to use the word πάρεσις — ' pretermission ' — rather than ἄφεσις : thus indicating the provisional, unsatisfactory character of the forgiveness offered by the old dispensation. See Rom. iii. 26 and commentaries.

[2] Eph. i. 14 ; 1 Cor. vi. 20, vii. 23 ; Gal. iii. 13, iv. 5 ; 1 Tim. ii. 6 ; Tit. ii. 14.

[3] Rom. v. 1 ; Eph. ii. 14 ; Col. i. 20. Cp. also J. Taylor, *Duct. Dub.* bk. i. chap. 1, rule 2, on the signs of true peace.

[4] Rom. v. 10 ; Col. i. 20 ; Gal. iv. 5.

[5] Matt. i. 21 ; Luke i. 71 ; Rom. v. 10, vi. 2, 18, 22.

the change of feeling towards their past life produced in them by the cognizance of the fact that they were forgiven. This, however, was not all. They were conscious that they faced the future with prospects very different from those which had been theirs so far. They took up their pilgrimage again, it is true, but this time they were equipped with a panoply of God— with *gifts* which would enable them to travel on their way in a very different spirit from that they had known. Here again they multiplied phrases in the attempt to express the variety and abundance of these gifts; and their experience was so vivid that each new phrase contributes some touch of its own to the picture.

The sum of it all is expressed in the conception of the *new life* of the forgiven Christian—his birth from above.[1] This life is a life of *grace*—an ambiguous word covering both God's transcendent favour towards His forgiven children, and the gifts which that favour confers.[2] More specifically the new life is characterised by the possibility of unlimited spiritual progress—to which the name *sanctification*[3] is given; by a supernatural *joy*[4]; by *zeal*[5] for good works—for he who has once experienced the joy of forgiveness must be inspired by the desire to extend the same experience to others; and by *intellectual enlightenment*.[6] And each of these gifts is specially mentioned as being one of the fruits of redemption.

Unlimited progress and purification; an unfailing supply of superhuman joy; zeal for good works; the stimulus of a unique intellectual enlightenment[7]—here are combined motives for a grateful, humble, tender, enthusiastic service of God and man far more enduring

---

[1] John iii. 3; cp. also Rom. vi. 4, vii. 6, xii. 2; 2 Cor. v. 17; Eph. iv. 24, &c.

[2] On χάρις, *grace*, in the New Testament, see J. Armitage Robinson, *Epistle to the Ephesians*, pp. 221 ff.

[3] 1 Cor. vi. 11.   [4] Rom. v. 11; 1 Pet. i. 8, 9.

[5] Eph. ii. 10; Tit. ii. 14.   [6] Eph. i. 9, 18.

[7] Dr. Gore characterises as 'one of the greatest and most illuminating of intellectual experiences' the perception of 'the coherence in one indiscerptible body of truth of all the articles of the Christian faith.' 'Nothing can be a substitute for this intellectual experience' (*National Mission Report on the Teaching Office of the Church*, p. 92).

and potent than sympathy alone or a desire for adventurous
activity. The latter indeed may serve until penitence
and faith have so developed as to produce, by their
combined influence, the sense of forgiveness; but if once
that sense becomes dominant in character no other influence
can possibly be so powerful.

There are, however, two gifts which forgiveness does
not bring ; and it is all the more important to emphasise
them because too often the Christian who is intoxicated—
no other word is graphic enough—with the first experience
of forgiveness, expects to receive them among his other
privileges, and may suffer bitter disillusionment when he
finds them lacking. One is *freedom from the consequences
of sin*; the other is *freedom from renewed temptation*. It
is important that converts or penitents who have just tasted
the joys of redemption should be warned on both these
heads.

(*a*) Forgiveness does not exempt the sinner from the
temporal consequences of his sin. This is expressed in
moral theology by a somewhat artificial distinction between
the *poena aeterna* and the *poena temporalis*—the ' eternal '
and the ' natural ' consequences of sin. Of these the *poena
aeterna*, we are told, is entirely remitted by absolution,
consequent upon contrition, confession and amendment ; the
poena temporalis remains unremitted, though its degree may
be lessened by works of *satisfaction*[1]—that is, by penance.
But we need no formal definition of theology to convince us
of a fact which is explicit in all Christian experience—that,
however deep a man's contrition may be, he will yet have
to pay the natural price of his sin : the price of ill-health,
of public disgrace, of loss of position or friends, or whatever other form it may take. Even the most spiritually-
minded are not exempt from this rule : ' Moses and Aaron
among His priests, and Samuel among them that call upon
His name : they called upon the Lord and He answered
them. . . . Thou answeredst them, O Lord our God ; Thou

---

[1] *Summa*, iii. q. 86, a. 4 ; Suppl. q. 10, a. 2 ; cp. Schieler-Heuser,
op. cit. p. 38 n. ; W. W. Williams, *Moral Theology of Sacrament of
Penance*, p. 53. But on the artificial character of these distinctions see
A. Chandler, *Cult of the Passing Moment*, pp. 95–97.

wast a God that forgavest them, *though Thou tookest vengeance upon their iniquities.*'[1]

It is true, no doubt, that God in His goodness often lightens the consequences of sin to those who repent and make willing amends. It is true—and far more important—that repentance and the sense of forgiveness enable them to pay the penalty, where it is unremitted, in a very different spirit from that with which they would have faced it with a still hardened heart. True repentance gives them the power ' in sufferance to rejoice.' They find in their punishment and expiation new opportunities of proving their devotion and of reasserting their position as Christians which by their sin they forfeited. The supernatural grace given to the penitent in forgiveness transforms the consequences of his sin into occasions of virtue ; and punishment becomes not merely remedial, but even a means by which he can reach a higher place than that from which he fell.

Yet among ill-instructed Christians this fact is commonly ignored ; and penitents are continually found who expect to obtain, with God's forgiveness, the forgiveness and complaisance of man as well. They have to be told that this expectation springs from a misunderstanding of God's methods and laws—that it is in itself a sign of imperfect penitence, of an attempt to bargain with God by the offer of apparent, but not real, contrition. They must be led back to consider the true origin of contrition—the love of God and not the fear of punishment—and urged to take that as their starting-point and banish every other motive from their minds.

(*b*) The same mistake is often made with regard to *recurrence of temptation* ; it is supposed that forgiveness will involve freedom from temptation in the future. The first assurance of forgiveness is commonly followed by a period of intense joy, peace and spiritual exaltation, which the beginner naturally thinks will continue all his life.

---

[1] Ps. xcix. 6–8 ; cp. Lev. xxvi. 41, 42 : ' If their uncircumcised heart be humbled, *and they then accept of the punishment of their iniquity*, then will I remember my covenant.' See also Num. xiv. 20–23 ; Deut. xxxii. 50 ; 2 Sam. xii. 13, 14 ; 1 Kings xxi. 29.

'When we begin to give ourselves entirely to God,' says Father Grou in his 'Manual for Interior Souls,'[1] 'He treats us at first with great kindness to win us to Himself; He fills the soul with an ineffable peace and joy; He makes us take a delight in solitude, in recollection, in all our religious duties; He makes the practice of virtue easy to us—nothing is a trouble to us, we think we are capable of everything.'

Such a halcyon period does not last long. Temptation soon recurs, often in a form more bitter and subtle even than that in which it appeared before. But the Christian may now look forward to it as one of God's methods of proving his new-won confidence and power, and leading him on to higher things. 'As soon as He is once certain of a soul, immediately [God] begins to enlighten her as to her defects; He raises by degrees the veil which concealed them from her, and He inspires her with a strong will to overcome them. From that moment such a soul turns against herself; she undertakes the conquest of self-love; she pursues it relentlessly wherever she perceives it—and when she is thoroughly illuminated by the Divine light, where does she *not* perceive it? She sees in herself nothing but misery, imperfection and sin; self-seeking and attachment to her own will; her very devotion appears to her full of defects.'[2]

It is therefore one outcome of the full sense of forgiveness, one sign of the zeal of Christian love, to be ready for punishment, temptation and trial; and not merely to be ready for them, but to welcome them, to run eagerly to meet them, to 'be joyful in tribulations,' to 'glory in weakness.'[3] It cannot be too clearly or too often emphasised that what is sometimes called 'Christian resignation' is not in any sense whatever a Christian virtue. It is inspired indeed by a spirit the very reverse of Christian zeal. The true attitude of the converted Christian towards temptation is an active, not a passive resistance; towards suffering, trial and punishment, the resolve to endure not meekly but heroically. He goes to meet whatever befalls not as one making the

---

[1] Chap. 5.   [2] J. Grou, *loc. cit.*
[3] 2 Cor. vii. 4, xi. 30, xii. 5, 9, 10; Phil. ii. 17; Col. i. 24.

best, as we say, of a bad business ; but as one intending to prove himself more than a conqueror. ' The Patience who *really* smiles at grief usually stands, or walks, or even runs ; she seldom sits.' [1]

(c) There is one other phenomenon connected with the sense of forgiveness of not infrequent occurrence, which requires wise treatment. Cases arise in which there can be no doubt of a man's true penitence and faith ; in which there is every readiness to confess sin and accept to the full its consequences ; but the joys associated with forgiveness are not experienced even after forgiveness has been assured by the most solemn means at the disposal of the Church. Here, as in the case of those who cannot feel the emotions of penitence, the cause lies somewhere in the man's natural constitution. He must remind himself that the feelings he desires, but cannot experience, are not of the essence of forgiveness. In this case also they are an ' overflow' which he cannot control or command, though he should hope to realise them ; they are doubtless withheld by God for some good purpose. Their absence throws no real doubt upon the reality of his forgiveness—*that* is assured to him by the atonement of our Lord and his own contrition. He is not to waste time in vain quest of a joy which others have but he has not, but rather to persevere in Christian zeal in the hope that some day the new feelings of release and of power will come to him. ' Beloved, if our heart condemn us not, then have we confidence towards God '—but ' if our heart condemn us, God is greater than our heart, and knoweth all things.' Only let us persevere in zealous love—' Let us love not in word or in tongue, but in deed and in truth ; and hereby we know that we are of the truth, and shall assure (*or*, persuade) our hearts before Him.' [2]

2. *The Signs of Christian Zeal*

It would seem almost superfluous to enumerate the signs accompanying that Christian zeal which springs, upon

---

[1] J. Ruskin, *Ethics of the Dust*, Lect. iv.
[2] 1 John iii. 18-21.

the foundations of faith and penitence, from a deep sense of forgiveness. It manifests itself in a humble, unselfish, tactful, unsparing life of love to others, showing forth the whole company of the cardinal virtues and their derivatives. We may, however, quote two such enumerations which deserve, for the mingling of fervour with sound common-sense which characterises them, to take their place as classical in the literature of Christian ethics. One is Bishop Jeremy Taylor's *Eight Signs of Purity of Intention* (which are here condensed) : the other, the most signifi-cant sentences in Father Grou's picture of the *Truly Devout Man*.

(a) *The Eight Signs of Purity of Intention* [1] are :

    i. That a man ' values religious ends before tem-poral.'

    ii. That he is ' not solicitous of the opinion and censures of men.'

    iii. That he ' does as well in private as in public ; in the church as in the theatre or market-place.'

    iv. That he ' is not solicitous and troubled con-cerning the effect and aspect of actions.'

    v. That he is ' not envious or angry at the per-fection and excellency of his neighbours.'

    vi. That he ' despises sensual pleasures, secular honours, and worldly reputation.'

    vii. That he ' uses the means God has laid before him with resignation, indifference, and thank-fulness.'

    viii. That he ' rejoices in the failure of a temporal end consisting with a spiritual but sub-ordinate to it.'

(b) *The Truly Devout Man.* [2]

' The truly devout man studies to fulfil perfectly all the duties of his state, and all his really necessary duties of kindness and courtesy to society. He is faithful to his devotional exercises, but is not a slave to them ; he in-terrupts them, he suspends them, he even gives them up for a time, when any reason of necessity or of simple charity

---

[1] *Holy Living,* chap. i. sect. 2.   [2] Grou, *op. cit.* chap. i.

requires it. Provided he does not do his own will, he is always certain of doing the will of God.

'The truly devout man does not run about seeking for good works, but he waits until the occasion of doing good presents itself.[1] He does what lies in him to secure success ; but he leaves the care of the success to God. He prefers those good works which are obscure and done in secret to those which are brilliant and gain general admiration ; but he does not shrink from these latter ones when they are for the glory of God and the edification of his neighbour. The truly devout man does not burden himself with a great quantity of vocal prayers and practices which do not leave him time to breathe. He always preserves his liberty of spirit ; he is neither scrupulous nor uneasy about himself ; he goes on with simplicity and confidence.

'He has made a determination once for all, to refuse nothing to God, to grant nothing to self-love, and never to commit a voluntary fault ; but he does not perplex himself ; he goes on courageously ; he is not too particular. If he falls into a fault, he does not agitate himself ; he humbles himself at the sight of his own weakness ; he raises himself up and thinks no more about it. . . . If he were to fall a hundred times a day he would not despair ; but he would stretch out his hands lovingly to God, and beg of Him to lift him up and take pity on him.

'The truly devout man has a horror of evil, but he has an even greater love of good. He thinks more about practising virtue than about avoiding vice. . . . In one word, he loves better to do what is good even at the risk of falling into some imperfection, than to omit it through fear of the danger of sinning.

'No one is so amiable in the ordinary intercourse of life as a really devout man. He is simple, straightforward, open as the day, gentle, solid, and true. His conversation is pleasing and interesting ; he can enter into all innocent amusements ; and he carries his condescending kindness and

---

[1] This does not, of course, mean that zeal is satisfied with merely taking opportunities of good as they come. That is excluded by the whole context. It is intended rather as a protest against excitability and mere nervous activity and energy.

charity as far as possible, short of what is wrong. Whatever some persons may say, true devotion is never a melancholy thing, either for itself or others. How should the man who continually enjoys the truest happiness, the only happiness, be ever sad ? '

From these two catalogues of the outward signs of Christian zeal we may deduce as well the signs of its absence. For it is of real importance to be able to discern between genuine zeal and its counterfeit. Men constantly devote themselves to apparently high ideals from mixed motives. There is no harm in this alone ; it is better that a man should serve God and his neighbour from an unworthy motive than that he should not serve them at all. But there *is* harm if no one perceives that he is wrongly motived, and consequently no attempt is made to inspire in him the true motives of zeal—that love of God which leads to penitence, that sense of forgiveness which strengthens and ennobles love. All other motives must fail to produce the finest effects of character, and may even produce distortions and caricatures of the Christian ideal which will bring the name of Christ into disrepute, ridicule or contempt. It is impossible to scrutinise another man's motives ; but we can at least by noting the outward characteristics of his life reach some degree of conjecture as to his inward dispositions.

Thus we may say that wherever a man's zeal is *purely outward* or *purely inward*, it is ' not according to knowledge.' Whether he concentrate his effort upon the welfare—spiritual or bodily—of others, or upon his own purity of heart alone, he is missing half at least of the Christian ideal, and may even miss it altogether ; for the outward and inward of the soul cannot be separated with safety to either. Whereever, again, in a life of service, he is found to be jealous of the success of others, or of their position and influence; wherever he speaks of himself as being ' unable to do his best work ' as he is ; wherever he seems to play for popularity, even though it be with the avowed purpose of using it to the glory of God ; there lurks the possibility that his zeal is motived not by self-surrender but by self-satisfaction.

There is no class of Christians more exposed to temptations of this character than the clergy themselves. A priest who gives part of his time to worldly pursuits, however harmless and justifiable they may be, is in perpetual spiritual danger from them. If they form a natural and beneficent outlet for his love of God, all is well; but if he takes part in them in order to achieve a prominence or position from which to commend his ministry, there is danger—if nothing more—of their stimulating a strain of worldliness in his character which he should have discarded for ever. Not that he will ever necessarily regard success in such secondary things as *more important* than the due discharge of his duties; but that he may come to rely upon them as essential, and not superfluous, aids to his ministry; that he will plan more for them than for his real mission.

The plain truth is that the ministry commends itself without any adventitious aids. The spread of the gospel does not depend on the popularity of the evangelist. A simple preaching of the message of forgiveness and a childlike purity of life may in the end prove a greater force than successful organisation or social popularity. Gifts of this character—powers of organisation, charm, athletic ability, literary interests—where God has given them, can be and should be used to His glory; but they carry with them their own temptations; and the priest must be on his guard lest in using them he exploit them to the detriment of his own soul and of the welfare of his people.

So, too, among the signs of a defective or distorted zeal we may number the instances in which generosity or charity is exerted, as with Sir Willoughby Patterne, on behalf of those whose gratitude can be perceptibly felt by the benefactor; but withheld from the vast masses who are too remote or too poverty-stricken for him to see visible results from his efforts. Conversely, cases are found—Mrs. Jellaby and Mrs. Pardiggle spring to the mind as examples—in which the enthusiast is so absorbed in a cause that he or she forgets entirely the claims of individuals, even if the individuals in question are those of his own home. It seems strange that such a perversion of zeal should be possible, yet it is far from uncommon. We may even suppose that one reason why St. Paul wished his 'bishops' to be chosen from the ranks of those who 'ruled their own households well'[1] was not merely that they should have given proof of ability to rule, but also to ensure that they should be animated by a zeal which would not exhaust itself in its efforts out of doors, but would penetrate the home as well.[2]

One other sign of defective zeal may be mentioned— the enthusiasm which absorbs itself in forms and ceremonies and the pedantry of religion.[3] Often enough enthusiasm of this character may be combined with complete callousness to the needs of others or to genuinely spiritual interests : wherever it is met with in an unbridled or undisciplined excess it should be carefully watched, as being a possible indication of spiritual poverty.

3. Declaratory Acts

A soul which is embarking—either for the first time, or after a lapse into sin—upon the life of conversion, will often wish to *declare* or *testify* to its new resolve by some action of an outward or public character. Even where natural timidity or hesitation holds it back, it should as a rule be urged to an act of this kind ; nothing stiffens resolve and tests reality so much as a first step. It is something to which the soul has committed itself more tangible than an internal resolution ; it marks an advance ; it provides a standard from which it would be disgraceful to go back.

Most religious bodies provide for the novice in religion some such declaratory act—as we may call it—often of public or semi-public character. In the Church of England, confirmation (though its meaning, of course, is in no way exhausted by that which the candidate does and says) has such a character for the boy or girl whose heart

---

[1] 1 Tim. iii. 4.

[2] Dr. McDougall gives the following signs of ' enthusiasm which is merely egoistic ' : (a) It ' will not go to the length of absolute sacrifice.' (b) It ' only extends to those with whom the man is brought into contact.' (c) It ' exerts a deleterious effect upon the recipients, encouraging flattery and toadying in some ; but provoking the scorn of men of sterner fibre ' (*Social Psychology*, p. 205).

[3] See F. Paget, *Christian Character*, pp. xviii, xix.

K

is moved towards God ; confession and penance are available in the case of those who after confirmation fall away and wish formally to be restored.[1] Often enough, however, the priest will be asked to advise as to such a step to be taken in addition to these ' official ' ones, or will feel it incumbent upon himself to recommend one. Declaratory steps, indeed, must occur at intervals all through the soul's spiritual progress. It should signalise each new access of grace, each new token of divine love or providence, by a new offering of itself to God, expressed first and foremost —as was its original dedication of itself—by something outward and irrevocable.

The greatest care is needed in the choice of such declaratory steps to be recommended to any individual. His needs, his capacities, his interests, must all be taken into account. ' Goodness,' in Sir Thomas Browne's phrase, is a ' funambular track ' ; a false step may lead to an issue from which recovery is not easy. If the Christian undertakes an act which overtaxes his spiritual strength, it may produce discouragement and despair.[2] If one which is too easy for him, the result may be a lessening, not a heightening, of zeal. If one which ministers to some secret weakness, the effect may be the very reverse of what was desired. Confirmation and confession, indeed, when the person who presents himself for them is alive to their gravity and has earnestly prepared himself for them, are not open to any of these dangers. But the offering of the soul in confirmation is of a very general character ; and the spiritual effort which the candidate makes in it requires to be supplemented by others of a more specialised kind, to determine the force and bent of his future progress. Confession, again, is incomplete without a penance, the object of which is just the same ; to fix and concentrate the new aspiration for holiness in some special act of service or devotion. Both these sacraments, therefore, find their natural completion in a declaratory act.

[1] This does not, of course, imply that, where confirmation (as in the Church of England) is separated by a period of some years from baptism, the sacrament of penance is not available for those who are baptised but unconfirmed.

[2] St. Thomas Aquinas, *Quodlib.* iii. a. 28.

We need, then, to consider the principles upon which such an act should be chosen or advised. For our guidance we may take, first of all, the qualities which are laid down in moral theology as marking a good confession ; secondly, the qualities which should characterise a wisely-imposed penance. From the first we may infer the *qualities which every soul should exhibit in performing declaratory acts* ; from the second, *the considerations which must influence the priest in prescribing a particular act to a particular person* so as to ensure his exhibiting the qualities in question.

(a) *Qualities of a good confession.*

The ' Summa ' [1] gives a list of sixteen qualities of a good confession. It must be simple (that is to say, without irrelevant matter) ; humble ; pure (that is, arising out of the sole motive of love to God) ; faithful (or true to fact) ; frequent ; candid (*nuda*—without reservations) ; discreet (that is, accusing no one else by name) ; voluntary ; reverent (*verecunda*) ; integral (that is to say, reaching to every mortal sin committed) ; secret ; remorseful (*lacrimabilis*) ; without delay (*accelerata*) ; brave (*fortis*) ; self-accusing ; and ready to obey the requirements of the confessor.

Several words in this list are more or less co-extensive ; and some of the requirements laid down are more suitable for the Roman than for the Anglican communion. When we have made allowances for both these factors, and also have discarded, for our immediate purpose, those qualifications which are required by the specific character of the act of confessing sin (that is, that it should be remorseful, self-accusing, &c.), there remains a catalogue which is of real value in enabling us to estimate the internal conditions which should characterise an act of declaration. It should be something *simple and straightforward* ; *unostentatious*, yet *making real demands upon character* ; entirely *voluntary* ; and *not ministering to any weakness or sinful tendency* (as, for example, self-assertion or a desire for concealment). Lastly, though it need not be an act demanding frequent or regular repetition, it should if possible make *some genuine and permanent contribution to character*.

[1] Suppl. q. 9, a. 4 (from *Sent.* iv. d. 17, q. 3, a. 4). Cp. W. W. Webb, *op. cit.* pp. 35–37.

We may compare with this summary the three ' Measures and Rules of Divine Love ' given by Jeremy Taylor [1] :—

(i) ' That our love be sweet, even, and full of tranquility . . . proportionable to our condition and present state. . . A new beginner in religion hath passionate and violent desires, but they must not be the measure of his actions.

(ii) ' Let our love be prudent and without illusion. . . . Love turns into doating when religion turns into superstition. . . . We cannot love God too much, but we may proclaim it in indecent manners.

(iii) ' Let our love be firm, constant and inseparable.' [2]

(b) *Characteristics of a wisely-imposed penance.*

These, it will be remembered, are considerations which will guide the priest in his choice of a penance for one whose confession he has heard. Their object is to ensure that the act prescribed shall elicit, in its performance, the dispositions just considered. The characteristics of a wisely-imposed penance are usually given as follows [3] :—

(i) It should be *proportionate* both to the gravity of the sins confessed, and to the ability and condition of the penitent. Men and women, adults and adolescents, that is to say, all require separate treatment.

(ii) It should be *remedial*—should aim at eradicating whichever of the weaknesses or sinful tendencies of the soul are most dangerous to it. It is not enough to select a penance which will advance the spiritual life in general, it should have special relation to the sins confessed.

(iii) It should be *secret*, except possibly for open and scandalous sin. This is, of course, a necessary condition arising out of the ' seal ' of the confessional ; it has no application to declaratory acts as a whole.

(iv) It should be *simple* (easily remembered) and to be performed within a certain time.

(v) As a rule the penance should be *light*, but especially so in the case of penitents who are of an emotional or

---

[1] *Holy Living*, chap. 4, sect. 3.

[2] Cp. also : ' That zeal only is good which in a fervent love hath temperate expression,' *ibid*.

[3] Webb, *op. cit.* pp. 60–67, and authorities there quoted. Schieler-Heuser, *op. cit.* § 33.

deeply contrite character, or are known to be physically or spiritually weak.

Most of these principles can be generalised so as to form a guide for all kinds of declaratory acts. There is an infinite number of different acts which may be of use in different cases—such as a specific kind of reparation for injury done ; the undertaking of an act of charity which (in addition to the benefits it confers) will be of spiritual value to the person performing it ; special prayers, meditations, or acts of self-restraint ; the acceptance of some office, small or great, in connection with Church work; the incorporation in character of a new form of devotion or worship. Some such act should follow, not merely each lapse into sin and consequent repentance, but equally, if not to a greater extent, any consciousness of special grace, favour, or protection received from God. We may generalise from what we have learnt, adding one or two other obvious considerations, and set down among the principles which should help to determine the nature of an act of declaration the following :—

(i) The priest should use all his ingenuity and imagination to discover the appropriate act to recommend in each case.

(ii) There is no harm in urging a slight delay before the act is undertaken—a delay sufficient to test the resolution, but not so great as to risk loss of will. Such a delay will serve to convert a passing emotion into a fixed impulse.[1]

(iii) The instinct for heroics, or for martyrdom, should never be allowed to assert itself.

(iv) With persons of an emotional character, the step proposed should be of a practical, matter-of-fact kind.

(v) With those to whom self-assertion or ostentation comes naturally, it should be of a humble and even a secret kind.

(vi) The priest should regard whatever step he recommends, not as a thing wholly isolated, but as the first of a series of steps stretching out into the future. It should therefore contain within itself the possibility of further

---

[1] ' The milk of human kindness should be allowed to stand overnight to test its quality.'—Seton Merriman, *The Velvet Glove*.

development or enlargement. It should be chosen, in fact, not with reference to the needs of the moment, but to those of the whole life.

(vii) Wherever possible the declaratory act should touch every department of character. It should contain elements which will kindle true desires or suppress bad ones, stabilise faith, and fix the will more firmly upon the love and service of God.

(viii) In the case of diffident or immature characters, it is useful to recommend a step which will bring them into relation with others who are striving after the same ideals. The joining of a Guild or Bible Class, or the like, is often the best action that can be recommended.

(ix) Allowance must be made for the extreme shyness of most of the laity in religious matters, and especially of boys. What to others appears a trivial step, may to them assume momentous proportions, and demand a very real effort of will.

(x) A warning should always be uttered as to the possibility of a renewal of temptation—*usually in an unexpected form*, often in those matters where the person thinks himself most strong [1]—after any important resolution has been taken in the spiritual life.

[1] Thus Moses, the meekest of all men, fell through pride ; Peter, the courageous, through cowardice. Each was tempted, and fell, at his strong point, not at his weak ones.

CHAPTER VI

THE EDUCATION OF THE SOUL

1. *Progress through Union with Christ*

So far we have considered separately the various elements which go to make up the Christian character ; the respective parts they play in it ; their results ; and the signs from which their presence or absence may be inferred. It remains to consider their interplay in the growth and expansion of that character as a whole. For this purpose we must abandon the analytic in favour of the synthetic method. Regarding the soul as one and indivisible we must trace the stages of its development, and estimate the part which the priest can play, by advice, influence and instruction, in bringing it as far as possible on its way.

It is, perhaps, not sufficiently emphasised in the Church of England that the Christian life does not spring into being fully equipped and perfect in all details. With the exception of the devout few, churchmen as a whole have failed to realise that the test of their religion is that it should exhibit fresh graces and achievements year by year. Yet this is sufficiently emphasised in the Bible to make it obvious even on the most casual of readings. The life of the disciple is spoken of as a pilgrimage,[1] a race,[2] a contest,[3] a warfare,[4] a building [5]—metaphors all of them which express effort, progress and achievement. To the conventional English

---

[1] Gen. xlvii. 9 ; 1 Chron. xxix. 15 ; Ps. xxxix. 12 ; Heb. xi. 13 ; 1 Pet. ii. 11.

[2] Eccles. ix. 11 ; 1 Cor. ix. 24 ; Phil. ii. 16, iii. 14 ; 2 Tim. iv. 7 ; Heb. xii. 1.

[3] 1 Cor. ix. 25 ; Eph. vi. 12 ; 2 Tim. iv. 7.

[4] Eccles. ix. 11 ; Rom. xiii. 12 ; Eph. vi. 11 ; 1 Tim. i. 18 ; 2 Tim. ii. 3, 4.

[5] Matt. vii. 24 ; Rom. xv. 20 ; 1 Cor. iii. 10.

point of view, on the other hand, Christian virtue appears as a static condition of not too exalted goodness to which the normal man can without overwhelming exertion attain, and beyond which no progress is expected of him.

This point of view is wholly untrue to the teaching of our Lord and His apostles. The Christian should be one continually going from strength to strength, reaching out to that which is still before him. He should test his progress from time to time by asking himself the question, How far have I advanced in holiness since I last reviewed my condition ? And it will effectively prevent complacency and self-satisfaction in his answer, if he remembers that the standard at which he is to aim is nothing less, in external things, than the example given by Christ in His earthly life ; and, in internal things, than the full dedication of desires, intellect and will to the service of God.

Our brief survey both of the mystic doctrine of the threefold way, and of the psychology of adolescence, led to the conclusion that the dedication of these three elements in life goes on—or should go on—concurrently ; though at various stages one or other of them comes into such prominence that for the time it attracts the greatest attention, and puts the other two into a subordinate position. Thus, whichever scheme we adopt as our guide, it entails first of all a period in which the desires have to be regulated according to the Christian ideal ; then one in which the mind is illuminated by, and brought into accord with, the dictates of faith ; finally, the development of a Christian will and purpose strong enough to subordinate all other purposes of life to itself. Yet in each of these periods the development of the whole character should go on at the same time. The enlightening of the mind and the strengthening of will may not be neglected even when the contest with desire is at the highest ; the purifying and ennobling of desire must continue even after the most vehement passions have been brought under control and the soul is at liberty to devote its main effort to the higher stages of life.

The same conclusions emerge from a third scheme of Christian progress, which goes even deeper than the other two, and which can reasonably be deduced from St. Paul's writings as dominating his conception of the spiritual life. The peculiar value of this new scheme is that it treats that life from the objective rather than from the subjective side. It concerns itself, not with the *efforts*, but with the *experiences* which mark the various stages of our pilgrimage ; it states progress, not with reference to its *distance from the starting-point*, but to its *approach to the goal*. And the goal of the Christian life is nothing less than union with Christ.

St. Paul uses four phrases or ideas to express various degrees of *nearness* or *union* between the Christian and his Lord. They are never formally arranged in order ; it is never even suggested that they form a sequence illustrating the stages through which Christian experience passes from the lower to the higher. But we can hardly reflect upon their implications without finding that they do arrange themselves in such a sequence ; it is at all events a legitimate speculation that they had this value in their author's mind. The fact that he never explicitly gives them such a form illustrates once more what we have already seen to be true : that the Christian life is an indivisible whole, and that the merest beginner in holiness may, for a moment, share in the most sacred experience of the saint—and by sharing in it receive a foretaste of his state to be, an inspiration to guide him through the darker stages of struggle, an ideal which, though fugitive and evanescent, remains yet as something ultimately to be achieved.

There are four such phrases in St. Paul. The first, which seems to represent the very beginnings of the spiritual life, is that of the *imitation of Christ*.[1] Here the Christian has parted company from the standards of this world ; he has accepted a higher and different ideal to which he will

---

[1] See Rom. xv. 1–3, 7; 1 Cor. xi. 1 ; 2 Cor. viii. 9; Eph. v. 2 ; Phil. ii. 5–11; 1 Thess. i. 6 ; and cp. Matt. xi. 29, xx. 26–28 ; John xiii. 14 ; Heb. xii. 1, 2 ; 1 Pet. ii. 18–24, iii. 17, 18, iv. 1, 2 ; 1 John iii. 16. Cp. also Clem. Rom., *Ep. ad Cor.* 16 ; Ignatius, *Eph.* 3, 10 ; *Trall.* 8 ; *Rom.* 6 ; Polycarp, *Ep. ad Phil.* 8, 10. It is therefore untrue to say that ' the imitation of Jesus, in the strict sense of the word, did not play any noteworthy rôle either in the apostolic or in the old Catholic period ' (A. Harnack, *History of Dogma* (Eng. tr.), vol. i. p. 67 n. ; *Expansion of Christianity* (Eng. tr.), vol. i. p. 107 n.)—unless the reference is to the voluntary acceptance of poverty and celibacy alone.

endeavour to conform. His greatest effort in this stage, no doubt, will be to bring his passions into conformity with this ideal ; but he will not fail to allow its influence to play upon mind and will as well. By degrees, however, as he meditates upon his example (for how else can he imitate it ?) and moulds his conscious life upon it, there cannot fail to come upon him an experience which marks the beginning of a higher stage. In his struggle to be like Christ, he meets with temptation, worldly loss perhaps, scorn, suffering and trial ; and all of these he tries to encounter as his Master encountered them upon earth. So there springs up in him a sense of sympathy or oneness with the sufferings of Jesus ; he thinks of himself as *suffering* or *dying with Him*, even as *making complete His sufferings*.[1] Here is a thought which is a very real illumination of the mind ; an explanation—the only explanation—of the troubles of the world, as well as a great incentive to further effort and achievement.

This achievement is in part accomplished when those around him, when even he himself, see that in one respect or another he is actually becoming, what he set out to be, visibly like his Master. They see *Christ in him*.[2] Here is indicated a third stage—a stage in which the Christian becomes conscious of a supernatural inward power which has taken possession of him, which—though perhaps intermittently only, at moments of high inspiration—enables him *to do all things*.[3] His will is identified with the will of Christ, and from that will draws by the channel of the Holy Spirit powers hitherto undreamt-of, of victory in prayer, in communion, in self-control, and in external acts of goodness.

This is not all. An even higher possibility is suggested by the change to a new phrase—the change by which the Christian characterises his condition no longer as *Christ in me* but *I in Christ*.[4] To most of us this change of phrase

[1] See Rom. viii. 17 ; 1 Cor. xv. 31 ; 2 Cor. iv. 10 ; Gal. vi. 17 ; Phil. iii. 10 ; Col. i. 24 ; and cp. Rom. vi. 3–5, xiv. 7–9 ; 2 Cor. iv. 11, v. 14 ; Gal. ii. 20, v. 24 ; Phil. i. 29 ; 1 Thess. ii. 14 ; 2 Thess. i. 5 ; 2 Tim. ii. 10, 11 ; 1 Pet. iv. 1.

[2] See Rom. viii. 10 ; 2 Cor. iv. 11, xiii. 3, 4 ; Gal. i. 16, ii. 20, iv. 19 ; Eph. iii. 17 ; Phil. i. 20 ; Col. iii. 4.

[3] Phil. iv. 13 ; cp. 2 Cor. xii. 9, 10 ; 2 Tim. iv. 17.

[4] See Armitage-Robinson, *Ephesians*, pp. 24, 32, 57, 58 ; Sanday-Headlam, *Romans*, pp. 160–166, with references there given.

is almost unmeaning; we have not penetrated far enough into the spiritual world to appreciate its tremendous significance. Yet we can get some glimpse of it by analogy. There is a difference between *sin in me* and *I in sin*. 'Sin in me' means briefly that I am cognisant of a power for evil active in my nature, and at times at least dominant there. 'I in sin' means much more—it means that sin has taken so complete possession of my every faculty that *I*, as a separate personality, have virtually ceased to exist—I exist only as an automatic instrument of sin; I am absorbed in sin, swamped by sin—it permeates every fibre of my being.

The difference between *Christ in me* and *I in Christ* has exactly the same significance. 'Christ in me' represents a high stage of Christian experience—higher than many of us attain except at rare moments. 'I in Christ' represents a stage infinitely higher. It is no longer the case even that the Christian is conscious of a sublime power *within* himself; he has ceased to be conscious of himself altogether, so supremely cognisant is he of the other Personality Which has laid hold upon him. Of this experience we may perhaps doubt whether there are many Christians so spiritually-minded as to know it as an abiding possession; but there are few earnest souls who, at least, at one or two moments in a lifetime, have not felt something akin to it. It represents a completeness of personal identity with Christ through the Spirit—impossible for long, we may conjecture, under the conditions of earthly life, yet possible for just long enough, to those who earnestly look for it, to give them a glimpse of what shall be their eternal reward.

These four phrases, then, present a picture of the successive stages of the Christian life expressed in terms of union with Christ. At times, mainly in the beginnings of that life—in the stage of conscious and strenuous compulsion upon the desires to bring them into conformity with the Christian law—but also at other times, Christ as a living Master and Friend is far from us; all we know is that we are trying to imitate Him. At times, again, mainly in a maturer stage of the soul's development, but occasionally also during its first struggles, our Lord is nearer; we feel that He shares in our sufferings and troubles, and we in His. Even so He is still far off—our community of experience with Him may be little more than our community of experience with lesser masters of the spiritual life of whom we have heard and read, and whose examples have inspired us—St. Francis, it may be, or George Herbert, or William Law. There is yet a closer degree of communion with Him to be experienced—a communion in which He manifests Himself within us, guiding and strengthening the will, and carrying it triumphantly through difficulties that otherwise must be insuperable. And there is one further state of communion which we can hope for as the abiding characteristic of our eternal life—a state of which in this life we catch indications only, rare and transitory, yet vouchsafed to most persevering souls—a state in which we ourselves seem as nothing, because we are lost in Him, whilst He is all in all.

There are many, it must be confessed, to whom phrases like these, expressing communion with Christ, are no more than picturesque metaphors of the pulpit. They correspond to no thought-out experience of the soul. It is not necessarily the Christian's fault if such phrases perplex and confuse him. He needs help to look for and to recognise evidences of union with Christ as a personal Friend in his daily religious experience. ' Have you never reflected,' he might well be told, ' in your struggles with temptation or your suffering for what is right, that Jesus passed through the same experience ? —Reflect upon that and you will realise that you are *suffering with Him*. Have you never known times when you were enabled to do something altogether beyond your normal powers ? It was *Christ in you*, the hope of glory, Who enabled you at such a moment. Do you not remember moments, at the Eucharist, or in private prayer, when you were lost in adoration, aspiration and holy desire ? when all earthly pleasures, cares and sorrows were alike forgotten ?—*You were in Christ then ;* He possessed you wholly ; your self was merged in His. Remember these things ; and when next such moments come to you reflect that you are suffering with Him and He with you ; or that the strength within you of which you are suddenly aware is Christ and none other ; or that you are in Him. Make yourself conscious at these times of His fellowship and presence and the mastery He has ; rejoice in the sense of His nearness ; try to recognise something of His character, love and care for you.'

It may be said that this is the merest subjectivism, the encouragement of self - suggestion and religious emotionalism. So it would be, if it were not for the objective truths of Christianity—the truths of the Incarnation, of the Resurrection, of the gift of the Spirit, of the indwelling of Christ. As we have already said, the *proof* of these truths is the work of dogmatic theology and Christian apologetics. Their acceptance, after due examination, is a necessary preliminary to all pastoral work ; and once accepted they are not lightly to be doubted. For a single doubt as to the reality of Christianity invalidates the whole of Christian theology and of Christian ethics. If the Resurrection is a myth and the gift of the Spirit an illusion, the *whole* of Christian experience is the purest self-suggestion ; even if momentarily justified by its results it remains a delusion which, because untrue, must end in ruin. Moral theology accepts unhesitatingly the data of Christian dogma. It assumes the reality and possibility of communion with a personal and living Saviour ; and therefore claims the right to interpret the phenomena of Christian experience in terms of that communion.

The scheme of Christian progress which we believe ourselves to have detected in St. Paul's four crucial phrases is obviously much deeper than either that of the mystic or that of the psychologist. And it emphasises a truth of the greatest practical importance, which is less clearly indicated in either of the others. This truth, to which allusion was made in the first chapter, is that the Christian life is *not so much a life of following rules, as a life of following Christ.* 'Character,' said F. W. H. Myers,[1] 'is largely a resultant of the direction and persistence of voluntary attention ' ; and the Christian character can in no way better be formed than by acts of attention concentrated upon our Lord.

[1] Quoted, K. Saunders, *Adventures of the Christian Soul,* p. 97.

It is true that He must be thought of and realised in His *full* nature, so far as the Christian can grasp it ; and that He should be thought of too *in relation to the thinker's own character*. Thus, in the first of these two matters, He is to be thought of as an example of zeal, of practical altruism, of unfailing energy, as well as of quiet happiness and tender friendliness ; in the second, the soul must compare His perfections with its own imperfections and stir itself to emulate His greatness, especially in those points where its own littleness is most manifest.

Rules, indeed, have their value in such a life ; but they are secondary only to this point of fundamental importance. We shall recur to it again ; but important as it is, it is not even so the whole truth. For the disciple is not merely one who *thinks about Christ*, but *one who knows Him*, and who can point out, in his own religious experience, those moments when his personal communion with Christ was highest and most fruitful. To the masters of the spiritual life it is ' not merely an intellectual reasoning upon finite data,' but the ' ontological presence of the Holy Spirit,' which marks the highest stage in Christian development.[1] Attention, that is, must be directed not merely to the idea, but to the *living person*, of the Lord. It is through attention and experience of this kind that desire, intellect and will are most readily and effectively ' made captive '[2] to the will of Christ ; that penitence, faith and zeal are brought to maturity ; and that the full manifestation of the Christian virtues is realised.

2. *The Priest as Director*

From this conception of the Christian life, as above all a life of growing and conscious union with the living Christ, emerges a second conclusion, no less firmly founded for the Christian believer, no less ludicrous and even repugnant to those who doubt the objective truth of his creed. It is, that the principal agent in the development of spiritual power must be, neither the soul itself, nor the priest who directs

[1] F. von Hügel, *Mystical Element of Religion*, vol. ii. p. 282.
[2] 2 Cor. x. 5.

it, but the Holy Spirit. It is He alone Who mediates to men the experience of union with Christ, and through that experience moulds the desires, illuminates the mind, strengthens and directs the will, and fuses all together in a life both of inward and of outward virtue. It is He even, innate in every man, who first stimulates the soul to that unconscious striving after the beautiful, the true, the good, which we have previously called *conscience*, and have seen to be present in germ in every human consciousness. Penitence may be akin to the normal stirrings of adolescent life ; faith may appear a process not confined to spiritual things alone, but operative in every human judgment ; zeal may betray resemblances to other forms of effort of activity ; but although these factors in the spiritual life have connections with what we call (loosely and without clear definition) 'natural phenomena,' it would be false to one of the deepest of Christian principles to suggest that they will develop of their own accord by 'natural' means. All Christian experience corroborates the doctrine that they are the free gift of God.

It follows, then, that one of the highest duties of moral theology should be to trace the methods by which the Holy Spirit normally leads men on from the first glimmers of religious aspiration to the full sense of union with Christ and the full practice of the virtues. Within a limited sphere—that of the operations of the Spirit through sacramental channels—this has been done,[1] though perhaps too much from the *a priori*, too little from the empirical point of view ; but the laws of His free and uncovenanted operation have never been carefully traced out. There is scope here for an inquiry, of the most reverent and humble kind, into one of the mysteries of religion.[2]

Such an inquiry, however, would lead to issues beyond

---

[1] E.g. *Summa*, iii. qq. 60–*fin.* ; Suppl. qq. 1–68.

[2] It would be unfair not to notice that mystical and ascetic theology do indeed treat constantly of this subject, though in the main implicitly and indirectly only. See, for example, the quotations from Scaramelli, Grou, Baker, &c., on pp. 51, 113, &c. Such books as Swete's *Holy Spirit in the New Testament, Holy Spirit in the Early Church*, again form an admirable and necessary introduction to the study suggested. See also Chandler, *Ara Coeli*, chap. ix., 'The Grace of Contemplation.'

the scope of the present chapter. Concerned as we are with moral theology on its ascetic side—that side which deals mainly with the practical rules which guide the priest in his work—it is enough for us to notice the omission and pass on. This at least may be said : that nothing can inspire and hearten the priest more in his difficult task than the constant recollection that he is not unaided ; that he is co-operating—in the humblest possible sense—with a Paraclete as perfect and all-wise as he is himself faulty and ignorant. Where he fails, the Holy Spirit must succeed ; where he makes mistakes, the Holy Spirit will rectify them ; where he falters, that Other is unfaltering. In the work of salvation the priest's part is at best small and secondary.

But it is important to emphasise that he *has* a part, and an essential one.[1] The conventional English view of the spiritual life—that it is comparatively easy to acquire— is responsible for an almost universal assumption that a sermon once a week, with a casual glance at the Bible from time to time, and a few fragmentary reminiscences of the catechism and early Sunday-school teaching, is all that a soul needs in the way of guidance. The rest may be left to the individual conscience. There are few points on which English Christianity is more fatally at variance with the spirit, not merely of the greatest saints, but of the New Testament itself. Timothy and Titus were men of rare spiritual gifts, but St. Paul thought it necessary to direct them not merely as to the details of their office, but as to the regulation of their own characters. The universal testimony of the saints is that the Christian soul cannot pursue its journey successfully without the help of a director. ' Seek the companionship of spiritual men, ' wrote St.

---

[1] Cassian (*Collat.* ii. 14, 15) makes the interesting observation that the Holy Spirit is not wont to reveal directly to men anything that may be learnt through human teachers. Thus Samuel, though directly called by the Holy Spirit, must go to Eli for an interpretation of the voice. Saul, on the Damascus road, is converted by the vision of our Lord, ' yet Almighty God, notwithstanding that He sees him so well disposed, does not disclose His designs. And why ? Because there is in Damascus a priest, Ananias by name, to whom he can make application. " Go to him," says our Lord, " and learn from him what I will have you to do." ' See Scaramelli, *op. cit.* Treat. i. §§ 93 *sqq.*

Jerome to Rufinus ; ' place yourself under their direction, and by no means presume to be your own master in perfection.'

Modern religious thought is permeated on this head by a spirit closely akin to that which in educational theory is called *naturalism*—the doctrine of Rousseau that so long as the growing child is kept in a favourable environment his natural impulses and interests will lead him on in a steady and unfaltering development. There is much that is true in this theory. Without a growing co-operation and sense of responsibility on the part of the child, the teacher can do little ; just as, in an allied sphere, ' every doctor knows that however great a share he may have in a cure, he is only co-operating with the patient.' [1] But the theory is defective. It overlooks the fact that a child's impulses are neither all of them good nor infallible. Indolence, one-sidedness, even a perversion of taste, may enter in and distort or impede his growth. More than this, the theory is wasteful. Centuries of experience have taught the race many things which can be imparted to the individual as, at all events, a sound working basis for life ; there is no need for him to epitomise, in his own person, the laborious discoveries, the mistakes, checks and discouragements, through which his forefathers passed in the garnering of knowledge. Teachers have a real part to play in education ; their duty is to ' *interfere* with natural development so as to produce a richer experience and a fuller exercise of the higher powers.' [2]

It is the same in the education of the soul. ' The *initiative* of healthy direction comes straight from the penitent, enlightened by the gift of God the Holy Ghost, as to his special need. The mission of the priest (this is Fénelon's view) is to aid, to perfect, to complete. He is to take for his basis that of which the individual soul is capable ; not that which he puts there, but that which he finds.' [3] But though we recognise the primary part thus assigned to the individual conscience in initiating progress, we must not

---

[1] P. Dearmer, *Body and Soul*, p. 73.
[2] J. Welton, *Psychology of Education*, p. 28.
[3] J. Skinner, *Synopsis of Moral and Ascetical Theology*, p. viii.

L

assume that it is at the same time *sufficient*. Were conscience, indeed, always alert and vivacious, never impeded by impulses detrimental to spiritual growth, it might be left to itself to guide the soul aright—though even then the experience of the masters of spiritual progress would be of infinite value in accelerating its approach to perfection. But conscience, as bitter failure has taught us all, is no longer such an ideal instructor. In many men it is—almost from infancy, it would seem—' seared,' ' darkened,' or ' defiled.'[1] ' Had we continued perfect,' wrote William Law, 'as God created the first man, perhaps the perfection of our own nature had been a sufficient self-instruction for everyone. But as sickness and diseases have created the necessity of medicines and physicians, so the change and disorder of our rational nature has introduced the necessity of education and tutors.'[2]

Confirmation of this position comes from an unexpected source. When Froude dismissed the second part of the ' Pilgrim's Progress ' as no more than a weak imitation of the first, he failed to observe that in one important particular the two are wholly divergent. In the first part the pilgrims receive only occasional advice and direction on their journey to the Celestial City ; in the second part their successors have a guide—a human guide—who does not leave them, except to ' return to his Lord at night.' It is impossible to read the account of Mr. Greatheart, and the pilgrims' dependence upon him, without hazarding the guess that Bunyan, in his second part, deliberately introduced the character to insist upon something which the first had overlooked—the advantage which the soul may derive from the guidance of experience. The guide, moreover, is not merely a man of experience, but one specially equipped for his task. For, ' tho' when it was *light*, their Guide could well enough tell how to miss those ways that led wrong, yet in the *dark* he was put to a stand ; but he had in his Pocket a Map of all the ways leading to or from the Celestial City ; wherefore he struck a Light (for he never goes also

---

[1] 1 Tim. iv. 2 ; Eph. iv. 18 (cp. Matt. vi. 23) ; Titus i. 15.
[2] *Serious Call*, chap. 18 ; cp. also J. Taylor, *Holy Living*, chap. iv sect. 9 ; *Summa*, i. 2, q. 95, a. 1.

without his Tinder-box) and takes a view of his Book or Map, which bids him be careful in that place to turn to the right-hand way.' ' Then thought I with myself, Who that goeth on Pilgrimage but would have one of these Maps about him, that he may look when he is at a stand, which is the way he must take ? ' [1]

The English Church needs renewed emphasis upon this truth. The use of spiritual direction can indeed be carried too far—so far that the director may stand, in an adverse sense, between the soul and God ; so far that the dependence upon direction may weaken the moral fibre and sense of responsibility. Neither of these dangers, however, are imminent in English Christianity. There, the use of direction has not in any degree gone far enough, so that many of us have lost the conception of spiritual progress, of the delicacy and intricacy of Christian virtue, altogether. ' The art of living is in itself a vocation, and needs a training as specific as that for any of the recognised modes of earning a livelihood ' ; [2] and this training, like any other training, can best be acquired under the guidance of an expert.

It may be said in reply that the English clergy, as a whole, are *not* expert in the matter of the spiritual life. This may well be true, for it cannot be supposed that the clergy would remain uninfluenced by the general trend of English thought. If the Christian public ceases to demand expert guidance, its ministers will, as a natural result, cease to be experts : cease perhaps even to exercise that reflection upon spiritual experience which is the necessary foundation of expert knowledge. But the converse is also true. If clergy and laity alike demand guidance in the spiritual life, and refuse to be content without it, the necessary experience will again be gathered together, analysed and formulated, and the demand supplied.

We may assume, then, that the Christian soul, in its pilgrimage from this world to the world to come, can be greatly helped by a human guide and director. The priest has a genuine work to perform in the shepherding of

---

[1] *The Pilgrim's Progress*, part ii.
[2] J. Adams, *Development of Educational Theory*, p. 243.

individual souls ; and if—as in modern English conditions
is unfortunately the case—they only rarely turn to him
as a director, he must with all humbleness but without
remission offer his ministry to them in that capacity.
Of the character requisite in a good director we shall speak
later ; we may notice here Father Grou's summary of
the signs by which a soul may recognise the director whom
God has selected for it. We are to know him as God's
choice for us by three indications : an ' irresistible attraction leading us to confide in him ' ; a ' peace which takes
possession of us when he speaks to us ' ; and an ' ardour
or strong desire of giving ourselves to God, with which
his words inspire us.' [1]

How, then, is the priest to discharge his function of
directing individual souls ? This is the question which
animates all ascetic theology, and leads the inquirer into
every ramification of the spiritual life. The abundance of
methods is so great that it is difficult at first sight to find
a principle according to which to group them. It may,
however, be best to think of them under two heads—as
methods suggesting *ideas* to the Christian, and methods
suggesting *habits*.

3. *Ideas and Habits*

The primary importance of ideas and habits [2] in all
educational method—not in the education of the spiritual
life alone—is of course a commonplace. Only a combination of great ideas with good habits will produce mature
and well-balanced characters. Ideas are necessary, because
without the stimulus of an alert and vivacious mind the
soul must quickly stagnate and be content with the bare
repetition of formal and mechanical acts. Yet ideas alone
will not win the battle. There are impulses in the soul which
need sterner and surer methods of treatment ; wise and
inspired minds do not necessarily always co-exist with self-
control and altruism. There is, indeed, something in the
individualistic freedom of an active mind which makes a

---

[1] Grou, *op. cit.* chap. 21.
[2] Or, as Jeremy Taylor calls them, *considerations* and *exercises*.

man a rebel; and a rebel not merely against uninspired conventionalism but against any system of matured experience, however wise and beneficent it may be. The stimulus of a great idea is often one-sided, the stimulus of many may be disruptive and nihilistic. Stability of character must be assured by other means to resist the inrush of intellectual enlightenment.

The danger of habits, on the other hand, is widely recognised. Not merely do they produce, too often, distaste and revolt when unintelligently enforced (as constantly with the enforced church-going of children); but where persevered in they ' grow stronger as life goes on. As intelligence develops they may become narrower, unless an impulse of feeling lead us to see that our duties are not cabined and confined within the strait limits of our immediate circle. Such narrow but intense habitudes . . . we know as prejudices.' [1] They lead to mental and spiritual stagnation ; in the religious life particularly, to a round of external uninspired conventionalism the very antithesis of the life of the Spirit.

Yet they cannot be dispensed with in the education of the soul, and that for three reasons. Habitude, whatever its dangers, *saves time, produces skill*, and *resists temptation.* It saves time because, once a habit has been formed, there is less tendency to consider whether, in any particular case, it shall be acted upon or not. It produces skill, for it sets the mind free from efforts of attention to the external form of what is being done, and allows it to concentrate upon the matter or essence of its activity.[2] Thus even the habit of repeating a collect known by heart has its value, though it has its danger too. The mind knows that the form of words employed expresses its meaning adequately ; it is no longer burdened with the choice of appropriate expression ; it is free to attend (though often it may not do so) more carefully to the meaning. No one who has realised the value of set forms of prayer would for a moment deny that they increase skill or facility in prayer, whatever their dangers may be. Lastly, habitude fortifies against temptation. Temptation

---

[1] J. Welton, *op. cit.* p. 177.
[2] Cp. *Summa*, i. 2, q. 56, a. 3 : ' per habitum acquiritur facultas.'

usually comes as a sudden unexpected onslaught; and the *habit* of turning to prayer, to an act of communion, to a recollection of Christ's example, whenever the soul is so surprised, will often intervene automatically at each new onset and so avoid that fatal hesitation which dallies with the temptation, and leads to a certain fall. ' You may always stand by Form against Force.' [1]

' There are then,' we may conclude with Dr. Welton,[2] ' two main classes of habitudes or life tendencies within us. The one makes for sterility and increases narrowness; it is a force of mental inertia. The other leads to fertility, increased breadth of outlook and of sympathy, a wider range of activities. . . . If a purpose is inspired, and by heedful reminders kept clearly in view, then a habitude grows up which finds expression in the desired acts. But such a purpose, like all purposes, implies not only an emotional spring of individual action—such as a desire to please a parent, or fear of punishment—but an intellectual grasp of the value of the required habit. . . .

' Purpose having been invoked, the new habituation can only grow in the ordinary way—by practice. The sooner occasion is sought for such exercise the better; for unfulfilled purpose grows cold and weak. Every repetition of acts which tend to the new habituation, it must be remembered, gives to the new purpose all the cumulative force of the growing habitude. So too any harking back to the old mode of behaviour must be avoided, or the old habituation is revived in all its force, and the work has to be begun over again.'

From what has been said we can draw certain con- clusions as to the choice of *rules of life*. Rules of life are necessary to the Christian. They mark a definite progress in his character; they form habits which he can use as a starting-point from which to reach out to higher achieve- ments; they fortify him against temptation.[3] But they

---

[1] J. Ruskin, *Ethics of the Dust*, lect. x.

[2] *Op cit*. pp. 177 ff.

[3] Thus the *Summa* on rules of fasting: ' Non sunt contra libertatem populi fidelis, sed magis sunt utilia ad impediendum servitutem peccati,' —ii. 2, q. 147, a. 3, ad. 3. Cp. the following: ' A rule of life banishes idleness; it braces and fortifies the soul by the discipline of regular

must be wisely selected with regard, not to their association with any passing religious impulse, but to their suitability for promoting the formed purpose of Christian virtue which the soul has adopted.   Every rule of life should be definitely justified by a progressive influence which it is known, or at least intended, to exert upon character.   Nothing is more regrettable than to see people unthinkingly adopt first one habit of devotion and then another ; burdening themselves with rules, few of which they have any real reason to believe in, in the pious hope that ' they will do them good.'   Each rule should be selected with some definite aim in view, consonant with the purpose of life as a whole : the acquisition of self-mastery in some new particular, the inauguration of a new habit of benevolence, the promotion of a new and higher practice of devotion.

It follows that every rule of life should have a practical bearing ; it must never become an end in itself, or it will lose all influence upon the real life of the soul.   It should have a *definite human interest*, the promotion of which will both inspire its observance and test its success or failure. This interest should always lie, in part, in its effect upon the soul of the individual who makes the rule ; but wherever possible should lie, also, in some benefit which the observance of the rule will confer on others.   Thus a rule of abstinence from some particular pleasure is of little value if it have no bearing at all upon character (if, for example, the pleasure abstained from is one to the attractions of which the person is wholly indifferent) ; it will have greater value if its bearing upon the encouragement of some special virtue is clearly seen.   But it will have greatest value of all—will be most eagerly embraced and inspire to the highest zeal—if in addition to the encouragement of virtue in the person practising it, it serves also to confer a benefit upon others ; as when, for example, the money saved by

hours ; it disallows the do-as-you-like procedure of self-will ; it renders every section of the day true to its appointed character ; the work becomes real tough hard work in the way of reading, business, prayer, meditation ; and the recreation is downright healthy amusement, than which there is nothing more wholesome for the human soul.   In neither case is there any room for that capricious, wayward, discursive laziness in which self-love runs riot.'—Chandler, *Ara Coeli*, p. 53.

Lenten abstinence is devoted to the relief of the poor or to other forms of altruistic endeavour.

Again, rules of life should be frequently passed in review and, if need be, revised or discarded. There are two reasons for this. In the first place, they may outgrow their usefulness, and require to be superseded by practices more suitable to a mature soul. Adults are to be found still adhering to the methods of prayer suitable for childhood ; the old habit, now altogether unfitted for the needs of life, has survived, and no new one has been chosen to take its place. They should be reviewed, again, to see whether they are still being obeyed with the same vivid zeal and clear grasp of their purpose as prompted their first adoption. Only by keeping alive the original aspiration of which they were at once the outcome and the means of realisation, can their observance be prevented from falling into a mechanical routine which may become a genuine spiritual danger. The *idea* from which the habit sprang must remain fresh in the mind if the habit is to retain its value.

The priest's work as director, then, must consist mainly in commending to his people individually such ideas and habits as are appropriate to the respective needs and state of maturity of each one of them. Two things must be said about the general character of such ideas and habits. First of all, they should be *positive* rather than *negative* ; secondly, they should be *capable of the greatest possible expansion*.

(*a*) They should be positive rather than negative. They should aim rather at adding to character than at taking away from it ; at developing what is good and harmless in it rather than at cutting off what has become, by constant misuse, a danger. In other words, they should direct the Christian's attention more to Christ than to sin ; more to God than to self ; more to the living future than to the dead past ; more to the joys of righteousness than to the punishment of evil. Consciousness cannot at the same moment be focussed upon two separate things ; and if the Christian's attention is fixed steadily upon Christ, sin must cease to attract him, or to have power over his character.

There are therefore two ways of ministering to character ·

the attention may be concentrated upon the beauty of holiness until it is inflamed with the desire of acquiring it, or it may be concentrated upon the repulsiveness of evil until it revolts from any contact with it. Both methods may avail, but of the two it is evident that the first is by far the better. For the second, while it may inspire a loathing of sin, does not provide any instruction in, or example of, goodness; 'it is one thing to escape out of a city ; it is quite a different thing to choose a path.' Indeed, the result may be even more dangerous : the spectacle of its own sinfulness may so fascinate and paralyse the soul that it despairs of ever escaping from it, or even rushes with renewed passion to its embrace.[1]

(b) They should be capable of the greatest possible expansion. It may be necessary at times to lay before the soul, especially in its less mature stages of growth, the great ideas of Christianity under the form of metaphor or parable. But these metaphors, while valuable for the moment, often contain the seeds of untruth as well as of truth. It follows, then, that as the soul grows older it either exercises free imagination about them and derives falsehood as well as truth ; or, recognising their faultiness, discards them, but discards their truth as well. Such results have often happened where a too literal teaching of the Bible has been in force. Those educated in such a school of thought have either accepted as truth much which we now recognise to have been no more than the metaphor of a child-like

---

[1] The following passage from W. E. H. Lecky (*Map of Life*, chap. 12) well illustrates the difference between positive and negative methods, though the writer's generalisation as to the ' old Catholic ascetic training ' is far too vague and sweeping :

' The great principle of modern moral education is to multiply innocent and beneficent interests, tastes and ambitions. It is to make the path of virtue the natural, the easy, the pleasing one ; to form a social atmosphere favourable to its development, making duty and interest as far as possible coincident. Vicious pleasures are combated by the multiplication of healthy ones and by a clearer insight into the consequences of each. . . . The starting-point of education is thus gradually changing. Perhaps the extent of the change is best shewn by the old Catholic ascetic training. Its supreme object was to discipline and strengthen the will ; to accustom men habitually to repudiate the pleasurable and accept the painful ; to mortify the most natural tastes and affections ; to narrow and weaken the empire of the desires ; to make men wholly independent of outward circumstances ; to preach self-renunciation as itself an end.'

race, unsuitable and even misleading in the atmosphere of more modern thought; or, rejecting the forms under which religion came to them, have rejected the truth as well which those forms contained. Both results are unhappy, and both spring from the same cause—that the original teaching was phrased in a form capable only of limited expansion.

Or again it happens that, with a particular need or weakness of character in view, the Christian adopts some habit of self-restraint, mortification, or devotion which, though valuable as a temporary measure and within a limited sphere, would be injurious if permanently incorporated in character or extended in other directions. Instances of such a kind will readily occur to the reader. Here again the habit is one *incapable of great expansion*. It is enough to say that habits and ideas of this character are dangerous, and should be avoided if possible. Only those ideas should be fostered which will lead the Christian on to the fullest truth without danger of misapprehension; only those habits which can be permanently adopted without fear of harm.

Force is given to these contentions—that the ideas and habits commended should as far as possible be positive and not negative, and capable of the greatest possible expansion—by the modern theory of subconsciousness. The theory in question, it must be admitted, has led to a great deal of absurd speculation on the part both of psychologists and of theologians. ' The words *subconscious* or *subliminal* self, as commonly used, are little more than words that serve to cloak our ignorance and to disguise from ourselves the need for further investigation.' [1] But the facts to which it bears witness cannot be questioned. It has long been recognised—it is fully recognised in the Bible—that whatever comes into consciousness passes out of it, not into complete oblivion, but into a region from which it may sometimes be recalled by an effort of memory, and from which it often returns to consciousness un-

---

[1] W. McDougall, *Psychology*, p. 213. For the various forms of the theory of subconsciousness see G. A. Coe, *Psychology of Religion*, pp. 202 ff.

summoned and undesired. To this subliminal region, so little under the control of consciousness, the Bible gives the name of ' heart.' [1]

What on the whole is new in the modern doctrine is its recognition, in simple language, that the subliminal region is not merely a *storehouse* but a *laboratory*. An idea which the mind dismisses casually as of little importance passes into subconsciousness, and there by some unknown chemistry of nature, the investigation of which is still in its infancy, combines with old forgotten ideas, discarded habits, desires inhibited but not altogether subdued ; until without warning it bursts back into consciousness, not as the trivial thing which was dismissed, but as an overwhelming and incalculable force. It follows, then, that any idea or habit which concerns itself *in the least* with the thought of sin may be the immediate cause of a swift and unprecedentedly fierce onslaught of temptation—it may be the last ingredient needed to consummate the subliminal explosion. Such unseen combinations, such unexpected explosions, can only be guarded against by the constant exercise of consciousness in habits and ideas not merely innocent but potent for good. By their means subconscious forces for good are steadily accumulated, sufficient to counterbalance, even to outweigh, the forces for evil of which we have all such bitter knowledge.

Thus a negative idea or habit, one which concentrates upon sin—*even with the purpose of eradicating it*—is not merely *not so good* as a positive one, but may even stimulate gigantic forces for evil. With some sinful tendencies this is more the case than with others ; to oppose lust, for example, by concentrating thought upon the loathsomeness of it, is almost to invite an overwhelming onslaught of passionate impulse towards the sin. The danger which we have already

[1] Cp., e.g., Prov. iv. 23, xxviii. 26 ; Matt. xii. 35, xv. 19 ; 1 Pet. iii. 4. The identity of ' heart ' with ' subconsciousness ' is further suggested by the fact that in Biblical psychology ' soul,' ' flesh,' ' spirit,' &c., are constantly used as synonyms for ' man,' whilst ' heart ' is never so used ; just as in modern terminology personality may be expressed in terms of ' mind,' ' consciousness,' ' will,' and even ' emotion,' but hardly in terms of ' subconsciousness.' See Hastings' *Dictionary of the Bible*, vol. iv p. 168, s.v. ' Psychology.'

seen to lie hidden in such ideas and habits appears, therefore, infinitely greater now than at first—so great, indeed, that it must be avoided in every case in which it is possible to do without it.

And this leads us back once more to a conclusion which we have already found to be fundamental—that the concentration of attention, by ideas and habits, upon the person of Christ and upon living union with Him, is beyond all comparison the best way of stimulating spiritual progress. In such a practice there is no danger : the mind will be engrossed with thoughts which can expand indefinitely into an ever-widening fullness of truth ; thoughts positive and not negative, supplanting even the slightest impulse towards sin ; thoughts incapable of being perverted to the use of any subconscious tendencies towards evil. We may summarise the work of the priest as director in something like the following terms : *he is to commend to the earnest Christian such ideas and habits, appropriate to his character and immediate needs, as will, by focussing attention upon communion with Christ, purify, ennoble and strengthen his desires, intellect and reason, and enable them to manifest their perfection in a life of Christian love.*

CHAPTER VII

THE EDUCATION OF THE SOUL (*continued*)

1. *Ideas Promoting Spiritual Development*

FOLLOWING upon what has been said in the last chapter, we must pass in review the various ideas and habits which can be recommended to the earnest Christian as helps to progress. Among them are some which stand out pre-eminently as focussing attention upon the fact of Christ, or promoting conscious communion with Him : these, it may fairly be said, are of universal application. Others appear which deal rather with secondary aspects of Christian faith or practice ; these are to be stressed in certain cases only, or for a limited period, and much care has to be exercised in commending them, lest they should monopolise attention or even lead to some perversion of character.

We may group both ideas and habits according as their primary influence is to purify the desires (or promote penitence and hope) ; to enlighten the mind (or kindle faith) ; or to inspire and strengthen the will to a life of zeal and love. Such a classification cannot be very rigorous, and if pressed at all might become wholly mechanical, absurd and un-Christian. Yet there are certain signs which indicate (in general) the presence or absence of the funda-mental dispositions of the spiritual life ; and the discerning priest will always at least attempt, from these and similar signs, to estimate the spiritual condition of anyone whom he proposes to advise. Therefore if he find him lacking in penitence, he will choose to prescribe for his con-sideration and practice such ideas and habits as will, in general, promote penitence in the soul ; and in the same way will select the appropriate methods where he conjectures lack of faith or lack of zeal. There are no heaven-sent rules for such a purpose; but we may hope to find at least traces of general principles to guide the work of direction.

The ideas which avail to promote the spiritual life are generally considered under the name of the *motives* or *sanctions* of Christian morality.[1] It is recognised that there is such a thing as a ' hierarchy of motives ' in Christianity; that some ideas may stimulate an undeveloped character to spiritual endeavour which would be ineffective and even repulsive if commended to a mature Christian. Of such is the motive of *fear*—the thought of the punishment of sin either in this world or the world to come. Even our Lord ' seemed to recognise the occasional need of appeals to fear, as likely to rouse the conscience and will ';[2] though the insistence of many Roman Catholic writers upon the efficacy of thoughts of hell-fire is without doubt utterly untrue to His method. The motive of the *reward* attending godliness, so long as that reward is regarded as ' the opportunity of exercising to the full our capacities for love and service,'[3] cannot be called a motive of self-interest, and may well be cherished by every Christian; but in less perfect forms it belongs to the lower stages of spiritual development and should be sparingly used. Neither of these ideas—of reward and punishment—seems to fit the temper of modern England,[4] though in the mission-field they are still of use in rousing consciences dead to any higher appeal. We may set them on one side and look for more convincing motives.

Of motives which will promote penitence we have already had some indication. Penitence covers a vast field of

---

[1] Thus Ottley in *Lux Mundi*, pp. 352 ff. The ideas which actually *embody* the laws of Christian morality, as distinct from those which inspire willing obedience to those laws, are discussed in Chapter VIII.

[2] Ottley, *loc. cit.*

[3] See the whole discussion in R. L. Ottley, *Christian Ideas and Ideals*, pp. 171–174. Cp. also H. Rashdall, *Theory of Good and Evil*, vol. ii. pp. 261–268.

[4] Though the *National Mission Report on the Evangelistic Work of the Church*, p. 13, says : ' There is evidence to shew that the impetus of fear is still needed to drive some to consider things eternal.'

emotions, any one of which may be its starting-point, though only one can bring it to perfection. The sinner may be urged to think upon his failure, his wasted opportunity, the harm he has done, the grief he has caused his friends. Any of these may touch his heart and set conscience in motion. But what is needed most is that his love to God should be stirred, and lead to grief for the injury done to a heavenly Father, and earnest desire and hope of amendment. One thought above all others is efficacious here—the thought of the Cross. In that agony the sinner may be taught to see not merely the price paid for his redemption, but also the measure of the grief his sin has caused to God ; so that sorrow for the sin and gratitude for the sacrifice shall be roused together.

It is more difficult to see what ideas or thoughts will promote faith and combat its antithesis—religious doubt. But the central theme of Christian faith is of course the existence, omnipotence and providence of God. Once grant the fact of an all-powerful, all-loving, all-enduring Father, and the rest of the creed follows. Even the Incarnation and Atonement become a necessity of the divine nature, without which it could not realise its own perfect love. The existence, power and love of God being therefore the central point in Christian belief, the seeds of doubt must be looked for in arguments which deny one or all of these attributes. Such arguments are those drawn from determinist postulates, from the continued presence of evil and suffering in the world, and—perhaps above all— from a personal impotence against temptation, even after devout and earnest struggles against it.

The specific form in which the hesitation of faith, springing from these causes, usually becomes a torture to the individual, is that of doubt as to the validity of his own spiritual experience. He begins to fear that God and religion are mere delusions—that he is simply hypnotising himself into a belief which has no ground whatever in fact. Therefore—whilst every argument which exposes the fallacies of determinism, or meets the difficulties of the continuance of evil in human society or personal life, may well be used, *provided always that its cogency is likely to be accepted by the doubting and troubled mind*[1]—wavering faith is best confirmed by an insistence upon every thought which emphasises the objective reality of God and spiritual things. Such thoughts in particular are the truth of the Incarnation, the influence of Christianity upon human progress, the efficacy of the sacraments, and the indications of God's love and foresight to be seen in His dealings with oneself.

In many cases the appeal of suggestions such as these will be stronger than any argument. In the end it is the effective faith of believers, rather than their logic, which God uses as a means of reassuring the doubtful mind; men come to believe because their neighbour's belief shows itself fruitful. Not proof, but conviction, is the demand of wavering faith; and the contrast between the effective service of a convinced Christian and the impotent vacillations of the doubter will lead many men, without further proof, to accept the Christian hypothesis. The mind must have some solid ground to stand on; and if it doubts the reality of the spiritual world, where is its doubt to end? Neither the love of friends nor the truth of moral ideals can be safe from suspicion—and if they go too, there is no hope of happiness, certainty, or relief of mind in any form whatever. A man must choose between doubting all things and accepting those which are best substantiated throughout history and in his own life—the value and truth of the spiritual element in experience.

One other consideration must not be overlooked. Too often intellectual difficulty is, in all honesty, allowed to become a pretext for refusing to accept the full postulates of Christianity, when the real and fundamental ground of hesitation is an unwillingness to fulfil the moral demands of Christ. Wherever the priest has reason to believe this

---

[1] This is an important proviso. Doubt as to the truth of religion usually involves doubt as to the *bona fides*—or, at all events, as to the intelligence—of those who teach it; and any argument advanced by them is suspect as being either sophistical or fallacious. It is often wiser, for this reason, to avoid being drawn into argument, and to be content with pointing out the inevitable bankruptcy, moral and spiritual, of deistic or atheistic thought, as compared with the practical fertility of Christianity.

to be the case, it is generally wise for him to say so frankly ;
to refuse to be drawn into academic discussion ; and to
concentrate upon an appeal to penitence—to the abandonment of some habit or cast of mind which refuses to give
up a cherished pleasure—or to zeal : to an exertion of
effort in the Christian cause. Weakness of faith is often
merely a cloak for weakness of aspiration or weakness of will.

It remains to consider the second of these points. Where
the soul needs a strengthening of will, an access of zeal
and fervour, what ideas and motives can be presented to
it as a stimulus ? First of all, no doubt, the example of
our Lord again—the thought of the self-forgetful enthusiasm with which He carried out His task without
regard for its inevitable consequences to Himself. Next
the example of the saints—particularly the saints of the
present day, meeting with conditions, difficulties and
temptations which the modern man knows all too well and
shrinks from, but which the best among his contemporaries
triumphantly overcome. In this connection, too, the
thought of the Communion of Saints merits greater emphasis
than it receives in modern English Christianity. Their
constant intercession for the Christian still on earth, their
anxious and absorbed interest in his progress, the spiritual
sustenance which in unknown ways they give him, should
all inspire a weak or passive will to greater effort. The
needs of others, the great conception of the kingdom of
God to be built up and brought to earthly realisation—
these and many other motives like them may be looked
to as productive of Christian zeal. But it must not be
forgotten that love springs above all from the grateful
sense of forgiveness, of freedom at last to love and serve ;
and the sluggish mind should be led to dwell upon that
until the inspiration to active and zealous service seizes it.

It is not enough that these fundamental ideas of
Christianity should be accepted by the mind—they will
not be really fruitful unless it reflects upon them, becomes
engrossed in them, uses them constantly. Faith is more
than the pigeon-holing of certain great truths ; it is the
habit of mind by which they are brought into daily contact

M

with the problems of life. The mind must be brought to busy itself about them, to explore their content, to find continually new implications in them. That this may be achieved, a great deal depends upon the manner in which they are presented. There is demanded of the priest what Phillips Brooks called the 'mental and spiritual unselfishness which always conceives of truth with reference to its communication.'[1] His continual care must be, 'How can I best present this thought to others so that it will inflame their minds and take hold upon their lives?'

Constant ingenuity and inventiveness is therefore required for the task of presenting Christian truth effectively. A turn of phrase, a happy illustration, a homely metaphor, is often far more incisive than elaborate argument. The parables of our Lord are a pattern for Christian teaching. Their simplicity and directness, their power of expressing even the deepest truths in phrases a child can understand, their immediate appeal to an active effort of imagination, their challenge to a fuller exploration of their mysteries— these are all characteristics which the Church cannot afford to neglect in her presentation of the gospel. It is not enough to ask, 'What ought I to say to this congregation or this individual?'—we must also ask, 'In what words shall I say it?' And often enough the second of these problems is infinitely harder to solve than the first.

It is only, for example, by emphasising, in the simplest and most detailed terms, the perfect humanity of our Lord in all His earthly relations that attention can be focussed upon two fundamental truths—the impossibility of its having been *imagined* by the evangelists; and the impossibility of its being *true*, unless the divine and human were united in Him in a manner infinitely higher and closer than that in which such union normally occurs. The teacher or director may well spend much loving thought upon the picture of Jesus which he will present to doubting minds; looking for those graphic details—of tenderness, initiative, humour, insight, tact, and the like—which mean so much more to all of us than broad generalisations about the main trend of His character and thought. Our teaching

[1] Quoted, R. L. Ottley, *Christian Ideas, &c.*, p. 361.

on His person is usually too abstract to make any strong appeal either to love or interest. It requires the detail, colouring and vividness which only earnest and devoted consideration can give before it will exercise its full influence upon the wavering mind.

The same detail and vivacity, again, should characterise any appeal to the lives of the saints or the history of the Church. The broad general statement that no other factor has equalled Christianity as an influence for good in the progress of civilisation only grips the attention when it is illustrated or substantiated by realistic appeals to historic fact. ' Particulars ever touch and awake more than generals.' [1] A wealth of evidence can be adduced to show that in no period of history and in no part of the world have universal education, the care of the infirm, diseased and destitute, the recognition of the duty of kindness to animals, and above all perhaps the sense of the dignity of womanhood and the suppression of slavery, ever become dominant social ideals except under Christian influences or (as in the case of modern Japan) in conscious imitation of Christian civilisation.

Any fair-minded history of civilisation, the records of missionary work throughout the world in all periods of Christian history, the lives of St. Francis, St. Vincent de Paul, and countless other pioneers, will furnish material more than ample for this purpose. The Christian teacher can afford to be impartial, and admit that often enough the Church has been slow to understand the implications of her own ideals ; that much has been done in the name of Christ that was wholly unworthy of it ; that Christendom as a whole, or some group among its leaders, has more than once opposed tendencies in essence Christian. But when he has granted all this and more, the verdict of history is triumphantly on his side ; there is not a village or a house in which the alert mind cannot find some token of the unique progressive impetus of Christianity.

Evidence of this character is of twofold importance. It counters the shallow but often attractive arguments of those who assert that the Church, so far from being in the

[1] G. Herbert, *Country Parson*, chap. 7.

van of progress, has always been a drag upon it. But more important still, it draws the mind irresistibly back to Christ again ; and, as we have seen, the Christian life develops most fully when its interest is centred upon Him. The line of argument we have been considering inevitably suggests the question, Who was it from Whose teaching and example such infinite progress sprang ? Must it not be true that He was what His friends claimed Him to be— what, if we are to believe their record, He claimed to be Himself ?

2. *Habits Promoting Spiritual Progress*

(*a*) From every point of view, *prayer* stands first among the habits to be commended to the Christian. It is extraordinary how little the ordinary Christian understands the character of prayer, despite an infinity of sermons and books about it. To him the word still means, on the whole, no more than petition and intercession ; beyond that, he has little conception of the true extent, degrees and varieties of prayer. That must be a justification for repeating here the outlines of the doctrine of prayer, of which the full content has been described in countless books.[1]

Christian prayer covers the whole range of intercourse with God. Petition and intercession no doubt occupy a place in it—a place large enough to demand earnest effort in both of every Christian. But its full extent is far wider than that. It includes every aspiration of mind, desire and will towards God. As such it is usually considered under three headings : *meditation* or mental prayer ;[2] the *prayer of aspiration* or of the affections ; and the *prayer of contemplation* or of quiet. These three correspond to the three stages of the mystic way ; but as we have already found those stages to be in reality concurrent in spiritual

---

[1] See, for example, Augustin Baker, *Holy Wisdom* ; V. Lehodey, *Ways of Mental Prayer* ; A. Saudreau, *Degrees of the Spiritual Life* ; A. J. Worlledge, *Prayer* ; A. Chandler, *Ara Coeli*, &c.

[2] The distinction between *mental* and *vocal* prayer is not of any importance, though vocal prayer, in the sense of the use of set verbal forms, may be regarded as the more elementary of the two. See Baker, *op. cit.* Treat. iii sect. i. chap. 1.

experience, so it follows that the Christian should at all times practise all three forms of prayer, giving prominence now to one of them, now to another.

Meditation is the consideration of spiritual things with a view to progress in devotion to God. The subjects of meditation may be the character, or earthly life, or heavenly condition of our Lord ; the great doctrines of Christianity ; any passage of the Bible or of spiritual books. The method has been so often described [1] that it seems unnecessary to do more than recapitulate its main principles. It involves the preparation of the material (that is to say, the work of pure intelligence beforehand in the use of books and commentaries, the division of the subject and so on) ; the invocation of the Holy Spirit at the time of meditation ; the representation of the subject or incident chosen as vividly as possible by the imagination ; the consideration of its spiritual meaning and its bearing upon life ; and the resolution or dedication of the will in some particular direction suggested by the course of reflection just completed.

No real advance in holiness or spiritual strength is possible to the Christian unless he is continually practising meditation by some such method as the above. He may prefer to call it Bible-reading ; but if he does, he must beware of that magical view of the Bible which seems to imply that a chapter casually read through at night will be of spiritual profit. He may recoil from the form of the method given above, but must realise that nothing less than its spirit conscientiously carried out will be of value to him. He may wish to read the Bible in other ways—to arrive at its historic truth, for example, by processes of ordinary criticism—but he must learn that, valuable as such ways of reading the Bible are, they are not in any degree of the same spiritual importance as Bible-reading in the sense of which we are speaking.

Every earnest Christian, therefore, needs a rule of life which will ensure his giving time to regular Bible-reading

[1] See *Holy Living*, chap. 4, sect. 4 ; Busaeus, *Brevis Orandi Methodus,* in Avancini, *Vita et Doctrina Jesu Christi* ; St. Bernard, *De Considera-tione*, Book v. ; D. Jenks, *Study of Meditation*, and authorities already quoted. A. H. McNeile, *Self-Training in Meditation*, is a most valuable little introduction to the whole subject.

for spiritual purposes—for to most laymen meditation comes most easily by means of the Bible. The time should be employed in some degree by reference to formal rules such as those suggested ; it is easy enough to spend time in idle day-dreaming with an open Bible, but there is little profit in it. Therefore some definite understanding of the methods of meditation, as practised by those who have benefited by it most, is essential ; though the Christian must always hold himself free to vary the method according to his own personal requirements, so long as he omits none of those elements which experience has shown to be of the essence of the habit.

It is impossible to prescribe *how often* or for *how long* a layman should meditate. This depends almost entirely on his circumstances and character. It will be sufficient to say first of all that his periods of meditation should be *regularly* observed ; and then that they should be frequent and long enough for the results of his meditation to bulk largely in his mind in the intervals. He should be taught to use his spare moments—in going to and from his daily work, for example—in recapitulating or even developing the main heads of his meditation ; and he will quickly find that this demands a considerable degree of frequency and application in the practice of meditation itself.

Meditation is mainly an operation of the intellect, leading up to an effort, or as it is technically called an *act*, of resolution and petition. In the second stage, that of *aspiring* or *affective* prayer, the intellectual element is regarded as preliminary only, and the soul is asked to concentrate upon *acts of will*, which are wholly under its control, with the concurrent object of stirring up the emotions that centre, or should centre, around the thought of God.[1] Such acts are those, for example, of hope, contrition,

---

[1] On the other hand, ' none of these acts need be made with a feverish ardour, nor in a tone of enthusiastic fervour. When protestations of friendship, gratitude, &c., are made to ourselves, the more simple and natural they are, the more they please us ; the moment they appear forced their sincerity becomes suspected. . . . It is the will that makes the prayer. Though our heart be in desolation and coldness and devoid of all feeling, yet as long as our prayer proceeds from an upright and resolute will, it is pleasing to God, who beholds our interior dispositions ' (Lehodey, *op. cit.* pp. 99, 100).

resig.ation, worship and desire ; and—though it is not usually counted among them—intercession, which is no more than a particularised form of Christian desire, ought certainly to be included.

It is clear that this form of prayer, whilst continually gathering material from successive meditations, is yet of a higher order, as it brings into operation all the various powers of the soul. It has also this advantage, that it tends to counteract what is always a potential danger in meditation—the possibility of its degenerating into a purely intellectual pastime. The prayer of aspiration is the means by which every reflection upon spiritual things is brought into relation with conduct, and made to bear fruit, first of all in the development of spiritual desires and purposes— in the strengthening of contrition and zeal—and so, finally, in new manifestations of Christian virtues.

'Aspiring' prayer comes nearest to that which the ill-instructed Christian knows by the name. But it makes far more demands upon character than he realises ; and he needs continual teaching and help before he learns to practise it with any fullness. It may be considered under the two heads of ejaculatory and formal. *Ejaculatory prayer* can be and should be employed at all times and in all places, and especially on the stimulus of any new experience or sudden temptation. It consists in a momentary act of recollection, in which the Christian either thanks God for some new mercy, or asks Him for special grace in sudden temptation or spiritual danger, or offers a brief intercession for someone or something of whose needs at the moment he is suddenly conscious. There can be no doubt of the value of such a habit of ejaculatory prayer throughout the day. Often it may be no more than a repetition of some phrase of Scripture or some attribute of divinity ; as St. Francis, for example, spent a whole night in simple repetition of the words ' My God and my all ' ; or the Curé D'Ars, even in the midst of a sermon, ' ceased not for a quarter of an hour to repeat : "We shall see Him, we shall see Him ! " ' To many Christians the mere repetition of the name of Jesus in sudden joy or sorrow brings back the sense of their spiritual vocation, affording them the strength or consolation they need, and throwing new light upon their difficulties and problems.

But no soul will be able to recollect itself at will for the purpose of ejaculation unless it has also a *formed habit* of aspiring prayer. Such a habit, resolutely and devoutly pursued, is as essential as meditation to spiritual progress. Regularly and methodically day by day, wherever possible, the Christian should find time for a catena of prayer, in which acts of faith, hope, love, contrition, intercession and thanksgiving find their place. The daily prayers of Lancelot Andrewes supply an example ; so do the ' acts ' given in de Cressy's appendix to ' Holy Wisdom,' and the various devotions of ' Holy Living ' and the ' Golden Grove.' None of these several exercises (if we may so call them) can be omitted, though one or more may be reduced to a minimum every day to allow, in orderly succession, due practice of them all. Carefully placing himself, in thought, in the presence of God—preparing, perhaps, for his task by a brief meditation and reflection upon the beauty of God's holiness and the seriousness of what he is about to undertake— the Christian should reassert his faith in His Father, Redeemer and Sanctifier ; his desire for all spiritual graces ; his sorrow for the past ; his eagerness for the coming of the Kingdom ; his thanksgiving for mercies received. One day, if need be, the greater part of his time may be given to the act of faith ; on other days, other parts of prayer should have the greatest prominence.

Contrition, intercession and thanksgiving are so definitely personal things that no one with even the slightest genuine desire for God's service can omit them even for a day. The beginner in the spiritual life should be encouraged to direct his attention to them from the first. But he must add to them, as soon as he can, the other and more abstract ' acts ' as well—faith, hope, love and worship ; using first of all simple sentences (such as those selected by Bishop Andrewes for his personal use from the Bible), and going on to acts of prayer which transcend clear verbal expression. Without these, contrition, intercession and thanksgiving may deflect the mind from thoughts of God to thoughts of self ;

and the essence of prayer is to forget self and remember God alone.

The prayer of aspiration is impossible without genuine and careful preparation. For one of ripe spiritual experience it may be possible to kneel down and at once pour out the heart in acts of affection towards God ; though it is to be noticed that it is the most saintly souls who are most careful in ordering their prayer towards Him. But for the ordinary Christian it is essential that before entering upon aspiring prayer he should have a clear conception of what he intends to say. For contrition, self-examination is necessary ; for faith and worship, a review of the certainties and mysteries of the spiritual world ; for thanksgiving, a recollection of God's mercies ; for intercession, a consideration of the causes and persons who are to be made its subject. And so vast is the range of every one of these activities that memory is rarely strong enough to do what is necessary ; some written or printed heads of prayer, with details filled in under each, are absolutely necessary. Some will find Bishop Andrewes' 'Private Prayers' give them all they need as a general outline of this character ; others will choose 'Sursum Corda' or some other manual ; others, again, will prefer to draw up their own scheme. Whichever method is chosen, it will be found that some regular arrangement is essential to a full Christian habit of prayer.

The use and continual revision of heads of intercession, contrition, thanksgiving, self-examination, with carefully arranged details under each, gives an unprecedented interest and impetus to affective prayer. It supplies it with material and converts it from what may be no more than a shallow emotional outpouring into a genuine spiritual force. Without going into details as to all of these points, we may consider, as an example, what is required of a good self-examination.[1]

That it should be *regular* and *methodical* goes without saying. To a certain extent, at all events, it should take place daily—at least with reference to those points in

[1] *Holy Dying*, chap. i. sect. 2 ; Webb, *Cure of Souls*, pp. 49–52 ; Williams, *Moral Theology of the Sacrament of Penance*, pp. 50–51.

character which are at the moment a cause of anxiety or special effort. Again, it should be, like all ideas and habits of the spiritual life, *positive* rather than *negative*—should concern itself more with excellences to be acquired than with sins to be eradicated.[1] The importance of this we have already seen ; there is a danger in allowing the mind to dwell upon sinful thoughts, even with a view to their suppression. Especially is this the case with self-examination, which commonly appeals with particular force to characters of a scrupulous and introspective turn—characters more than usually liable to depression and despair.[2] Frequent self-examination should be discouraged for such persons ; when, however, it does take place it should be of a positive kind. For the same reason, it should be *purposive* —that is to say, directed not merely to the satisfaction of a psychological interest, still less to that of an unnatural emotionalism, but to the practical end of spiritual growth. With this in mind the soul will approach its task of self-examination with a humility and sincerity of infinite importance for its purpose.

To the same end, all *vagueness* must be avoided ; the examination should concern itself with concrete details rather than with generalisations. If the soul is considering, let us say, its advance in humility, it is not enough that it should accuse itself, in general terms, of pride ; it should look for the particular occasions on which it has fallen short of the ideal, and find the causes which operated in each case to bring about that result. It may be that examination of a detailed kind takes place too rarely for this to be possible ; morbid and sentimental natures, as we have seen, should be restrained from too frequent

---

[1] This is usually disregarded in most schemes of self-examination, based as they are upon lists of *sins* rather than upon lists of *ideals*.

[2] ' It may be said with some truth that the self best realises itself when it thinks least about itself. . . . In aiding the self-realisation of the educand the educator proceeds more healthily when he avoids an appeal directly to the conscious self. . . . Occasionally it is necessary to call upon an educand to take official stock of himself, but this ought rarely to be done, and should be made an opportunity for vigorous emotional discipline. Nothing is so unhealthy for either child or adult as continual introspection and self-analysis.'—J. Adams, *Development of Educational Theory*, p. 343.

inquiry into their shortcomings. In such cases the examination can be conducted by considering conduct on selected typical occasions.[1] The questioner may ask himself, ' How did I behave on such and such a Sunday ? ' to lead him to conclusions as to his use of Sundays in general as times of worship and rest ; or his behaviour in a particular business difficulty will guide his thoughts as to his attitude towards business as a whole.

It need hardly be added that, as all this is preparatory only, the self-examination must conclude with confession,[2] resolution of amendment and prayer for grace.

The same principles should be applied both to intercession and thanksgiving. In both of these regularity and method are required ; in both a preparation of the material, as definite and detailed as possible. Thanksgiving is by nature positive, for it deals with the special graces and mercies given by God ; and it is well that intercession should as far as possible be made so too. That is to say, intercession should centre rather upon the ideal of God's purposes—the redemption of humanity, the coming of the Kingdom, the reign of love—than upon the present need of the world : the darkness of heathendom, the horror of social conditions, the prevalence of suffering. This will give to intercession, and through it to life as a whole, the character of a conquering optimism rather than that of a despairing struggle. It is perhaps important to emphasise this, for the need of the world is so commonly

---

[1] Schieler-Heuser, *op. cit.* p. 220.

[2] For the specific purposes of ascetic theology (as distinct from moral theology proper), confession to a priest and confession to God alone need not be distinguished ; though it must be recognised that the latter requires a greater degree of spiritual effort than the former to produce the same *immediate* effects upon character. The act of confessing in the hearing of a fellow-mortal (especially in his official character as a minister of reconciliation) usually produces the greater degree of shame and contrition ; it is arguable on the other hand, that if frequently resorted to it may easily result in callousness and hypocrisy. The considerations on both sides are, however, sufficiently discussed in most books on confession and penance ; and we need more evidence as to the effect of sacramental confession upon various types of character before we can say with certainty *how often* it should be employed by the normal Christian. That it is almost certainly required by all Christians, at all events occasionally in a lifetime, and by many much oftener, cannot be doubted. See also *supra*, pp. xvi, 23, 73 ; *infra*, p. 255.

presented as a stimulus to Christian effort, both in prayer and action, that we fail to recognise that it is a motive leading as much to despair as to confidence.

It may be thought that too much stress has been laid upon the form and method of affective prayer, and too little upon its spirit. Formalism is no doubt a very real and great danger. Regular habits of prayer, conducted according to fixed rules, will not *produce* a spirit of prayer—they may even tend to deaden it. The priest, therefore, must adapt and select the rules of prayer which he recommends according to the needs of the individual. They should indeed be appropriate and adequate, but they must not be excessive or burdensome. He must not ' heap too much wood upon the fire, otherwise he will only stifle the spark of goodwill which glows within the heart.' [1] ' Cassian relates that the Egyptian monks did not approve of a multitude of vocal prayers, but preferred to recite their prayers with great attention and penetration of their meaning. . . . Should the director then meet with persons who have burdened themselves with a huge weight of prayers—which they recite hurriedly, without attention or feeling, caring much more for the completion of their self-imposed task than for the interior devotion of the heart—he should reduce the prayers to a third, fourth, or even a fifth part, as he shall judge expedient. But he must remind them meanwhile to make up for the number by the strictness of their attention, in order to relish the affections which the prayers express, not as something learnt by rote, but as the expression of a feeling proceeding from the heart and made vocal by the tongue.' [2]

On the other hand, we may remind ourselves that vagueness, not formalism, is the besetting danger of English religion. Few people have any conception of the application of methodical principles, except on the most exiguous scale, to the spiritual life. Habit, as we have said, avoids waste and develops skill ; and without method, habit is impossible. Without definite rules in prayer the spirit cannot progress in intensity and effective-

---

[1] Scaramelli, *op. cit.* Treat. iii. § 43, from St. Thomas Aquinas, *Quodlib.* iii. a. 28.   [2] *Ibid.* Treat. i. § 267.

ness. It follows, therefore, that Christian men and women should be urged to adopt and apply definite methods in their prayers ; and advised not to relinquish those methods because they appear burdensome or fruitless, until they have been fairly tried. The value of a practice does not manifest itself until some degree of facility has been attained.

A certain latitude of experiment must be allowed to the individual. He may even be encouraged to test for himself various methods of prayer, provided always that he does so in no spirit of religious dilettantism, but with the genuine intention of finding as full and fruitful a method as his character can assimilate. Once he has found rules adequate and appropriate to the fullest possible expression of his spiritual aspirations, he must resolve to adhere to them and use them to the best advantage ; and only to alter or add to or subtract from them if he sees the promise of real benefit from such a course. But in present-day teaching, it is the lack of definite and effective rules, rather than their multiplicity, which deadens spiritual effort.

Contemplation, or the *Prayer of Simplicity* or *Quiet,* is the highest interior activity of the spiritual life—indeed, it aims not at being an activity at all, but at reducing the soul to a purely passive condition in which it may listen, unimpeded by thoughts of self or the cares of the world, to the voice of God alone. ' As rest is the end of motion, so contemplation is the end of all other both internal and external exercises ; for to this end, by long discourse and much practice of affection, the soul inquires and tends to a worthy object that she may quietly contemplate it and . . . repose with contentment in it.' [1]

This is not the place to consider the varied experiences which the mystics have recorded as taking place in the prayer of quiet, nor their consequent formulation of its diversities. Our purpose is simply to see in what way it can be commended to the ordinary Christian as a practice necessary to his spiritual progress. In essence it is simplicity itself. At the end of a meditation, or of a period of aspiring prayer, the soul remains perfectly still,

[1] Baker, *op. cit.* Treat. iii. sect. iv. chap. 1.

its attention fixed upon God and His goodness, and waits for Him to reveal to it some new beauty in Himself. Often enough such revelation does not come, often enough it comes merely in the guise of a formless peace which fills the heart and leaves it ready to go out again to serve God in all simplicity. This is that *Practice of the Presence of God* of which Brother Laurence wrote. Sometimes the answer to the prayer of quiet comes in a new inspiration from God which changes the whole tenour of a life. The soul must still itself without any special expectation of what is to happen. Union with God through Christ is the end of the spiritual life ; and the prayer of quiet is the attempt to taste the joy and power of such a union in perfect dependence upon God.[1] Here is something which He alone can give ; our effort, *at the moment when we look for it*, will merely obtrude a disturbing element. After we have given of our best in meditation or aspiration, it remains simply to be still, and let Him give of His best in return.

Thus contemplation corrects, as it were, the emphasis of the other forms of prayer. *They* manifest themselves in human effort ; *this* recurs to the fundamental truth of religion that we can do nothing of ourselves, that all comes from Him.[2] If at any given time of contemplation the soul experiences nothing, it has no reason to be disturbed. We have opened our eyes to see the vision of God, we have opened our ears to hear His words ; if for this turn He withholds Himself, it is His will that it should be so. We have at least witnessed to Him and to ourselves once again that all things come from Him, and without Him there can be nothing.

This high spiritual expectation, which is content to wait upon God in absolute quiet, is essential for all who wish to advance in the spiritual life. It is only in this way that they can have experience not of God's words,

---

[1] ' It is an affectionate remembrance of God, a simple loving look at God, at our Lord, or at such and such a mystery of our Lord . . . *we look and we love.*'—Lehodey, *op. cit.* pp. 191 *sqq.*

[2] Hence Bishop Chandler's description of contemplation as the ' hardest work in the world ' (*Ara Coeli*, p. 93) is more true of affective prayer than of the prayer of quiet.

or of His providence, or of His power, but of Himself.
Once again it must be repeated that, to any except those
who have objective faith in spiritual things, such a practice
must be an absurdity, the crudest form of self-suggestion.
But to those who have such faith the prayer of quiet can
become not merely a reality, but the greatest reality of
all—that in which God and the soul merge wholly into one.

It need scarcely be pointed out that every one of these
forms of prayer finds its consummation in the *Holy
Eucharist*.[1] Meditation, indeed, should not be practised
at the time of the Communion unless the soul is content,
and well-advised, to withdraw its attention from the
greater part of the service ; and for the most part this
should only be encouraged where the Christian is able to
attend celebrations very frequently. But meditation upon
the subjects suggested in the Collect, Epistle and Gospel
for the day is a most helpful and desirable preliminary, and
should be regarded by every Christian as a practice not
lightly to be set aside.

The service abounds in opportunities for acts of aspiration and affection ; and the more these have been carefully
prepared for, the greater will be the spiritual profit in the
Communion itself. But here, as in prayer in general,
the Christian must be warned not to tie himself too closely
to his preparation, but to be ready, if his mind or affections
are moved in some unexpected but wholly good direction,
to embrace it willingly as a special indication of God's
purpose, and abandon his preconceived plan.

Lastly, the Consecration and the Communion itself
bring with them the Christian's greatest opportunity for
the prayer of quiet. If he has meditated beforehand upon
the truths presented to him by the special service of the
day, prepared the acts of contrition, faith, intercession
and thanksgiving which he is to offer up as a part of his
share in the Eucharist, and earnestly made those offerings
at appropriate moments in the service, he is ready for a
supreme act of contemplation of the Godhead of Christ
veiled in the Holy Mysteries. At this moment, all his

[1] Cp. Lehodey, *op. cit.* pp. 214 *sqq.* ; *Holy Living*, chap. iv. sect. 10.

acts of will or affection may cease, and he should still his soul so that Christ may come to him in the fullness of all spiritual blessing.

To be present at the Holy Eucharist, therefore, and receive the sacrament, is the central moment of the spiritual life. It must be prepared for, not merely in the special ways we have enumerated, but by a continual life of prayer and Christian holiness ; and the priest should try to teach Christian men and women to co-ordinate all their spiritual effort and experience in this one central fact. He must insist upon careful preparation—much more perhaps than it is insisted upon nowadays. But he must also insist, and this is even more necessary, upon careful recollection of the sacrament afterwards—the carrying of it, in fact as well as in memory, into every corner of the daily life as an illuminating and cleansing influence.[1]

Only one other support of the spiritual life need be mentioned here—and that is the *Retreat*. Recent experience has shown the folly of confining retreats to the clergy or to educated Christians alone. It is now recognised that working men and women, soldiers, schoolboys, and every class of the community can find in a retreat an acceptable method of developing the spiritual life. In retreat they have time and leisure to practise and develop the various methods of prayer ; to review their lives in the light both of their failures and successes ; to strengthen their dispositions towards holiness and to discover new ways in which to express their zeal for Christ.

The priest should therefore lose no opportunity of setting retreats before them as a practice natural to every healthy Christian life, and not confined to the ' pious ' alone ; and of ensuring that wherever possible every Christian from time to time has the opportunity of spending at least a single day exclusively in the practice of prayer. ' Let him that is most busied set apart some *solemn time every year*,' says Jeremy Taylor wisely, ' in which, for the time quitting all worldly business, he may attend wholly to fasting and prayer, and the dressing of his soul by con-

[1] Cp. Chandler, *Ara Coeli*, pp. 65–69.

fessions, meditations, and attendances upon God ; that he may make up his accounts, renew his vows, make amends for his carelessness, and retire back again from whence levity and the vanities of the world, or the opportunities of temptations, or the distraction of secular affairs have carried him. ' [1]

We have not attempted to classify the various forms of prayer according to their influence in developing penitence, faith and zeal respectively. Their psychological effect is too far-reaching for such an attempt to be wise or possible. Prayer is so intimate a communion with the Father through His Son that it must affect every fibre of the religious life. But we may notice that certain forms of it, quite apart from their ultimate spiritual value, have distinct psychological effects.[2] Meditation, for example, stirs and strengthens the mind and so makes for vivacity of faith. Self-examination deepens contrition ; thanksgiving for God's goodness increases zeal and confirms faith.[3] Intercession is a great power in fostering zeal ; *intercession for one's enemies*, in particular, tends to produce humility, charitableness and a forgiving spirit. These various parts of prayer may therefore be suggested as remedies for specific spiritual

---

[1] *Holy Living*, chap. I, sect. I.

[2] For the purposes of ascetic theology the psychological effect of prayer is more important than its character as an ultimate spiritual force. Thus intercession is considered as an influence upon the soul which uses it, rather than as a power contributing to the fulfilment of God's purposes. But it must not be forgotten that the latter, rather than the former, is its *true* purpose. ' He who rises from prayer a better man, his prayer has been answered,' expresses only a part of the truth, and the lesser part at that.

[3] We should do well to notice that few parts of prayer are more neglected by the ordinary Christian than thanksgiving. He may feel and express gratitude to God for special manifestations of His goodness, but he rarely takes trouble to examine his daily life for the continual instances of divine providence which it is bound to afford ; still less to render constant thanks for His ' inestimable love in the redemption of the world by our Lord Jesus Christ ; for the means of grace ; and for the hope of glory.' A great deal of exhortation and instruction upon this point is needed in the ordinary Christian community. The psychological value of thanksgiving, as well as of the other forms of prayer, is well indicated by Bishop Wilson's phrase : ' He knows little of himself who is not often in prayer ; he knows little of God who is not often in praise.'

N

defects, according as each promises to be most efficacious.

(b) *Fasting and almsgiving* are classed with prayer by our Lord as a supreme trinity of spiritual habits. As prayer is the fullest expression of the Christian's attitude towards God, so fasting summarizes his attitude towards himself, and almsgiving his attitude towards his neighbour. We need not deal fully with either of the latter, for what has been said as to acts of declaration applies in general here as well. Regularity and method are important in each case, in order to develop the habit and give it sufficient strength and vitality to react to sudden stimulus. *Fasting*, of course, covers all forms of self-control ; the contented endurance of petty troubles and irritations ; the power not to resent injury ; the refusal to allow pleasure or self-indulgence to interfere with the moral purpose ; as well as more considered and deliberate forms of discipline. It is obvious that self-control *must* be most diligently observed in all matters in which there is danger of imminent or grave temptation ; but to enable it to be an effective characteristic of life it may well be practised, from time to time and in moderation, in harmless things. A weekly self-denial on Friday, a more rigorous observance during Lent, has real psychological value ; but in each case it must involve an effort of abstinence or will sufficiently real to enter into consciousness.[1] In conformity with a principle previously noted it is better if such forms of abstinence are chosen as will produce some benefit, however slight, to others. There is less danger in such a case of their becoming irksome or indifferent, or of their being relaxed on trivial excuses. The general question of the subjugation of the passions will be dealt with when we come to consider the problem of sin.[2]

(c) *Almsgiving* includes all forms of loving effort on behalf of others—both ' corporal ' and ' spiritual ' works of

---

[1] *Holy Living*, chap. iv. sect. 5. The whole section is of the greatest importance. Cp. also Geo. Herbert, *Country Parson*, chap. 10 ; A. Chandler, *Ara Coeli*, pp. 34-39.

[2] *Infra*, pp. 262-264.

mercy.[1] Opportunities for it in its wider sense occur at every hour of the day ; yet it is of value, here as in other matters, not merely to wait for occasions on which it can be practised, but to adopt and observe certain rules of life in connection with it. The commonest and best of them is the devotion of a certain part of one's income to the needs of others. Such ' charity ' must, of course, be on a scale to demand some degree of self-denial from the person exercising it, otherwise it has no religious value whatever, however much good it may do. Nor is a mere natural kindness or good-temper or geniality to be regarded as a form of spiritual almsgiving. It has its place—and an important one—in the world, but unless it helps to develop the character of the man or woman exercising it, it cannot count as of value for ' ascetic ' purposes. This fact is commonly ignored, and many Christians are of opinion that an occasional contribution to some charitable fund, making no real call upon their purse, or a general habit of tolerance and good nature, is all that is required of them as an exercise of love towards their fellow-men. It must be made clear that the love which lays down its life for its friends is something of an altogether different calibre, which can be and should be exercised in all departments of life.

Setting aside, therefore, the ' corporal ' works of mercy, of which it may be said that every Christian should be as deeply engaged in them as his income and his circumstances allow, and that nothing short of this fulfils his duty either to God or to his neighbour, we may select two of the ' spiritual ' forms of almsgiving as of special importance, both as regards the resultant benefit to the Christian community, and for the difficulty which they usually present to the individual who tries to practise them.

The first is *forgiveness of others*. This, in our Lord's

---

[1] The *corporal works of mercy* are : to feed the hungry ; to give drink to the thirsty ; to clothe the naked ; to redeem captives ; to visit the sick ; to entertain strangers ; to bury the dead. The *spiritual works* are : to teach the ignorant ; to counsel the dubious ; to admonish sinners ; to comfort the afflicted ; to pardon offenders ; to succour the weak ; to pray for all men. Jeremy Taylor (*Holy Living*, chap. iv. sect. 8) enumerates many others.

own teaching, is set down as a primary condition of winning forgiveness for ourselves.[1] Remembering what the sense of forgiveness means to the Christian, we must insist that in forgiving others he should attempt to produce the same effects in them. There must be something bracing, inspiring, creative in his attitude towards them—something to make new men of them. To forgive is not merely to ' overlook,' or to ' forget,' or to ' say no more about ' the past ; it is to inspire a new effort by an act or attitude of unexpected graciousness. Forgiveness of others, therefore, can only come from an overwhelming zeal for their spiritual welfare ; if that zeal be impeded by consciousness of injury done by them, it must be roused to activity by a consideration of their infinite value in God's sight.

The normal Christian scarcely realises this. Forgiving others, to him, means wiping out their past score ;[2] it does not mean seeking for opportunities to set them up in a new spiritual life. In another respect, also, he ignores the full meaning of forgiveness. He regards it as extending only to injury consciously inflicted. This, however, is an untrue limitation of its content. Springing, as it must do, from genuine and untiring zeal for the welfare of others, it involves a deliberate disregard for everything on their part which tends to alienate that zeal. Not merely intentional injury, but bad manners, dullness, irritating habits, general unattractiveness, must all be *forgiven*—that is to say, must not be allowed to interfere with our zeal for the spiritual progress of those who exhibit them.

Allied to forgiveness in this wide sense is a second ' work of mercy,' which goes by the singularly unfortunate name of *brotherly correction*. Unhappy though the name is, it yet denotes a habit of mind incumbent upon the Christian; and singularly difficult for him to put into effective operation. He has to learn that he is, in a very real sense, his brother's keeper ; that he is responsible, as far as in him lies, for the development of the spiritual life of his

---

[1] Matt. vi. 14, 15, xviii. 35 ; Mark xi. 25, 26.

[2] Sometimes not even that. ' You ought certainly,' wrote Mr. Collins to Mr. Bennett, ' to forgive them, as a Christian ; but never to admit them in your sight, or allow their names to be mentioned in your hearing ' (*Pride and Prejudice*, chap. 57).

neighbour. To the majority of Englishmen this suggestion is singularly uncongenial : any ' interference ' with the point of view or ideals of another appears to them an unwarrantable impertinence. To a minority, it is distressingly congenial ; they constitute themselves judges of the character and conduct of others, and exercise their chosen function in a manner devoid of tact, delicacy or insight. The Christian has to learn a habit of mind free from the defects of either of these extremes. On the one hand, he must never be content until he has put at the disposal of those who come within his influence all the experience of Christ, all the comfort and inspiration of religion, at his command. On the other, he must recognise, that nothing is more difficult than to do this tactfully and with effect ; and must, as a layman, give some study to that art of guiding souls which is the special duty, but by no means the monopoly, of the priest.

Once again we have to emphasise the importance of *definiteness* with reference to these two habits. The Christian must learn to ask himself, ' Is there no one who irritates me—no one who fills me with such dislike or contempt that I find it hard to realise that he has a soul to be saved ? If so, though he has done me no conscious injury, I must *forgive* him : that is to say, must overcome my natural feeling of repugnance, and work and pray for his welfare.' So, too, he should consider, whether in his home or business circle, there are any for whose spiritual benefit he might conceivably exert himself ; should face the fact that there are such people around him, and exercise his insight and imagination until he discovers the best and most tactful way of saving them from sin, or promoting their love for God and desire for goodness. In helping men to *define* their good intentions in this way, to fix them in clear-cut rules of conduct towards specific individuals, the director can do a great deal towards leading them on to a strong life of active Christian love.[1]

---

[1] Under the heading of almsgiving may perhaps be included such duties of religion as are due to God and the Church ; e.g. attendance at public worship, the observance of holy days, &c. These are so frequently treated of that it is unnecessary to discuss them here.

3. *Interest and Environment*

(*a*) Ideas and habits such as the above are those to which the attention of Christian people may be drawn, to secure the progressive growth of their spiritual experience and power. It is, however, a recognised principle of psychology that attention, unless it is to involve an overwhelming effort of will, is best sustained by *interest*. The director therefore requires some knowledge of the ways in which he can interest others in the ideas and habits he commends to them.

A first principle, of course, is that he must consider individuality. He must select for each of those to whom his advice is given such ideas and habits as will elicit the most immediate response on their part. This selection must extend even to the details of the thoughts or methods he recommends. Some Christians, for example, will find their appropriate sphere of zeal in public life, others among boys or men, others in the Sunday school or some other form of Church work. Some will find prayer easy and delightful ; others difficult and irksome. To each the method most needed for the development of his character must be introduced in the manner most likely to commend it to him.

But it is dangerous to suggest too much at first. Although saintliness is without doubt a matter of long progress, a beginner is often deterred if presented with too wide or difficult a task. It is safer to suggest to him that with the conquest of early difficulties there will come such an access of vision as will reveal innumerable fresh fields for activity, and at the same time such an increase of zeal and strength as will enable them to be faced without fear or discouragement. ' When desires of perfection begin to awake in the soul,' says Scaramelli wisely, ' the director must take care not to exact too much, as though he were anxious to make a saint in a single day ; lest if he be eager for too much, he run the risk of losing all.' [1] And again : ' It is better to begin with the correction of outward defects,

---

[1] *Op. cit.* Treat. i. § 79.

both because these are commonly occasions of scandal, and because they are more easily corrected than inward defects, which are rooted in our souls and are as it were a part of our nature. Common prudence dictates that it is better to begin with the more easy tasks ; and to make these a stepping-stone to more difficult and arduous under-takings.' [1]

Interest, too, is sustained often enough by relaxation and variety. Starbuck, whose principles of religious education are singularly in accord with those of ascetic theologians, tells of ' a certain music teacher who says to her pupils, after the thing to be done has been clearly pointed out and unsuccessfully attempted, " Stop trying and it will do itself." ' [2] ' Nervous energy,' he explains in another place, ' when vigorously directed in a certain way, completely expends itself, and must then have a period of recuperation. Rhythms in the supply of avail-able energy are coming to be a universally recognised phenomenon. If with the proper apparatus one tries continuously to lift a weight at successive intervals of a second, one can lift it to a less and less distance, until finally it cannot be lifted at all. But suddenly the ability to perform the work is almost completely regained, and it continues to come and go at intervals.' [3]

This principle is of great importance. It frequently happens that an earnest Christian complains of spiritual dryness, of loss of enthusiasm. Where the cause is not to be looked for (as often it is) in physical ill-health, relief may be found in abandoning all except the lightest spiritual exercises for a time, in the surrender of the personal will and the acceptance of a placid enjoyment of life. This, of course, must not continue for long ; only for long enough to ensure that the spirit has its necessary rest, and can take up its activities again with new enthusiasm.

Where complete relaxation appears undesirable, variety

---

[1] *Op. cit.* Treat. i. § 387.

[2] *Psychology of Religion*, p. 117.

[3] *Ibid.* p. 357. Cp. William James' paradox that ' we learn to skate in the summer, and to swim in the winter ' (*Principles of Psychology*, vol. i. p. 110). The importance of this principle in fixing the alternation between aspiring prayer and the prayer of quiet should not be forgotten.

—a change in methods of prayer, a change even of spiritual work : from Sunday school to boys' club, for example— often produces the desired renewal of interest. Where the soul is ' languid and benumbed,' the director should try some ' little expedient ' of this kind to rouse it again.[1] But if possible this variation should be of such a kind as to lead on gradually to a new stage of the spiritual life, and introduce the soul to higher privileges.[2] In such a way not only will attention be relaxed as it needs to be, but the interest of religion will be maintained and even heightened.

(*b*) The importance of *environment*, not only in sustaining interest, but in the development of every faculty of the soul, cannot be over-emphasised. There are natures so constituted as almost certainly to resent advice or admonition, however lovingly or tactfully administered. In such cases, the best—perhaps the only—practical solution of the problem presented is to make no overt appeal to them, but to ensure that in the most natural way possible in the circumstances they are brought into touch with men and women who will create around them a new and more favourable atmosphere. In most cases of this kind the priest himself will not be of much use ; a prejudice against his profession will prevent his making any but the slowest progress in gaining respect or confidence ; the work must be left to the laity. Their influence and example, however, may be of the greatest value, particularly if it appears that they are acting spontaneously and not according to any preconceived plan.

Such cases—and there are many of them—remind the priest that the laity also have a unique part to play in the ministry of reconciliation. They have not his authority, indeed, or his position as an expert ; he, on the other hand, has not their opportunities, their freedom from the suspicion attaching to his ' cloth,' nor—except perhaps in rare cases— their community of interests with laymen less religious than themselves. Where the indirect influence of environment

---

[1] Scaramelli, *op. cit.* Treat. i. § 76. Cp. *Holy Living*, chap. iv. sect. 7 : ' Eleven Remedies against Tediousness of Spirit.'

[2] J. Welton, *op. cit.* p. 346 ; E. D. Starbuck, *op. cit.* p. 417.

is to be exerted on the soul—and psychology is daily attaching greater importance to it—the priest must hand over his task to the laity, and be content to watch their work, to make intercession for them, and to help them—occasionally, but not by any means always—with such advice as fellow-workmen can give to each other without offence.

It is scarcely necessary to say more as to the supreme importance of surrounding every struggling soul with the best possible environment, with or without its cognisance. The principle lies at the back of all boys' and girls' clubs, and all parochial guilds and societies. It is, in fact, a fundamental principle of a religion in which no one lives or dies to himself—in which all are members of one another. It should be a great consolation to any director, painfully aware of his own continual mistakes and failures, to realise that the Holy Spirit, through the unconscious influence of men and women, boys and girls, each in his or her degree leading an eager upright normal life, may often touch the souls he fails to reach and guide them in the right way.

CHAPTER VIII

CONSCIENCE, LAW AND CASUISTRY

1. *The Nature of Conscience*

FROM the interminable controversies which have raged round the problem of conscience, there have emerged two main opposed points of view. One is that which regards conscience as primarily emotional, and speaks of it as a *moral sense* or *faculty* ; the other that which treats it as primarily rational, and calls it *reason* or the *practical reason.* Any discussion of these two theories, with their respective variations, would be irrelevant to our purpose ; it is enough to notice that modern writers on the whole, in spite of individual preferences in one direction or the other, do not hesitate to admit a measure of truth in both points of view. They allow, that is to say, both a cognitive and a conative element in conscience. Thus Dr. McDougall[1] speaks of it as containing both ' an ideal and a sentiment for the ideal.' To Cardinal Newman,[2] it is ' a mental act ' with both a ' critical and judicial office,' but is also ' always emotional.' Dr. Rashdall,[3] whilst contending that the 'moral faculty' is ' essentially reason,' goes on to admit that ' conscience may be held to include not merely the capacity of pronouncing moral judgments, but the whole body of instincts, feelings, emotions, desires, which are presupposed by and which influence those judgments, as well as those which prompt to the doing of the actions which they prescribe.' ' Conscience,' he adds, 'is a name for a particular aspect of the single self which is thought and feeling and will.

[1] *Social Psychology*, p. 228.
[2] *Grammar of Assent*, part i. chap. 5.
[3] *Theory of Good and Evil*, vol. i. pp. 175, 176.

Morality would be impossible and meaningless, or at least defective and one-sided, for a being in whom any one of these elements were wanting.'

We may conclude, then, that it is not wrong to assign, as we have previously done,[1] the name of ' conscience ' to that tendency of human nature which leads both conative and cognitive elements to seek unsparingly for satisfaction in the good, the beautiful and the true.   Its influence is felt in every sphere of conduct—emotional as well as intellectual. But the customary use of the word is slightly different. It attaches itself particularly to the operations of this tendency *on specific occasions*, to the sense of peace or un-easiness, of relief or shame, consequent upon some act being performed ; to a restlessness which cannot be appeased until in some manner or another reparation or confession has been made.   Conscience, in this narrower sense of the word, comes into operation only in connection with *particular* actions contemplated or committed.   In connection with these acts it reveals itself as a sense either of approbation or disapprobation, producing in the agent either satisfaction or unrest.

It is unnecessary here to attempt to trace these sensa-tions of conscience to their psychological origin.   However much the psychologist may find their source in the maternal instinct, the self-regarding sense, or other primary emotions singly or in combination,[2] moral theology is concerned not with their origin but with their outcome.   It assumes, as a first principle, that conscience is no mere system of con-ventions or prejudice, however much convention may have contributed to its developed form, or prejudice have warped and invalidated its operation.   Taking conscience—this sense of relief or uneasiness attending either the contem-plation or performance of an act, and called out by the *moral* qualities of that act—as a fact of life, it seeks to discover within what limits its dictates are valid, and by what means it may be checked, regulated and brought to fullness of operation.

----

[1] See p. 47.

[2] Thus W. McDougall, *Social Psychology,* chap. 9 ; and cp. Hume, *Treatise on Human Nature,* book iii. part i. §§ 1. 2 ; and part iii. § 1.

The practical problems connected with conscience arise the moment that its tendencies are translated into intelligible judgments. Along with the sense of uneasiness, shame or self-reproach, in every case will go the judgment, implicit or expressed, ' I ought not to have done this ' ; along with the sense of peace and restfulness, the judgment, ' I was right in doing that.' It is a matter of individuality alone that decides whether the judgment precedes or follows the sentiment, or whether the latter is strong or weak. The important point to observe is, that in a rational being this feeling, like every other, must have its counterpart in thought. We notice, further, that the judgment finds its ultimate vindication not in the feeling, but in some general law of morality which in the particular case is being violated or upheld. A penitent thief does not say, ' I ought not to have taken the money, because my conscience pricks me.' He says, in effect, ' I ought not to have taken it, because the action constituted a theft, and theft is wrong.' And this leads to a conclusion anticipated by all the great moralists, that conscience, at all events on its intellectual side, operates in two fields—the field of general principles and the field of particular actions.

The power by which we pass, or hold, general moral judgments is known to theologians by the name of *synderesis* [1]—from that συντήρησις or ' phylactery,' as Jeremy Taylor [2] paraphrased it, which St. Jerome [3] described as the *scintilla conscientiae* remaining in Cain ' after he was expelled from Paradise ' [*sic*]. The application of these general judgments to particular moral problems is the work of *conscientia* properly so-called. The distinction is of formal rather than of practical value ; for in this, as in all matters

---

[1] *Summa*, i. q. 79, a. 12. Cp. *De Veritate*, qq. 16, 17.

[2] *Duct. Dub.* book i. chap. 1, rule 2. He also uses the equivalents ' repository ' and ' preserver.'

[3] In *Ezek.* i. 7. For a suggestion that the original reading was συνείδησις see *Athenæum*, 1877, vol. i. p. 798. Albertus Magnus connected it with συναίρεσις (*Summa de Creat*. pt. ii. tr. 1, q. 71, a. 1). The derivation and original meaning of the word is however a complete mystery. There is a full discussion in H. Appel, *Die Lehre der Scholastiker von der Synteresis* (Rostock, 1891). For a complete survey of the doctrine as a whole see O. Renz, *Die Synteresis nach d. hlg. Thomas v. Aquin* (Münster-i.-W., 1911).

of reasoning, the syllogism by which the particular judgment is referred to the general principle is usually the last stage of the mental process concerned with the act in question. In practice, at all events in simple cases, the first movement of conscience is the feeling either of satisfaction or of uneasiness ; the second—which often accompanies it simultaneously—the thought ' This is right ' or ' This is wrong.' It is only on reflection that the question, ' *Why* is it right or wrong ? ' is asked, and answered by reference to some general principle of morality.

It is a first principle of morals that wherever conscience gives a clear ruling for or against an act, it must be unhesitatingly obeyed, even though impartial criticism holds that the conscience is ' erroneous '—that is, that the agent's judgment as to what is right or wrong in the matter is at fault.[1] Error of this kind may arise from more than one cause. The agent may be genuinely at fault in his first principles—he may, that is, be ignorant of one or more of the rules of right action, or may assume that one or other of these rules points to a type of action which as a matter of fact does not really come under its scope : error arising from these causes would more strictly be referable to the *synderesis*, or grasp upon first principles. Or the agent may have mistaken for the voice of conscience some other tendency or desire at work in his soul—prejudice, it may be, or convention, or self-interest. Two questions of practical importance are therefore presented at once : the first, what are the principles of right action which should be operative in every mature and vigorous conscience ?—the second, how may the voice of conscience be distinguished from that of prejudice, convention, and the other influences which tend to mould our actions ?

---

[1] *Summa*, i. 2, q. 19, aa. 5, 6. By ' erroneous ' in this connection is meant ' *invincibly* erroneous '—i.e. the principle stated above does not cover cases where further inquiry is possible and would reverse the judgment of conscience. In such cases the conscience is said to be in a state of *vincible error*. A conscience *permitting* something in a state of vincible error must not be followed ; on the other hand, if it *forbids* something in a state of vincible error its dictates may not be disobeyed until the error is discovered ; for conscience errs more often through laxity than through rigour. See J. P. Gury, *Compendium Theologiae Moralis* (5th edition, Ratisbon), vol. i. §§ 37, 38.

The first of these is important because, as we have already seen,[1] the individual conscience is not infallible. It needs direction, education, correction even, before it can acquire and retain a true vision of the full possibilities of the Christian life. And though we have considered[2] the principles of Christian truth which will act as a stimulus to moral and spiritual effort, we have yet to examine the principles of *action* upon which the Christian must fall back whenever his relations to others have to be analysed or readjusted. As to the second, it is clearly of the utmost importance that there should be certain rough and ready tests of conscience by which the individual may assure himself that he has, as far as possible, emancipated himself from the insidious influence of unworthy motives masquerading as worthy ones. Even so, however, we have not exhausted the problems with which the fact of conscience presents us.

It is evident that in innumerable cases in which it has to be decided whether an action completed or contemplated is right or not, more than one general principle of morality will be involved, each pointing to a different conclusion. The counter-claims of public and private or domestic duty, of justice and mercy, of courtesy and truthfulness—these and many others are continually producing ‘cases of conscience’ of the most difficult and even painful kinds.[3] How is the Christian to decide such cases ?—or by what rules shall his spiritual adviser help him ? He can, indeed, assure himself that he is not unduly influenced by personal motives or desires, and so act in full confidence that God will bless the result—but is that enough ? Such a principle —the one, no doubt, most commonly called in in cases of the kind—would be adequate, were it not for the fact already established that every act has a permanent effect upon character in tending to the formation of a habit. Whilst, therefore, a single act, if free from unworthy motive, may in itself be unexceptionable, as one of a

---

[1] *Supra*, pp. 136 f.   [2] *Supra*, pp. 148 ff.
[3] It is surely untrue to say (T. H. Green, *Prolegomena to Ethics*, book iv. chap. 2, § 313) that ‘ the margin within which such perplexities can arise in a Christian society is not really very large.’

chain it may lend itself to the formation of habits of real danger. It is at least allowable to look for some principle of guidance in cases of conscience—some general agreement, based upon Christian experience, as to when the primary laws of conscience admit of mitigation, and when they do not.

2. *Conscience and Law*

Our first problem is to ascertain what may be called the *content of synderesis*—that is to say, the body of moral principles which should be at the command of every mature and conscientious Christian, so that he may, by reference to one or more of them, vindicate his action in any given circumstances, or use them as guides in perplexity. The *validity* of general principles of morality is no more here in question than is their *origin*. For just as moral theology assumes that its principles, whatever their immediate source, have their ultimate origin in the self-revelation of God to man, so too it assumes that these principles, as formulated by the Church under the guidance of the Holy Spirit, have a validity which will be unquestioned by the normal Christian conscience. If that validity be challenged, either on the grounds of origin or for some other reason, it is the task of apologetics to establish it. The moralist, as such, confines himself to the attempt to indicate the scope and application of the principles in question.

The accepted Christian belief then is, first of all, that we may postulate a body of *natural law* which—whatever its immediate source—is of universal validity, and is either implanted in, or acceptable to, the normal human conscience. That the moral standards of different races and different epochs vary almost indefinitely, is doubtless the case ; [1] but it is equally the case that, quite apart from the Christian revelation, the normal progress of human thought reduces all these variations to one more or less common standard. This general standard of opinion as to the right and wrong of human conduct—as evidenced,

---

[1] Compare the story of the Greeks and Indians before Darius (Herodotus, iii. 38), and *supra*, p. 26.

for example, in the Greek philosophers or the normal principles of decency and mutual regard operative among civilised, even though non-Christian, communities—is commonly spoken of as the law of nature ; and it is legitimate to assume that it represents the standard of moral principle which could be attained by the ordinary conscience without any special enlightenment either from within or without.[1]

In attempting to determine the general content of natural law, St. Thomas pursues a severely *a posteriori* method which has the closest affinities with modern thought. ' Reason,' he tells us, ' naturally apprehends as good all those things to which man has a natural inclination,' and consequently, as the first precept of the law of nature, he sets the rule : ' Good (in this sense, of that for which we have a natural inclination) is to be sought for, evil avoided.'[2] According to this rule, self-preservation, the reproduction of the species, the care of offspring and so forth, stand first among the laws of nature ; in the second place come those ' laws ' which man does not share with the animal creation—to ' know the truth about God,' and hence ' to shun ignorance ' ; ' to live in society,' and hence ' to avoid offending those among whom one lives.' Natural law, in fact, means simply the satisfaction, in harmony one with another, of the natural human instincts, as much on their intellectual as on their physical sides. A modern psychologist could scarcely better this statement.

It is evident, therefore, that a statement of natural law based upon this psychological principle will not differ very much from that summary of human duty which we have already seen to be deducible from the equally psychological classification of the four cardinal virtues. Indeed

---

[1] Its recognition by conscience is, of course, a gift of God, but a gift common to all men—' Nihil aliud est quam participatio legis aeternae in rationali creaturâ ' (*Summa*, i. 2, q. 91, a. 2). ' Lumen rationis naturalis, quo discernitur quid sit bonum et quid malum quod pertinet ad naturalem legem, nihil aliud est quam impressio luminis divini in nobis ' (*ibid.*). Its principles are ' communissima ' and ' omnibus nota ' and cannot wholly be obliterated in any conscience (*ibid.* q. 94, a. 6), though they may be darkened and corrupted—' Sicut apud Germanos olim latrocinium non reputabatur iniquum ' (*ibid.* a. 4 ; cp. q. 99, a. 2, ad. 2 ; q. 100, a. 5, ad. 1 ; ii. 2, q. 22, a. 1, ad. 1 ; &c.).

[2] *Summa*, i. 2, q. 94, a. 2.

the expanded consideration of the cardinal virtues given by St. Thomas and other moralists would serve very well for an exhaustive account of the content of natural law.[1] But just as the Christian consciousness could not satisfy itself with the cardinal virtues alone, and therefore, partly by expanding their meaning and partly by adding the theological virtues, set forth in the end a very different account of Christian excellence ; so, too, it could not rest content with this summary of natural law as being all that the Christian conscience is required to recognise. Natural law is completed in *divine law* ;[2] and the essence of the divine law is first of all that it is of internal conditions rather than of external acts,[3] and secondly that it is in the main a *lex non scripta*, a law implanted in the soul.[4] The gospel precepts indeed, the Beatitudes, even the decalogue in its Christian re-interpretation, are a part of this new law ; they prepare and fit the soul to receive the power of the Holy Spirit ;[5] but in essence it is a law of liberty. The ideal Christian, in other words, would be one who, while fully possessed of the principles of morality, need never call them to mind. He would be so full of the Spirit, so intimately in communion with his Lord, that his actions would spontaneously correspond with the Christian ideal ; he would have no need either to consider them beforehand or to review them afterwards.

It is in passages such as this that St. Thomas Aquinas shows himself to fall short neither of the thought of the New Testament nor of the highest Christian experience. But with an eminently practical mind he goes on to point out that the new dispensation, though substituting its ' law of liberty ' for both the law of nature and the imperfect revelation of the Old Testament, does as a matter

---

[1] St. Thomas's actual opinion seems to be that the *general principles* of the cardinal virtues belong to the law of nature, but not all their *implications*, ' multa enim secundum virtutem fiunt ad quae natura non primo inclinat ; sed per rationis inquisitionem ea homines adinvenerunt quasi utilia ad bene vivendum ' (*Summa*, i. 2, q. 94, a. 3).

[2] *Summa*, i. 2, q. 91, a. 4. In strict thought, the divine law has two parts, the Old and the New (q. 106, a. 2), the latter being the completion of the former (*ibid.* a. 3) ; cp. also q. 107, aa. 1–4.

[3] *Ibid.* ; and cp. q. 98, a. 1 ; q. 100 a. 9.

[4] *Ibid.* q. 106, a. 1 ; q. 108, a. 1.   [5] *Ibid.*

O

of fact enjoin certain outward acts. These are, first of all, such acts as lead to the receiving and maintaining of spiritual grace—prayer, the Eucharist, and the like ; second, such habits of ' faith working through love ' as alone can give it outlet.[1] These, therefore—the due performance of such actions as are known to lay the soul open to the influence of grace, and the continued effort to give that grace more and more effective expression in thought and life—should be principles recognised by the conscience of every Christian man or woman.

The practical importance of this conclusion lies in its inevitable corollary, that wherever an individual is not alive to the urgency of these duties—the duty, on the one hand, of taking every opportunity, sacramental or otherwise, of receiving grace ; and the duty, on the other, of giving grace received full power of manifesting itself in the virtues of the new law—whilst no blame is necessarily to be attached to him, whilst no suspicion of *mala fides* on his part need arise, he is yet not to be considered as a person of mature or fully developed conscience. It remains for the priest, in such a case, to persevere in the work of instructing or assisting conscience to its full development.

A mature and sensitive conscience, then, should recognise as authoritative the promptings both of natural law— the complex of principles leading to a useful, progressive, and benevolent life in the society of others ; and of divine law—the reinterpretation of natural law according to the teaching and example of Christ, as well as the rules by which a Christian life may be brought most fully under the influence of the Holy Spirit,[2] and may express the inspira-

---

[1] *Summa*, i. 2, q. 108, a. 1.

[2] Or may avoid special scandals and dangers. The formulation of these rules is the task of *ecclesiastical law*. The six so-called ' precepts of the Church '—observance of Sundays and holy days, of days of abstinence, the rules of confession, communion, and the support of pastors, and the prohibition of marriage within certain degrees (see Webb, *Cure of Souls*, pp. 100, 207 ff.)—form a convenient summary of this part of the divine law. Less convenient is the list of sixty-nine ' precepts of the Gospel ' given in *Holy Dying*, chap. 4, sect. 8. On the nature, scope, and degree of obligation of ecclesiastical law, see *Duct. Dub.* bk. iii. chap. 4 ; Sanderson, *De Oblig. Consc.*, prael. vi. § 26 ; prael. vii. § 27 ; Hooker, *Ecclesiastical Polity*, bk. iii. ; Elmendorf, *Moral Theology*, p. 507.

tion thus received in the most perfect forms. In ideal, a life actuated by such a conscience will be spontaneous and unreflective ; but until the ideal is reached, the Christian must live by the law of conscience, unless his liberty is to become licence. Even when the ideal has to some degree been attained, the law has still a part to play. The Christian may be challenged to give a reason for his actions, or thrown into perplexity by some more than usually difficult problem. In both these cases he will need to recall the principles which have guided his progress so far. To such a man these laws—both of nature and of God—will be *binding* ; that is to say, wherever, upon reflection, a case is found to fall wholly and clearly under one of them, there will be no room for further discussion and questioning. The law will be obeyed.

But, if we are to follow St. Thomas a little further, a conscientious Christian will also recognise as principles— if not to be obeyed to the letter at all events to be held in high esteem—the ' evangelical counsels '—poverty, celibacy and obedience.[1] ' To every law there are counsels attached. A law may be said to be a nucleus of precept, having an envelope of counsel.' [2] St. Thomas speaks of these ' counsels,' which of course can only be fully obeyed in the monastic state, with interesting moderation. He affirms indeed, apparently as a matter of abstract theory, that ' a man will attain more speedily to eternal happiness ' by adopting the counsels in full, and so giving up the goods of the world entirely. But he makes it clear that such a life is only for those who are ' able to receive it,' and that the Christian can realise eternal bliss without any violent breach with secular cares and employments ; and he further insists that the counsels can be observed in spirit, though not perhaps in the letter, by any Christian however placed—thus ' when anyone gives alms to the poor, not being bound to do so, he is following the counsels in that particular case.' [3]

We cannot leave this question of the laws to be observed by a well-regulated conscience without considering briefly

[1] *Summa*, i. 2, q. 108, a. 4.
[2] J. Rickaby, *Moral Philosophy*, p. 128.
[3] *Summa, loc. cit.*

one of the most complex subjects with which moral theology presumes to deal. What are we to say of the relation between conscience and human law ? How far must the conscientious man hold himself *bound* to obey the laws of the state in which he lives—morally bound *in foro conscientiae*, that is to say ; not merely legally bound *in foro externo* ? Few problems have been so widely canvassed in the whole realm of Christian morals, and the three great English casuists—Bishops Jeremy Taylor, Sanderson and Hall—all of them dealt with the subject at great length. We cannot here do more than summarise as briefly as possible the principal conclusions which appear to bear upon the matter, without following our authorities into the intricacies of discussion as to the nature of human law in general.

It appears, then, that human law, in its ideal, is no more than the application of the principles of natural law to the circumstances of ordinary life in society. If, then, laws conform to the principles of natural law in three main respects [1]—as being for the common good, as not exceeding the lawgiver's authority,[2] and as imposing no disproportionate burden upon any member of the community—they must be regarded as binding *in foro conscientiae* ;[3] that is to say, the conscientious Christian will regard it as an integral part of his scheme of morality to obey them willingly and promptly. Where these conditions are not satisfied, the law in itself has no claim upon conscience, though it may be part of the Christian's duty to obey in order to avoid scandal or disturbance, ' for which cause a man should even yield his right.'[4] It need hardly be added that even

---

[1] *Summa*, i. 2, q. 96, a. 4.

[2] *Ibid.* a. 5.—Thus it is beyond the authority of civil law to make enactments about religion and conscience ; or beyond the authority of school or college law to regulate the ways in which pupils shall spend their holidays.

[3] Yet according to modern Roman Catholic teaching there is ' a probable opinion of long standing ' that positive laws ' do not bind under sin ' (i.e. in conscience).—T. Slater, *Manual of Moral Theology*, vol. i. p. 127. Hence Fr. Slater can maintain (*Cases of Conscience*, vol. i. p. 91) that one who has made a false declaration of income to avoid payment of tax, though ' his action is not to be praised or imitated,' is not bound in conscience to make restitution.

[4] *Summa*, i. 2, q. 96, a. 4.

Just laws are only binding when framed by a competent authority—'either the whole people or some official who is vice-gerent of the whole people'[1]—and when duly promulgated;[2] and to this Bishop Sanderson adds that the consent of the people to the law is required,[3] though it is enough if this consent is tacit or implicit.

On the question of the right of rebellion, authorities, as is natural, differ. Thus St. Thomas allows rebellion against tyrants, unless it involves more suffering for the subject people than did the tyrannical rule.[4] Jeremy Taylor, on the other hand, concludes that it is not lawful for subjects to rebel, or to take up arms against the supreme power of the nation, upon any pretence whatsoever;[5] and this he argues from Scripture, from the Fathers, and from experience. ' Many subjects have laid aside their supreme princes and magistrates, and have exchanged them for liberty and justice,' but all that they gained was, in effect, ' words in present, and repentance in reversion.' His condemnation of the opposite opinion is sweeping to a degree : ' No man who can think it lawful to fight against the supreme power of his nation, can be fit to read cases of conscience '—after which there seems little more to be said! Sanderson, writing at the same troubled time and from the same point of view, is rather less dogmatic. ' I cannot say,' he concludes in his sermon on the rebellion of the people against Samuel,[6] ' that the greatest tyranny or corruption imaginable could have warranted such an attempt *in toto*.' The problem is so much bound up with historical and political questions that a clear solution is scarcely to be hoped for[7] : it may, however, be assumed that the modern tendency is to ascribe to the citizen, with T. H. Green,[8] not merely the right but even the duty of

[1] *Summa*, i. 2, q. 90, a. 3.
[2] *Ibid.* a. 4.
[3] *De Oblig. Conscientiae*, praelect. 7. Cp. Hooker, *Ecclesiastical Polity* book i. § 10 : ' Laws they are not therefore which public approbation hath not made so.'
[4] *Summa*, ii. 2, q. 42, a. 2, ad. 3. Cp. *De Reg. Princ.* i. 6.
[5] *Duct. Dub.* book iii. chap. 3, rule 3.
[6] *Sermo vi ad Magistratum* (Nottingham, 1634).
[7] See J. N. Figgis, *Divine Right of Kings*, esp. chaps. 7–9.
[8] *Works*, vol. ii. pp. 424–426.

resistance in certain cases, provided that there is some real prospect of a happy issue.

3. *The Tests of Conscience*

Such, then, is the moral scheme with which the well-equipped conscience should be furnished—a scheme embracing natural, divine and human law. The conscientious Christian will at least have thought out the main principles comprehended in this scheme, both that he may establish some valid rule of life for himself, and that he may have some general guidance in case of perplexity. Where such cases arise, he will attempt to bring them under one or other of the principles of Christian action, and direct his effort accordingly. Yet even here there is a danger. Suppose that he decides that such and such an action is required by the law of conscience, or that such another is not required—how can he be certain that he is unbiased in applying the particular law to the question in dispute, or in exempting the suggested course of action from the veto of all known law ? How may he assure himself that his intention to act has been framed simply and solely by the valid process of bringing it into conformity with law, without suffering any perversion under the influence of prejudice, personal preference, or convention ? Are the dictates he recognises in any given case those of conscience or of self-will ?

It is right that a man should examine himself with a view to securing purity of motive—should assure himself, that is, that he has decided his problem purely on the grounds of the law of conscience and without reference to other impulses. The habit may indeed become a disease ; when it does so it takes the shape of what is known as ' scrupulosity,' and presents a very difficult problem indeed to any priest who may have to deal with it.[1] But in moderation it is a habit to be commended, subject always to the limitation that true Christian action should spring spontaneously from continuous communion with God, and that no degree of reflection can prove a satisfactory

[1] *Infra*, p. 213.

substitute for that one supreme source of morality.   Rules
for such examination of conscience cannot be laid down
with any hard and fast distinctness; but here, as always,
Bishop Jeremy Taylor showed a sympathetic knowledge
of human nature with which some of his contemporaries
scarcely credited him, and we may well follow his guidance.
By far the most readable parts of 'Ductor Dubitantium' are
the two short passages in which he discusses how to avoid
mistaking 'prejudice or passion, fancy or affection, error
or illusion' for conscience; [1] and lays down the 'signs of
difference whereby in a mixed or complicated intention
we may discern which is the principal ingredient.' [2]

Under the first of these heads are included such principles
as the following. 'We are to suspect our conscience of
being misinformed when we are not willing to enquire into
the particulars . . . for we are not to choose the way
because it looks fair, but because it leads surely; and to
this purpose the most hearty and particular inquest is most
prudent and effective.'   And, as a corollary to the foregoing, 'He that resolves upon the conclusion before the
premisses, (only) enquiring into particulars to confirm his
opinion at aventures (i.e. *at all costs*) not to shake it if it
be false or to establish it only in case it be true, unless he
be defended by chance is sure to mistake, or at least can
never be sure whether he does or no.'   Again, in conduct-
ing such inquiry, and forming a conclusion upon it, we must
be guided not by 'the multitude that easily errs' in
preference to 'the wise guide of souls'; not by 'them that
speak by chance rather than them who have studied the
question'; not by 'him of another profession rather
than him whose office and employment it is to answer.'
There is a very human touch in this last piece of advice :
how often do men not satisfy conscience by obtaining the
concurrence and support of someone no more competent
to judge impartially than themselves ?

'That determination is to be suspected that does
apparently serve an interest, and but obscurely serve a
pious end; when that appears and nothing else appears,
the resolution and counsel is to be considered warily before

[1] *Duct. Dub.* book i. chap. 1, rule 3.   [2] *Ibid.* book i. chap. 2, rule 5.

it be pursued.' Jeremy Taylor illustrates this very aptly by criticising, *inter alia*, the arguments adduced by Roman controversialists for the temporal power of the Pope— ' in these things every man with half an eye can see the temporal advantage ; but how piety and truth shall thrive in the meanwhile, no eye hath yet been so illuminate as to perceive.' Yet he admits that cases will occur ' where both truth and interest may be conjoined ' ; in these cases the ' end of piety ' will not be obscure, and so long as the man's zeal ' be not bigger than the certainty of the proposition ' the fact that conscience and interest both seem to point in the same direction need not be regarded as a barrier.

Recognising, however, that cases of this kind will present real cause of uneasiness to delicate consciences, anxious never to allow to self-interest undue weight in any decision, the Bishop reverts, in the second passage to which allusion has been made, to certain considerations whose intention is obviously to relieve the uneasy mind. ' Whatever came in after the determination was made,' he says in the first place, ' though it add much the greater confidence, and makes the resolution sharper and more active, yet it is not to be reckoned as the prevailing ingredient.' The mere fact, that is, that a course of action, once decided upon, is found to be pleasurable, is no evidence that the pleasure to be derived from it was the prevailing influence which led to its adoption. Again, ' when the determination is almost made, and wants some weight to finish it, what soever then supervenes and casts the scales is not to be accounted the prevailing ingredient '—where a course of action otherwise considered to be right is only entered upon through the addition of some slight incentive of self-interest, we need not on that account accuse ourselves of having acted in pure selfishness. 'A child's finger may thrust a load forward, which being haled by strong men stands still for want of a little assistance.'

His next principle goes very deeply into the matter and is one of supreme importance. ' That is the prevailing ingredient in the determination which is most valued, not which most pleases ; that which is rationally preferred, not that which delights the senses. . . . He

that keeps a festival in gratitude and spiritual joy to do
God glory and to give Him thanks, and in the preparation
to the action is hugely pleased by considering the music,
the company, the festivity and innocent refreshments,
and in his fancy leaps at this, hath not spoiled the regularity
of his conscience by the intermixture of the sensual with
the spiritual, so long as it remains innocent ; for though
this flames brightest, yet *the other* burns hotter, and will
last longer than the other.' Two precautions only are
necessary—we must be ' infinitely careful to prescribe
measures and limits to the secular joy, that it may be
perfectly subordinate to, and complying with, the spiritual
and religious ' ; and we must be ' willing to suppress the
light flame, rather than extinguish the solid fire.'

Two things further remain to be guarded against. If
an action is proposed ministering both to a spiritual (or
conscientious) and a personal end, but manifestly more
adapted to the latter than the former, its motives are to
be suspected. Large subscriptions to charitable purposes,
unless anonymous, minister to self-advertisement as much
as to benevolence ; and the donor should be on his guard
against the predominance of the personal motive—' He that
serves a secret piety by a public panegyric, disorders the
piety by dismantling the secret ; it may still be piety, but
it will be lessened by the publication, though this publication be no otherwise criminal than because it is vain.' And
again, the moment any admittedly evil purpose is allowed
among the motives of an action otherwise creditable, ' the
conscience is neither sure nor right, but is dishonoured and
defiled.' In such cases the remedy is not so much to abstain
from the action proposed, as to attack the sinful tendency
which lies at the root of the unworthy motive.

4. *Cases of Conscience* [1]

We come now to a problem which has inspired and
exercised the subtlety of generations of theologians. Where

[1] For an important discussion of this question, containing a clear
account of the various casuistical schools (Probabilism, Probabiliorism,
Rigorism, &c.) see the article on ' Probabilism ' by the Rev. C. J. Shebbeare
in the *Church Quarterly Review*, vol. lxxiv. (July 1912).

a proposed action appears to fall under two of the laws of conscience, one of which approves whilst the other condemns it, is there any way by which the agent can be guided as to the course he is to take ? Let it be clear from the outset that this is a conflict between *law* and *law*, not between *law* and *liberty*. There can be no question of emancipating a Christian from any of the precepts of morality *except* at the instance of some other precept.

Cases, of course, will occasionally arise in which a Christian is perplexed because, though he is aware of a particular law whose authority he recognises, he is not able to decide whether it applies in the special circumstances in which he finds himself—cases, that is, in which the antithesis is genuinely one between law and liberty only. Such cases, however, are very rare, and will only occur, as a matter of fact, with reference to ecclesiastical precepts. ' Perplexity of conscience, properly so-called,' says T. H. Green,[1] ' seems only to arise from conflict between different formulæ for expressing the idea of good in human conduct.'

Yet this conflict between formula and formula, this antithesis between law and law, has become transformed, in much casuistical writing, into one between law and liberty, so that, of two opposed courses, one is commonly spoken of as *legi favens*, the other as *libertati favens*. There is a very simple reason for this. The agent is scarcely ever without a personal inclination in the matter. He naturally favours one course or the other ; and therefore, to him, the law which his inclinations lead him to invoke takes the shape not of law but of liberty ; and the question becomes, not ' Which of two laws—A or B—must I obey ? ' but, ' May I, by assuming my action to be under the ruling of law A, conscientiously hold myself exempt from obedience to law B ? '[2]

A practical instance will make this simpler. A conscientious Christian knows that he must exercise some degree of abstinence in Lent, and that abstinence, to be of any real

---

[1] *Prolegomena to Ethics*, book iv. chap. 2, § 314.

[2] This is fully developed by T. H. Green, *op. cit.* book iv. chap. 2, §§ 315-317.—It has to be remembered that such cases only arise where the contesting laws are *of equal obligation*. See J. J. Elmendorf, *Moral Theology*, p. 503.

spiritual value, must involve giving up something he is fond of. He chooses to abstain from tobacco, or theatres, or whatever it may be, and is at once assailed by the thought, ' This abstinence will make you irritable or dull-witted ; it will harm your efficiency.' Thus the rule of honest work is at once opposed to the rule of abstinence, suggesting exemption from the latter. But the man's natural inclinations all support the exemption ; and therefore to him the exemption means *liberty* (though he can only claim it on the ground of its value for efficiency—that is, in obedience to the *law* of work), whilst the rule of abstinence becomes the *law* from which he desires exemption ; and the problem is no longer, Which of these laws am I to obey ? but, May I conscientiously claim *liberty*, or exemption, from the law of abstinence ?

This point—that in the vast majority of cases of conscience, the conflict, though it appears as one between law and liberty, is really one between law and law—is rarely made clear in casuistical writings. The result is unfortunate, for it has led to the condemnation of *all* systems of casuistry (many of which are simply honest attempts to find guidance for perplexed souls) [1] as no more than a series of ' rules for the breaking of rules ' ; [2] and the debased Jesuitical sophistries pilloried in the ' Provincial Letters ' have been taken as the final and only issue to which the attempt can come. The process has been helped by a further antithesis equally dangerous—the opposition between the *opinio tutior* and the *opinio minus tuta*. This distinction, like the other, comes from the casuists themselves ; and suggests that the question is simply one of ' When is it *safe* to ignore a law of conscience ? ' thus taking the problem out of the sphere of morality into that of mere prudential calculations.[3] It must be admitted that by these two false distinctions Roman Catholic casuistry has laid itself open to the most damning indictments. It has substituted

---

[1] A common-sense view of the value of casuistry is taken by Geo. Herbert, *Country Parson*, chap. 5.

[2] C. F. D'Arcy, *Christian Ethics and Modern Thought*, p. 103.

[3] As Jeremy Taylor points out, the problem can never be one of safety *alone* ; we must consider whether an action contemplated is *laudable* as well as safe (*Duct. Dub.* book i. chap. 4, rule 3).

for the liberty of the Spirit a juristic system of the most rigorous and detailed kind, whose enactments have to be evaded by elaborate and sophistical special pleading, or a fully-developed system of dispensations.[1] We have already seen how completely this has warped the whole trend of moral theology.[2]

Once, however, it is recognised that the distinction *is* a false one—that there is no question, in reality, of opposing liberty to law, or of finding at all costs justification for leaving the safer path—we may extract principles of real value from the writings of the casuists. Our problem is simply to find the principles which justify in obeying that law of conscience to which we are naturally inclined at any given moment, even though another law appears to bear upon the case and enjoin an opposite solution. Such principles appear to be the following :

(*a*) There are certain laws of conscience which define the actions they condemn so clearly, that not even the applicability of another law can become an excuse for disobeying them. Such, for example, is the seventh precept of the decalogue, taken in its most literal sense, condemning an outward act ; and the tenth, condemning an inward one. This appears to be the meaning of the rule : ' Probabilism cannot be applied to cases . . . where some end *must* be obtained, or where there is question of the *certain* right of some other person which must be respected.' [3] (The italics are not in the original.)

(*b*) Beyond this, it seems true to say that, in cases of *bona-fide* doubtfulness, a probable opinion may be followed without fear of sin. The definition of a *probable opinion* is one, however, which requires the greatest care. According to Fr. Slater, it is one which ' rests on good or solid grounds such as would incline a man of prudence and

---

[1] On *dispensations* see T. Slater, *Manual of Moral Theology*, vol. i. pp. 111–115.

[2] See p. 11 n. In addition to the authorities there quoted for the causes of the juristic influence in Roman Catholic theology, see H. Sidgwick, *History of Ethics*, p. 144.

[3] T. Slater, *Manual of Moral Theology*, vol. i. p. 71 ; J. J. Elmendorf, *Elements of Moral Theology*, p. 500. For illustrations see Gury, *Compendium*, vol. i. § 57.

judgment to embrace it.' [1] These grounds may be either
intrinsic, that is to say, deducible from the nature of the
case ; or *extrinsic*, i.e. based upon the authority of experts
in the spiritual life. It is generally assumed by Roman
Catholic writers that no layman can decide the *intrinsic*
probability of any opinion ; he must leave this to the
experts, and must rest content with an extrinsic probability based upon the concurrence of their considered
judgment.

Few English Christians would, however, consent to
such an extreme of ecclesiasticism as this. The individual neither can, nor ought, to consider himself free
from the duty of weighing the intrinsic merits of every
case of conscience with which he is faced. But we may
well agree that it is wise, in every difficult problem, to take
the advice of experts in the spiritual life; and here the
rules of probabilism help us. Should the experts be in
agreement, there is a strong case for accepting their advice.
Where, however, there is no general agreement between
authorities, we must fall back upon some further principle
or principles to help us to decide between them. Such
principles are those, for example, quoted from Martinus
ab Azpilcueta (*c.* 1560) by Fr. Slater :

' Where there is a difference among doctors, that opinion
should be preferred which is confirmed by custom, or
grounded on a text of law, or which rests on an invincible
argument. If none of these rules serves, then the common
opinion should be followed, and that may be called a common
opinion which six or seven approved authors adopt. . . .
If that rule does not suit the case, then that opinion should
be chosen which is backed by more numerous authorities
and reasons ; then that which is more lenient, or which
favours marriage, a last will and testament, liberty, a private
individual against the State, the validity of an act, or the
defendant in an action at law. If in none of these ways
one opinion is better than the other, then that should be
adopted which the greater number of theologians follow
if the matter belong to theology, or canonists if it belong
to canon law, or civilians if it belong to civil law. To

---

[1] *Op cit.* vol. i. p. 69.

these rules Navarrus adds the note that in the forum of conscience it is sufficient to choose as true the opinion of a man of virtue and learning.' [1]

So far we have found nothing to which exception can be taken, except in the last sentence, to which we must recur. Navarrus' rules can indeed be summed up much more briefly in the four notes of a probable opinion given by Suarez : The opinion must not run counter to any truth universally accepted by the Church ; it must be in agreement with common sense ; it must be based on reason and supported by good authority ; and, if it has not the support of the majority of authorities, it must at all events not be an opinion generally abandoned.[2] There is nothing in this to suggest that the individual Christian is exempt from making searching inquiry, or may act upon any *obiter dictum* which seems to favour his personal feelings. The rules just quoted seem to presuppose on the part of the perplexed mind a genuine and earnest desire to reach the truth ; and, consequently, are of very real value.

The real danger of probabilism began when Bartholomew à Medina (1528–1581), taking up the hint contained in Navarrus' last sentence, laid down the rule that the probable opinion of a single doctor of the Church, provided that it was probable, was sufficient justification for an action, *even if more probable opinions could be alleged on the other side*. This is the characteristic feature of probabilism strictly so-called. Clearly, though no doubt a fair logical conclusion from what had gone before,[3] it opens the door for every kind of irregularity. It relieves the inquirer of the burden of making fair comparison between arguments and authorities. So long as he can find *one* probable opinion to support the action he wishes to take, he is exempt from all further moral responsibility in the matter.[4]

[1] *Op. cit.* vol. ii. p. 550. See Azpilcueta (Doctor Navarrus), *Manuale Confessariorum*, chap. 27, §§ 286–289.

[2] Suarez, *De Ult. Fin., Tract.* iii., *de bon. et mal.*, disput. xii. sect. 6.

[3] Both sides of the question are discussed in *Ductor Dubitantium*, book i. chap. 4, rule 5.

[4] It is to be noted that Roman Catholic apologists for probabilism claim only that it is a *safe*, not that it is the *best*, solution of difficulties of conscience. *Cf.* Slater, *op. cit.* vol. i. p. 74.

It would be foreign to our purpose to inquire into the tedious details of the controversies which probabilism aroused,[1] or of the practical excesses to which it gave birth. The real failure of the system lies in the irresponsibility with which it invests the individual Christian. On that account it can never be introduced as an ethical principle into English Christianity. The Englishman may be willing to take the *advice* of authorities and experts, but, quite rightly, he will never submit to a system which relieves him of the burden—and thereby deprives him of the privilege—of settling his own cases of conscience for himself upon their merits.

We must therefore consider the grounds upon which *intrinsic*, as distinct from *extrinsic*, probability can be established; that is, on which the conscience can be held to be exempt from obedience to one of two conflicting laws by reason of its duty to the other, even though the latter is supported by natural inclination.

(c) Jeremy Taylor sets himself the question : ' How shall the ignorant and vulgar proceed in such cases where their teachers are divided ? ' ; and answers with a tinge of asperity : ' In most cases it is best for them to let them alone, and let them be divided still, and to follow them in those things where they do agree ; but if it be in such cases where they must declare or act on one side, *let them take that which they think to be the safest*, or the most pious, the most charitable and the most useful '— and he adds certain ' collateral considerations ' which will help in coming to a decision.[2]

Here is embodied a perfectly simple principle—' Always take the safe course.' This principle is expressed in the doctrine called *Tutiorism*, and its watchword is *in dubio pars tutior est sequenda*. In those rare cases of which we have spoken, where there is a doubt as to the applicability of a particular law in given circumstances, it must mean, ' Obey the law ' ; in the commoner cases where law is opposed to law, it must be interpreted, ' So long as the

[1] For a full account, see Döllinger-Reusch, *Geschichte der Moral-streitigkeiten*, vol. i. part i.
[2] *Duct. Dub.* book iv. chap. 1, rule 9.

doubt remains, obey the law opposed to your natural inclinations, and not the one which they support.'[1]

Attractive as such a principle is, it would obviously be both intolerable and wrong if it were made a binding precept of morality. Jeremy Taylor recurs to it on a later page, and the best he can say for it is that it is 'good advice, but not necessary in all cases.' 'It is always an effect of piety and a strong will to do good, but very often an effect of a weak understanding'; it may even be merely a 'prudent compliance either with a timorous or with an ignorant conscience.'[2] The principle, conceived as a final rule of conduct, would be *intolerable*; for scrupulous consciences could always find some law of possible application to prevent any action however innocent. It would at times be *wrong* as well, because often enough the heroic course is *not* the safe course, and prudential calculations, as we have seen, are by no means the highest motives in the Christian life. If the best that can be said for an action is, 'I cannot be blamed for it, anyhow,' Christian morality would be reduced to a very low order indeed.

On these grounds, *Tutiorism*, or *Rigorism*, as it is also called, was condemned by Pope Alexander VIII,[3] and the principle *lex dubia non obligat* became established. We are not *bound* to obey a doubtful law, though we may certainly not act against its precepts unless we have good positive reasons on the other side for doing so.[4] If no such reasons appear, we may either obey the law, or we may look round for other principles to be our guide.

(*d*) Of such other principles,[5] the first is expressed in the words *melior est conditio possidentis*. It may be interpreted thus: where a person is acting in accordance with some considered rule or right, and a doubt supervenes whether in any given case he ought not to alter his mode of action,

---

[1] Gury, *op. cit.* vol. i. § 52 (*fin*).

[2] *Duct. Dub.* book i. chap. 5, rule 5.

[3] Proposition 3 of Dec. 7, 1690. See Denzinger-Bannwart, *Enchiridion*, § 1160; Gury, *op. cit.* vol. i. § 53.

[4] Slater, *op. cit.* vol. i. p. 64; Rickaby, *Moral Philosophy*, p. 165; Gury, *op. cit.* vol. i. §§ 41, 42.

[5] Given in Slater, *op. cit.* vol. i. p. 65; Gury, *op. cit.* vol. i. §§ 75–80; Elmendorf, *op. cit.* pp. 500, 501. They are mainly derived from canon law.

he may conscientiously continue his original mode of action *unless and until the doubt becomes a moral certainty*. The law or right ' in possession ' has the strongest claim, until some other law or right is proved stronger. ' If a doubt arises as to whether I have said my breviary,' is a Roman Catholic interpretation of this maxim,[1] ' I must say it, for the law is in possession ; if on the contrary a doubt comes into my mind as to whether I have taken food after midnight, I may go to Holy Communion, because my right to receive is in possession.' Note that in each of these cases there is only a *doubt* as to whether the law or the right is abrogated by circumstances; the moment *moral certainty* supervened the Roman theologian, at all events, would be quite clear as to which way action should lie.

(*e*) A further rule is that which allows one to *presume*, in any given case, that he has acted or will act according to his usual custom in such a matter.[2] If, for example, a servant is in doubt whether his master has given him an illegal order, he may presume that it is in this case as in others ; if the master is habitually law-abiding, and there is no clear evidence that the command is illegal, its legality may be presumed. Or, again, if a man knows that certain associates always lead him into sin, he must presume that they will do so on any given occasion ; and it becomes a sinful action for him to go with them.

(*f*) *In dubio standum est pro valore actus* is a maxim of real value for priests who hear confessions—' You should take an action or intention at its face value unless there is strong suspicion to the contrary.' Thus a Christian who comes to make a confession should be assumed to be doing so in all *bona fides*, and with every intention of revealing everything and concealing nothing. Or, again, a scrupulous person who tortures himself as to his motives, even in cases where his action has all the visible signs of morality and honesty, may be reassured as to his doubt : so long as he has no clear evidence to the contrary he may assume that all is well. To much the same effect is another maxim : *in dubio favores sunt ampliandi, et odia restringenda* ;

---

[1] Slater, *op. cit.* vol. i. p. 66.
[2] *In dubio standum est pro eo pro quo stat presumptio.*

which may be rendered, 'Give the benefit of the doubt wherever you can.' [1]

(g) Cases may arise where the choice of action lies between two evils : 'The choice, e.g., may lie between continuing in a corrupt church and implicitly favouring apostacy and unbelief. Again, a wife may have to choose between condoning a husband's infidelity to her by living with him, or breaking up a family.' [2] Here the rule, ' Of two evils choose the least,' is of natural and obvious application. Jeremy Taylor and St. Thomas even apply this to a choice between *sins* ; where an individual is *absolutely bent* upon committing one of two sins, he may be advised to commit the lesser in order to avoid the greater.[3] But it is evident that this principle can only be applied in the most extreme cases imaginable.

We may therefore sum up the principles which should guide a conscientious Christian in any case of grave perplexity something as follows [4] :

(i) Do not allow any of your considered rules of life to be abrogated or altered without very strong reason based upon the obvious applicability of some equally binding or higher law.

(ii) Do not attach too much importance to your own inclinations in the matter. The fact that you favour a certain course of action as being the easier or pleasanter for you is not necessarily evidence against its morality.

(iii) Assume that what has happened before in your experience will happen again, and do not be frightened or influenced by unlikely possibilities.

---

[1] Cp. *Summa*, ii. 2, q. 40, a. 4.

[2] Elmendorf, *op. cit.* p. 502. *Cf.* Sanderson, *Praelectiones*, ii. § 18 ; Taylor, *Duct. Dub.* book i. chap. 4, rule 3 ; chap. 5, rule 8.

[3] *Duct. Dub.* book i. chap. 5, rule 8, where patristic instances are quoted ; *Summa*, i. 2, q. 101, a. 3, ad. 2. This maxim is satirised by Pascal in the *Lettres Provinciales* (letter 8)—the thesis chosen for ridicule suggesting that where a thief is seen to be ready and determined to rob a poor man, it is a virtuous action to point out to him a rich man whom he can rob instead.

[4] Cp. the ' collateral considerations ' given in *Duct. Dub.* book i. chap. 4, rule 9 ; and Hooker's ' four general propositions demanding that which may reasonably be granted concerning matters of outward form in religion ' (*Ecclesiastical Polity*, book v. §§ 5–9).

(iv) Where unhappy consequences are bound in any case to ensue, choose the course of action which, whilst satisfying the foregoing rules, will minimise the evil ensuing.

(v) Go for advice to conscientious and intelligent Christians who have real experience of *the particular kind of problem that perplexes you.*

(vi) Having chosen your course of action along these lines, with prayer for guidance, act boldly and firmly, though holding yourself ready to change your course if new evidence arises.

There is, indeed, nothing in this that is not corroborated by the ordinary rules of common sense.[1] But the rules we have suggested have reached their importance after long testing in the experience of the Church ; and for those who feel it their duty (as surely it is every Christian man's) to make up their own minds after due consideration of every available piece of evidence—who, like Pascal, ' are not content with the probable, but seek the sure '[2]—they will afford some principles of guidance by which to test and regulate the chaos of impulses that surround every intended action.

[1] So E. T. Churton, *Use of Penitence*, pp. 165, 166.
[2] *Provincials*, letter 5.

CHAPTER IX

THE HEALING OF THE SOUL

1. *The Character of the Director*

WE have regarded Christian progress hitherto as a development slow indeed, and not without periods of apparent stagnation, but unimpeded by anything more than the limitations of the normal man. If this were all, the work of the priest in guiding the soul would be comparatively simple. He would notice, at every stage of its development, whether each of the fundamental dispositions of the Christian life were growing steadily towards perfection, and wherever he found one of them languishing would bring forward one or more of the appropriate ideas and habits as a stimulus. If faith were weak, he would speak of those things which most confirm it, and urge the practice of meditation and of thanksgiving as a means of growth. Where penitence seemed lacking, he would advise a consideration of the sufferings of our Lord, and inculcate self-examination and confession of sin. Given a certain amount of insight, sympathy, imagination and tact, his work might indeed be arduous, but there would be no great fear that it would be unsuccessful.

The problem, as it is known to us, is not by any means so simple. The priest has not alone to foster the growth of souls moving steadily if slowly onward to perfection. He has to deal with souls into which every variety of distortion, perversity, and vice has obtruded itself. It is not merely that the ground in which the seed is to be sown is choked with stones and weeds. Often enough where seed has fallen upon good ground its growth is afterwards ensnared and strangled by tares of every description. The

priest is not like a trainer—to vary the metaphor—whose
pupils are all healthy in body and merely need a development of physique, and an increase of strength and agility ;
rather, he resembles a doctor attempting to restore health
to a sickly and diseased child, and to bring it up to manhood
despite the constant danger of new infection on every hand.

These metaphors are none too strong. There may
indeed be ' once-born ' or ' healthy-minded ' souls which
never fall very far from innocence ; but they are not many.
For the most part, men and women, when they first become
acutely conscious of the ideal of goodness and seek to
follow it, have already contracted habits of selfishness,
bad-temper, love of pleasure, if of nothing worse. Almost
all, again, are hampered by natural impediments to
righteousness : slothfulness, morbidity, cynicism, or the
like. And all are liable to fall again and again to the very
end of their days. It is easy to see how terribly this
multiplies the difficulties of pastoral work, and what
immense demands it makes upon the character of the
priest.

It is therefore at this point—where we approach the
gravest of all spiritual problems, that of the healing of
the soul—that we may consider the qualities required in
a good director ; for it is in this matter particularly that
he will be called upon to exercise them. In his public
ministry, as the Ordinal reminds him, he is to show himself
a *messenger, steward* and *watchman* to his people. Moral
theology sets against this a list of four capacities in which
he must minister to them privately : he must combine the
qualities of a *father*, a *teacher*, a *judge* and a *physician*.[1]

All manuals of ascetic and penitential theology deal
fully with these four qualifications, and we need do no
more than summarise their conclusions. Nor can we
consider the rules of life by which the clergy must fit
themselves for their task, except to re-affirm what has
been so often affirmed, that a priest who is not constantly
striving to increase his own holiness, and model it more

---

[1] See Scaramelli, *op. cit.* Treat. i. §§ 106–113 ; Gaume, *Advice on
Hearing Confession* (tr. E. B. Pusey), chap. 1 ; W. W. Williams, *op. cit.*
pp. 81–86.

closely upon the pattern of his Master, can never expect his work to be fruitful. For direction on this subject the reader must turn to the books specially written to help the clergy in the care of their own spiritual life.[1] It will be enough to indicate briefly what this fourfold character of the priesthood involves ; and its general intention becomes clear when we say that the priest, in dealing with individual souls, must exhibit a father's *love*, a teacher's *authority*, a judge's *equity*, and a physician's *skill*.

(*a*) *A father's love.*—It would be impossible to enumerate the forms in which this love—the first and most necessary of these qualifications, and the one in respect of which the director stands most especially in the place of Christ towards men—should manifest itself. Two functions of primary importance, however, may be ascribed to it. The first is, to elicit confidence ; the second, to inspire effort. The priest will be only a poor father to his people if he has not got their confidence ; equally poor, if by his fatherhood he does not lead them to a new dedication of themselves to the service of Christ. And neither of these results can be obtained except by a manifestation of love.

The love that inspires confidence must show itself first in *patience*. The director will hope to learn from their own lips of his people's needs and failures and troubles ; and to do this he must often listen with apparent readiness and interest to stories packed with irrelevant and trivial detail. Yet this very listening in itself may be the greatest help to those in trouble : ' It is some relief for a poor body,' said Isaak Walton, writing of Herbert's conduct on his first visit to Bemerton, ' to be heard with patience.' It is to be noticed, too, that a priest who thinks himself, or allows himself to be thought, a busy man, will lose countless opportunities of this kind. People will believe him too pressed for time to listen to their slow and badly-expressed account of their troubles, and will hesitate to open their griefs to him. One of the first characteristics of fatherly love is to

---

[1] For example Chrysostom, *De Sacerdotio*; Greg. Naz., *Oratio II.*; Gregory, *De Pastorali Cura* ; Arvisenet, *Memoriale Vitae Sacerdotalis*; Bossuet, *Panegyrics* ; G. Herbert, *Country Parson* ; Burnet, *Discourse of the Pastoral Care* ; &c.

exhibit to the world an apparent freedom from hurry, a complete readiness to attend to the longest and most involved recital, a spirit of calm expectancy.

A second requisite for the inviting of confidence must be a manner which *never betrays disgust or horror*. The priest has much to hear which will move him to indignation and revulsion, even though it moves to pity as well; but if he allows any feeling of this kind to be seen, it will at once alienate those who most wish to confide their sins to him. He must exhibit a sense of the gravity of sin, whilst at the same time extending an even enhanced sympathy to the sinner.

To inspire to effort those who seek his help, the priest's love of them must show itself first of all in *a personal interest*. It must never appear that he regards individuals as ' cases ' to be dealt with and then dismissed. He must give to each one who comes to him an utterly undivided attention, concentrating upon his problems for the moment as the only ones he has to consider. Nor must his interest subside when the trouble of the moment has been dealt with; sympathy has brought him into a new relation with a human soul—when the immediate need for sympathy has passed, he must not allow the relationship to lapse. Lastly, and most important of all, he must have no favourites in his parish; no one must be supposed to have his private ear, to be listened to more than others. This is not to say that approved Christians among his flock are not to have some share—perhaps a great share—in organising its welfare; what is meant is that he must be known as a man who judges in all things impartially and without prejudice, allowing personal considerations no more than their due influence.

Again, as an incentive to effort, he must always appear an optimist as to the spiritual possibilities of his people, even where he has, in fact, the gravest reason for doubt. In dealing with one whom you believe to be a hypocrite, says St. Augustine, treat him as the man he wishes you to think him, and make him feel how pleasant it would be to be such a man in reality as well as in seeming.[1] This advice, however, must be tempered by judgment—love may have to show

[1] *De Cat. Rud.* 6.

itself in sternness and rebuke as much as in kindness and praise. For the most part, however, it may be assumed that those who come for advice, whether sincere or not, will best be helped by encouragement ; even by deliberate praise of whatever good can be found in them. Queen Elizabeth's principle—to make men trustworthy by trusting them [1]—is on the whole a sound spiritual rule.

(b) *Authority* in spiritual things is a moral, not an official qualification. It is quite distinct from *commission*—the scribes were commissioned to explain the law, but it was our Lord, though He had no commission recognisable by His contemporaries, Who spake with authority, and not as the scribes. The priest has his official commission to deal with souls ; his authority he must acquire for himself.

Authority, as the derivation shows,[2] is a quality distinguishing the expert, which only expert knowledge can confer. Such expert knowledge comes from a combination of causes. Careful and diligent study is one of them ; a continually widening experience of human nature, a second ; constant reflection upon the material collected in these two ways is the third.[3] That the requisite study must extend to the main principles of moral theology and Christian ethics goes, of course, without saying ; and the knowledge of principles should be reinforced by instances of their application, drawn from the priest's own experience, from that of his brother clergy, and from the whole range of Christian literature. Thus equipped he will be able to advise those who seek his help, not indeed with absolute infallibility, but with a certain weight of evidence and precedent on his side which will give his words more than ordinary importance and gravity.

An authority of this kind—the authority of a painstaking and eager student who has achieved some degree of facility in his subject—can never be arrogant. It will always admit the possibility of error ; will always be on the alert for new types of character, new complexities of problem. It will never deliver summary judgment in

---

[1] J. A. Froude, *Reign of Queen Elizabeth*, chap. 25.
[2] Cp. A. E. J. Rawlinson in *Foundations*, Essay viii. pp. 366, 367.
[3] F. Paget, *op. cit.* p. 20.

any matter, however trivial it may appear, until the facts have been fully examined ; and it will always be willing to admit fresh evidence, to listen to doubts and hesitations, and to state the grounds of its own decisions. Its object will be to obtain the willing and considered assent of those in whose interests it exerts itself ; it will look not for an enforced obedience, but for a considered agreement with its conclusions. It will be the authority of a teacher, in short, not that of a tyrant.

It should scarcely be necessary to emphasise the importance of definite and continued study in this connection ; but there is reason to believe that it is. Experience of life is a great thing, but it requires the balance and guidance of the wider experience of the community before it can be regarded as in any degree final. There are some men so gifted that they can give the right advice in any case of difficulty almost by instinct ; but they are few in number only. For the most part, it must be insisted that the priest who wishes to help the souls of others can never intermit his reading of moral theology, ethics, psychology and Christian biography, however little time he may have to give to it. Without it, his practice will at best be by rule of thumb only, and will lack the weight and certainty that the laity rightly expect of him.

(c) In the confessional the priest acts as a *judge* in a specific direction—that of assessing the gravity of sins confessed to him and the consequent appropriate penance ;[1] and of estimating the reality of a penitent's contrition and deciding whether absolution can safely be given. But the art of spiritual direction, particularly in the Church of England, extends far beyond the limits of sacramental confession. We may say, then, that the director's juridical

---

[1] In traditional theology, penance is regarded both as a *satisfaction* and as a *remedy* for sin (Williams, *op. cit.* pp. 53, 54 ; Elmendorf, *Moral Theology*, p. 604). The former aspect belongs to a juristic conception of the relations between God and man which is singularly difficult for the modern mind to grasp, and is fruitful in unhappy results, unless equal insistence is laid upon the fact that no human effort of satisfaction can conceivably atone for sin. Whatever truth there may be in it, it has little bearing upon the ascetic side of moral theology ; and the general tendency even in conservative writers is to ignore it as far as possible. See also *Summa* Suppl. q. 12, a 3 ; q. 13, a. 1 (from *Sent.* iv. d. 15, q. 1, aa. 1, 2).

function, in its widest sense, consists in an ability to discern, in any particular case of difficulty or conscience, which spiritual principles are applicable; and to adapt them, where necessary, to the particular problem under consideration. The methods which experience has shown to be of use in such a connection have been discussed in the last chapter; it remains only to add a few words as to the manner in which they should be applied.

The first requirement, then, of the priest as judge is the ability to *assess evidence*, to decide whether the account he receives from a Christian of his own spiritual problem is true to fact or not; and if it is untrue or distorted, to explain the real facts of the case. He must help men, wrote Dr. Paget in a fine passage, 'to discern through the haste and insistency of the present, what is its real meaning and its just demand; help to give due weight to what is reasonable, however unreasonably it may be stated or defended; help . . . to adjust the claims of general rules and special equity; help to carry with one conscientiously, on the journey to decision, all the various thoughts which ought to tell on the issue; help to keep consistency from hardening into obstinacy and common sense from sinking into time-serving; help to think out one's duty as in a still pure air, sensitive to all true signs and voices of this world, and yet unshaken by its storms.'[1]

For such a work both sympathy and detachment are necessary; sympathy to enter into the inmost thoughts of those who confide in us, to understand their reticences, to know the significance of their laboured explanation, to grasp, and if need be to expose, their concealments; detachment, to sum up all the evidence thus brought to light into a consistent picture of character, and without regard to extraneous considerations of person or condition to bring

---

[1] *Christian Character*, p. 5. This characteristic is technically known as *epicheia* (ἐπιείκεια = equity). It is unwise to define it as a 'benign interpretation of the law' (Slater, *Moral Theology*, vol. i. p. 103); for this suggests that it is in some way opposed to severity, even where the latter is equitable—an interpretation specially rejected by St. Thomas (*Summa*, ii. 2, q. 120, a. 1). It is not a mitigation of the law in favour of privileged individuals, but rather a just interpretation of the law with due reference to the circumstances of the particular case.

it firmly into comparison with the general laws of moral and spiritual life. In gathering the experience necessary for such a task, countless mistakes will doubtless be made ; but the priest must go forward in the humble attempt to make himself a discerning and just judge of character and its needs, trusting that God will remedy whatever harm follows from his inevitable errors.

Something must be said here about *questioning* ;[1] for often enough it is impossible to get sufficient evidence for a wise decision without direct inquiry of the person who has submitted his problem to our notice. The questions asked should be as few as possible, and absolutely relevant ; there should be no hint of inquisitiveness. They must be discreet ; that is to say, must never suggest to the penitent sins of which he is not guilty—perhaps even sins of the existence of which he is absolutely ignorant. Yet they must be, where need requires it, incisive ; where a boy, for instance, is in trouble about impurity it is essential to know exactly to what point self-indulgence has carried him. Above all, they must be tactful and kindly ; put in the helpful spirit of a friend, not in the manner of an inquisitor. Lastly, where possible, they should be of such a kind as to reveal to the penitent, in the act of searching for an answer, the causes of his trouble. It is always best that, even at the last moment, he should find the truth for himself, rather than wait for it to be told him by another.

(d) All that has been said of the director as father, teacher and judge is summed up in the description of him as a *physician of souls*. Here we are face to face with one of the time-honoured metaphors of Christianity ; a metaphor which our Lord did not find inadequate to express the nature of His own mission.[2] In the earliest Christian literature it begins to be elaborated ; thus the ' Apostolic Constitutions '[3] contains the following penetrating account of the various methods employed in the healing of the soul : ' If it be a hollow wound or great gash nourish it with a suitable plaister ; . . . if foul, cleanse it with a corrosive powder— that is, words of reproof ; if it have proud flesh, eat it down

---

[1] See W. W. Webb, *op. cit.* §§ 46–48 ; Gaume, *op. cit.* chap. 4.
[2] Matt. ix. 12.   [3] ii. 41.

with a sharp plaister—threats of judgment ; if it spreads, cut off the putrid flesh . . . but if there is no room for a fomentation or oil or bandage, then with a great deal of consideration and the advice of other skilful physicians, cut off the putrified member, that the whole church be not corrupted. . . . Be not hasty with the saw, but first try lancing.'

The physician of souls must show his skill first of all in diagnosing, from the symptoms revealed to him or discerned by him, with or without inquiry, the *real cause* of any spiritual disorder which comes under his notice. There are many symptoms which arise alike from widely different causes. Spiritual sloth, apparent self-conceit, infrequent communion do not point each to any one defect at bottom. Symptoms must be grouped, every factor bearing upon the case must be considered, before a decision as to the real cause can be reached. Once that decision has been made, the priest must choose the method by which he proposes to remedy the disease. Nor does his task end here ; he must *apply* the remedy as well. If it involves some new rule of life for the person whom he is trying to help, it must be presented to him in such terms and argument as will lead him willingly to undertake it. Sometimes he must be informed of hidden causes of his trouble ; sometimes it is dangerous to make this revelation. The wise priest will have to decide *what* he is to tell, and *how much* he is to tell, to the people who come to him for advice.

There are, for example, men in the grip of dangerous passions who turn to the priest almost in a fit of despair. However grave he recognises their case to be, it would be madness to disclose the fact ; rather he must behave as though it were something which is certainly remediable, and insist upon the fact that he is undertaking responsibility for the cure, and that he will not desert the sufferer. Others again have a morbid interest in their sins ; others are almost proud of the peculiarities of temperament of which they are conscious. In either case their attention must be diverted from an interest in the fault itself. They must be led to believe that their case is nothing out of the common—that they are not the remarkable spiritual phenomena they think themselves. On the other hand, there are characters whose tendency is always to depreciate their failings, to find excuses for them, to think of themselves as better than they might have been ; with these the priest must speak sharply and sternly, driving home upon their consciences the gravity even of the slightest fall.

It will be seen, therefore, that not actual sin alone, but also temperamental conditions, must be taken into account both in diagnosing the causes of spiritual failure and in choosing and applying the remedy. We may indeed say that the causes of disorder in the soul are twofold—*innate* and *acquired*. By innate causes we mean those over the origin of which the soul has no control. They exist in it as permanent disabilities, challenges to action and effort ; they are not the result of voluntary sin. It is indeed sinful to pander to them, or to regard them as insuperable ; but for their actual presence the soul has no responsibility. It is responsible only for not allowing them to interfere with and impede its growth.[1]

2. *Temperament*

Psychologists have attempted, from time to time, an exhaustive classification of the varieties of human temperament.[2] Such a classification is in fact impossible. Human nature is too diverse to be contained within the limits of any scheme, however detailed. At the same time, it is possible to recognise certain well-marked general distinctions of temperament which cover, in a rough and ready way, most ordinary characters and suggest specific methods of approach in each case. It is to be noticed that these

---

[1] Cp. A. D. Sertillanges, *S. Thomas d'Aquin*, vol. ii. pp. 310, 311 : ' L'atavique ou le mal éduqué, à plus fort raison l'ignorant, ne sont pas immoraux avant d'avoir signé en pleine conscience et appliqué librement à l'acte les regrettables dispositions dont ils souffrent. . . . Les tares physiologiques ou psychologiques d'un sujet n'ont de caractère immoral que celui qu'elles revêtent par l'intervention de la liberté, qui les prend à son compte et les signe.'

[2] Cp. T. Ribot, *Psychology of the Emotions*, chaps. 12 and 13, esp. pp. 383, 384 ; G. A. Coe, quoted Starbuck, *Psychology of Religion*, p. 72.

temperamental disabilities only become a real danger to
the soul when they are highly developed in any particular
case ; in general they are no more than tendencies which
have to be taken into consideration in attempting to form
an estimate of the spiritual well-being of souls. Nor are
they altogether mutually exclusive ; two of them may co-
exist in a given character, or they may occur successively.[1]

Eighteen hundred years ago the physician Galen[2] noticed
and elaborated four such distinct character-tendencies ;
and his classification—without however the physiological
basis he found for it—holds good in general terms to-day.
He distinguished the four principal temperaments as the
melancholic (caused by a predominance of gall in the system),
the *choleric* (with the bile predominant), the *sanguine* (with
blood predominant), and the *phlegmatic* or *lymphatic* (with
phlegm predominant).

(*a*) To the *melancholic* type belong those natures whose
feelings, though deep and strong, are slow to express themselves outwardly. Such people are usually absorbed, either in
themselves, or in some interest which grips them so strongly
as to be almost an obsession ; and they do not give their
deep-seated emotionalism any adequate outlet. As a result
they often appear irritable, suspicious, intolerant and sullen.
' From bridling the tongue overmuch they suffer from a more
grievous loquacity of heart ; so that thoughts seethe in
the mind through being straitened' ;[3] and are apt to burst
out in sudden, though short-lived, gusts of intense passion.
The depth of their feelings often makes them both obstinate
and intolerant ; yet secretly they have a real distrust, often
even a contempt, of themselves. This is due to the fact
that however deeply they brood over whatever it is that
forms their main obsession, they are conscious of even
greater depths in it which they cannot plumb. Restless,
dissatisfied, pessimistic, their life is as unhappy to themselves
as it is painful to their neighbours.

[1] Welton, *Psychology of Education*, p. 14.
[2] Galen, *De Temperamentis* (περὶ κράσεων).
[3] Gregory, *De Past. Cur.* iii. admon. 15. Compare:

> ' *Julia :* His little speaking shews his love but small.
> *Lucetta :* Fire that's closest kept burns most of all.'
> *Two Gentlemen of Verona*, act. i. scene 2.

If the interest of a melancholic man is mainly intellectual, his temperament will show itself in an inability to make up his own mind, combined with a contempt for the opinions of others. In religious matters this usually results in a constant doubt of the truths of faith, which both envies and despises those who believe without difficulty. In moral matters, the melancholic temperament shows itself in what is known as *scrupulosity*[1]: a morbid habit of self-questioning which can never admit any pleasure, however innocent, through the lurking fear that it may be wrong, nor yet submit such a matter to the guidance of authority. The sense of forgiveness comes with difficulty to such natures, for they are always in doubt as to whether they have shown sufficient contrition to merit it ; and often enough they go from church to church, from director to director, in the forlorn hope of finding someone who will give them the assurance which they lack.

Distrust of oneself leads by an easy transition into distrust of others ; and once this becomes a habit of mind with the melancholic man, he naturally and insensibly becomes a cynic. ' He has gone far enough into his neighbours to find out that the outside is false, without caring to go farther and discover what is really true. . . . He has learnt the first lesson, that no man is wholly good ; but he has not even suspected that there is another equally true, to wit that no man is wholly bad. . . . He does not want light, because he finds the darkness more pleasant.'[2]

(b) If the melancholic habit of mind is self-centred yet self-distrustful, the *choleric* is self-assertive. These natures ' resemble spirited young horses,' full of life and activity, impatient of control, discipline or advice ; opinionated, active, self-confident, and often arrogant. Yet their very enthusiasm has its dangers. They are unstable, and a check in one direction will easily turn zeal into repugnance, and set them off on a new and even a contrary pursuit. They cannot brook opposition, and if thwarted will not persevere, but launch out into some different sphere of activity.

---

[1] An important analysis of *scrupulosity* is given by Chandler, *Ara Coeli*, p. 63.

[2] R. L. Stevenson, *Lay Morals, &c.*—' The Cynic.'

Characters of this description—eager, enthusiastic, visionary —are in youth, as a rule, particularly charming (Jane Austen's ' Emma ' is perhaps as perfect an example as one could wish) ; but in later years disappointment edges their enthusiasm with bitterness, and they may easily become narrow-minded zealots. Pharisaism and Jesuitry are only two of the forms of character into which the choleric type may easily develop.

(c) The *sanguine* type is usually one of particular attractiveness and charm. To it belong those childish, affectionate, optimistic and volatile natures whose fundamental characteristic is a passive selfishness. Harold Skimpole is to all time the example of them. With no moral stability, with no deep enthusiasms, they are ready to share in the pleasures and interests of all around them, provided always that no heavy call is made upon themselves. But their interests quickly pass, and they relinquish friendships or undertakings as easily and pleasantly as they make them. The ' trifling of their favour ' is—

> ' A violet in the youth of primy nature,—
> Forward, not permanent ; sweet, not lasting ;
> The perfume and suppliance of a minute ;
> No more.'

Their religion—and they have no aversion to religion so long as it demands no effort of them—is in consequence inarticulate, ' because a cheerful man does not care whether he is understood or not ; just as a man is less articulate when he is humming than when he is calling for help.' [1] Their ideals are never high, their moral reserve always small ; they fall into sin at the slightest temptation, through no innate tendency to vice, but through mere inability to resist. They have indeed this safeguard, that so long as their environment is healthy, they have little temptation to continued or passionate sin ; and they give up a bad habit as easily as they contract it through sheer loss of interest. Thus often enough they present the spectacle of a ' softened sinner,' like poor Fred Bayham ; pleasant, ineffective, faulty people, the despair of any who try to rouse

---

[1] G. K. Chesterton, *Victorian Age in Literature*, p. 147.

them to an ideal of manly independence, but without any dangerous vice.

This, however, is the best that can be said of them; where circumstances are against them they stand in very real and imminent danger. ' A weak nature which is naturally kindly, affectionate and pure, which floats through life under the influence of the feelings, with no real powers of restraint, is indeed not without its charm, and may attain a high degree of beauty ; but its besetting failings will steadily grow ; it has no recuperative power and will often end in a moral catastrophe.' [1] The sanguine character often presents the priest with one of his most difficult problems.

(*d*) Very different from any of the three we have considered is the *phlegmatic* type. The others all react to stimulus—the melancholic indeed not very readily, but with intense force of emotion ; the sanguine readily enough, but without strength or permanence. The phlegmatic type stands for those self-contained characters upon which it is apparently impossible to make any impression at all. Sometimes the cause of this is a genuine dullness of nature, extending to intellect, emotion and will alike. More often it appears to result not so much from dullness as from callousness and coldness. There seems to be nothing in character except a calculating self-interest, which yet reveals itself not in a single passion or in many, but in a complete lack of interest in everything and everybody. The heart is gripped, as it were, by ice. Such a character is well exemplified by Anne Elliot's rejected suitor in 'Persuasion.' He was 'rational, discreet, polished—but he was not open. There was never any burst of feeling, any warmth of indignation or delight at the evil or good of others. This was to Anne a decided imperfection. Warmth and enthusiasm captivated her still. She felt that she could so much more depend upon the sincerity of those who looked or said a careless or a hasty thing, than of those whose presence of mind never varied, whose tongue never slipped.'

It is obvious that wherever one of these temperamental

[1] W. E. H. Lecky, *Map of Life*, p. 251.

tendencies is strongly developed, it must result in a serious perversion of character, or at least a genuine hindrance to its harmonious development. The melancholic habit of mind may well exhibit an excess of penitence, but it will usually be of that imperfect type to which St. Thomas gave the name of 'attrition,' and will not easily be raised to the stage of contrite hope. Faith, again, is almost always weak and unstable in the melancholic man ; he is so absorbed in his own imperfections that he can scarcely spare a glance for the perfection and immutability of God. Nor will he be capable of any great zeal for others until his centripetal tendency of mind has been inhibited or corrected.

The choleric nature, if it accepts the service of Christ, has probably no lack of faith, though it may be of a narrow unreflective kind. Zeal, too, will be there in apparent profusion ; but it is more often the 'obstinacy of self-will' than 'steadiness of principle,' as is shown by the ease with which opposition or disappointment will divert it from its immediate purpose to another and even a contrary one. What is most lacking in the choleric nature is the disposition of contrition with its natural consequence of humility. This is all the more distressing because often enough the best church workers are drawn from people of this character ; and the quarrels which from time to time cleave a parish into two parties and wreck the work of the Church can often be traced to a clash of interests between two persons of this kind.

At first sight the sanguine character offers the best field for spiritual growth : there are no impediments or perversions to stultify regular and harmonious development. Unhappily, however, the impulse to religion, if it comes—as it often does to such a nature—is usually short-lived ; and the vast ranks of lapsed communicants who promised well at confirmation are mainly recruited from among the sanguine.

Lastly, the phlegmatic type—the 'stony ground' of the parable [1]—is almost the despair of every parish priest.

---

[1] The analogy of the various types indicated above with the parable of the Sower is too obvious to require more than passing notice.

There seems to be no joint in its impregnable armour, no lever or force by which it can be moved. It is not so much dullness as coldness that is the most terrible feature in this type—a coldness so intense that no warmth of human intercourse or friendship seems to meet it.

It is obvious that very different methods are necessary in dealing with these different types.[1] The essential thing with the melancholic or scrupulous man is to turn his attention from himself. Introspection and brooding, therefore, must be as far as possible discouraged. He should be treated with kindness and sympathy, but not condoled with upon the unhappiness of his spiritual condition. The best environment for him is the society of healthy, normal, non-reflective friends, provided always that they are not of such boisterous energy or self-expression that they repel his more complex nature. By little tasks of service for others he can gradually be weaned from his contemplation of himself.

His wavering faith should be confirmed by presenting to it, and by keeping before it, one or two clearly expressed ideas about God's goodness and providence ; and he must learn, by slow degrees perhaps, to refuse to doubt upon matters once accepted in this way. Argument will only minister to his doubt. What he requires is the example of others who have been through the same crises as himself but have come out with enhanced confidence. He should be led to believe that the same happy issue will some day be his, and urged to take hold of any sign that offers itself of the new light breaking in upon his soul. He should be made to admit the good points which he knows to exist in his character, to rely upon them and to thank God for them ; ' we may bring back the fainthearted to the way of well-doing, if we search for some good point about them and embrace it with praises.'[2]

Very different treatment is appropriate to the choleric type. There is no fear of disheartening him by reproof or rebuke. The danger lies in not making the rebuke strong enough to break down his self-sufficiency. Therefore if

<hr>

[1] Cp. Scaramelli, *op. cit.* Treat. iii. §§ 41-45.
[2] Gregory, *De Past. Cur.* iii. admon. 9.

his temperamental tendency is proving a real danger to himself or to the Church, he must be dealt with frankly, openly, and even brutally. All depends upon his being outfaced, and forced to acknowledge first of all his own spiritual failure, and then the vanity and ambition which lay at its root.

Where, however, the danger is less urgent, such violent means are unnecessary. He must be led to realise, first of all, that he is by no means so essential or so efficient as he thinks himself to be; this can be done—with a certain amount of tact, to prevent his taking too serious offence— by treating him as an ordinary individual and giving him work for the Church of a less prominent character than he might wish. But he can be frankly told that he needs greater humility and contrition; and his instinct for completeness and efficiency called upon to induce him to take up such habits of meditation or self-examination and confession as he needs. He may be advised continually to reflect upon his failures rather than upon his successes, and to compare them with the perfect ideal set before him in Jesus Christ.

Few types of character present less difficulty. They respond more than any others to plain speaking and a genial frankness, provided always that it comes as from man to man. There is little need for reticence, tact or caution. One danger only has to be guarded against in cases where the choleric temperament is combined with any high degree of nervous excitability: it must not be allowed to find an outlet for its energy in embracing martyrdom. Such natures are ready enough to brave public opinion, to ' testify ' or to champion an unpopular cause; but to allow them to do this in any but the strictest moderation simply ministers to their self-esteem, and may result in more harm than good. For the same reason, they should not be rebuked publicly, or put to any open slight, for fear they make it an occasion of posing as victims of petty jealousy or tyranny.

The transformation of the sanguine type of character into something more independent and purposive is a very difficult matter. People of this kind expect to be treated almost with the consideration given to a favourite child ; and their expectation appears so natural and artless that there is real danger that those who wish to help them may fall in with it. They must not be spoilt, petted or indulged ; their spiritual weaknesses must not be condoned. By gentle yet firm treatment they must learn that they are expected to show the virtues of manhood as well as the innocence of childhood. They must be led on by a steady, imperceptible pressure through successive stages of spiritual development. Progress will be slow—often even unnoticed—but the priest must be on his guard against attempting to hasten it. So long as the character is, to some extent by its own effort, keeping itself from new forms of sin or relapses into old ones, something is being gained.

'Weak and careless characters,' wrote St. Chrysostom,[1] with this type no doubt in mind, ' addicted to the pleasures of this world, may yet if gently and gradually brought to repent of their errors, be delivered partially at least if not perfectly, from the evils by which they are possessed ; but if anyone were to apply the discipline all at once he would deprive them even of this slight chance of amend-ment.'

There is, however, one point in the sanguine character that often gives genuine hope for the future. Its warm-hearted appreciation of what is good in others will some-times be stirred into a genuine hero-worship if the right person to inspire it can be found. In such a case, the result may exceed every expectation. The weak, pliant and vacillating nature, under the influence of something finer than itself, grows strong and virile, and, retaining as it does all its early charm, may not fall far short of a very high approximation to the Christian ideal. The influence of a mature and calm example of Christian goodness will often do more in such a case than much careful thought or considered advice.

There is only one rule in dealing with the phlegmatic type of person, whether his impenetrability comes from dullness or from callousness—that is, to examine his

[1] *De Sacerdot.* ii. 4.

character until some spark of human interest or spiritual fire be found in it, and steadily appeal to that. No other method offers much hope of success; but there are few natures so dead that they do not exhibit, though perhaps only at the rarest intervals, some sign of spiritual vitality. ' Fire can be struck from the hardest flints,' says Hazlitt;[1] though he adds, with undue optimism, that ' the most phlegmatic constitutions often contain the most inflammable material.' But until the fire has actually been kindled, the priest can do no more except maintain as friendly and cordial a relationship as circumstances allow. He must not forget, however, that natures impervious to individual appeal may yet be moved by a mass sentiment; and that the influence of a mission may be successful with the phlegmatic type of character where individual effort has wholly failed.

It is doubtful whether more than this can be said as to ways of dealing with temperamental impediments to Christian progress. Every combination of the temperaments mentioned can be met with day by day, and innumerable varieties of each. Detailed classification and analysis is impossible; the complexity of character defies scientific description. But something is to be gained by recognising the main types which exist, and without attempting to bring every individual rigidly under one class or another, by considering his affinities with that which he most resembles, and modifying one's treatment of him accordingly.

[1] *Table Talk*, Essay 31, ' On the Knowledge of Character.'

CHAPTER X

SIN

1. *Sin as a Practical Problem*

IN his capacity as missioner, pastor or confessor, the priest is primarily interested in sin as a practical problem. That it presents other problems as well—problems of a metaphysical and ontological character—he is well aware ; and for the purpose of teaching and justifying the Christian doctrine of sin he requires a true appreciation of the magnitude of these problems, of the way in which they present themselves to the normal thinking man, and of the manner in which they may reasonably be solved. These, however, are questions of dogma and apologetics ; moral theology is concerned so to state the facts about sin as to enable the shepherd and guardian of souls to deal with it most effectively. The questions of its compatibility with divine foresight and love, or of its bearing upon the problems of free-will, responsibility and punishment, are therefore from this point of view secondary, and do not concern us here. Our problem is intellectually a simpler one : sin exists as a fact of life ; by the sacrifice of Christ it has been overcome ; by the power of the Holy Spirit this victory can be repeated in the heart of the individual ;—how then can the priest co-operate with the Holy Spirit in the work of leading men to such a victory ?

To this end, sin must be looked on primarily as one of the influences which delay or inhibit the development of the Christian character, or even tend to hurl the soul back towards its unconverted state of darkness. These influences, as was indicated in the previous chapter, are twofold : those for which the individual cannot be held personally responsible, and those for which he can. Under the former heading fell the temperamental tendencies which so often originate distortions of character, but which come from hereditary sources ; innate disabilities, challenging the Christian to special effort, but not attributable to indolence or evil will on his part. Under the latter head we can class uncompromisingly all acts which the converted soul commits, all habits which it contracts, encourages or tolerates, *with the full knowledge that they are detrimental to its spiritual progress.* To such acts and habits the Christian consciousness has never hesitated to give the name of sin.

There remain, however, two other species of influence, both of them admittedly detrimental to the welfare of the soul, which at first sight appear to come under neither of the above heads. Among the first, we may class those habits acquired in the innocence of infancy, or even of later life, which were not adopted with any conscious knowledge of their detrimental character. Often enough the example or influence of some older person, some hero of childhood, will lead an immature character unconsciously astray : a chance suggestion of conversation or reading may have the same effect. With influences of this character, too, may be compared actions committed, or habits contracted, in good faith. A man may act, as he thinks, for the best : yet his action will be such as to lead him away from God. He may even adopt a religious practice which, though harmless for others, is detrimental for himself. Instances of this kind are innumerable ; are we to consider them as sins, or must we find some new classification under which to deal with them ?

Among the second, we must consider the many spontaneous reactions into which the soul is surprised by stimulus of an unexpected or overwhelming character : sudden outbursts of passion, sudden spasms of terror, sudden acts of evil impulse. Here, it may be said, the agent *had no time* to consider the quality of his actions. He could not *know* beforehand that what he was about to do would be harmful to his character, because the act was committed before ever the mind could get to work upon its implications.[1]

We cannot solve this problem unless we see clearly in what the difficulty really consists. The primary question for the pastor is not to fix *responsibility* (to assess guilt). This indeed he may have to do according to the light given him by the Spirit of God ; for he may have to urge the necessity of an act of confession, overt or secret, as a remedial means. As we have previously seen, such an act of confession, with its attendant disposition of penitence or contrition, and its effective consequences of reparation and amendment, is necessary for the renewal of the spiritual life after every sin ; though *sacramental* confession has never been held obligatory upon the sinner except in cases of ' mortal ' sin.[2] It constantly occurs that the priest has to point out to his penitent a responsibility of which the latter was till then unconscious ; to show him that some habit or act—whose harmful character may have altogether escaped him—arises from a condition of soul for which he must admit responsibility ; and to urge him in consequence honestly to assume that responsibility, and at the same time to free himself from its tyranny, by asking God's forgiveness for its evil effects, and adopting such means as are necessary for the renewal of spiritual progress.

In such a sense the pastor may be called upon to estimate the guilt of apparently unconscious habits or involuntary acts. But in his capacity as physician of the soul we have seen that often enough, among other things, he is called upon to treat a disease or ailment without revealing its character, perhaps without revealing even its presence, to the patient. The habits and acts we are considering are, without doubt, diseases of the soul, for they do it harm.

---

[1] In technical theology actions and habits of this kind are known as *material*, as distinct from *formal*, sin ; they partake of the *matter* of sin— the action, desire or habit—but not necessarily of its *form* (that which gives it its special character of *sin*) : i.e. the deliberate intention of doing what the agent knows to be wrong. See *Summa*, i. 2, q. 71, a. 6 ; q. 72 a. 6, &c. ; W. W. Williams, *Moral Theology of the Sacrament of Penance*. p. 175 ; W. W. Webb, *Cure of Souls*, p. 73.

[2] *Infra*, pp. 252 f.

What the priest requires to know is therefore this :—must they be dealt with by the methods suitable to *temperamental* or by those suited to *sinful* disorders ; or do they form a class of their own to which special methods, unlike those applicable in either of the other cases, will alone be found appropriate ?

The question then is : should such actions committed, or habits contracted, in ignorance, or under the sudden onslaught of passion, be considered and treated as *sins* ? It would be tedious to examine the elaborate arguments which this question has roused ; it will be enough to collect from St. Thomas [1] the answer to which he inclines, and which is altogether in accord with the moral consciousness. Whenever we can say, ' You ought to have known,' or ' You ought to have foreseen '—whenever, in technical language, ignorance is *culpable* and *vincible*—there the act or habit in question is a *symptom* of sin. The *sin itself*—the true danger to the soul—lies not in the act or habit, harmful though these may be, but *in the refusal to learn their character, the failure to foresee their possibility*.[2] A childish habit of evil import, surviving in a mature man, is a symptom of sin on his part, however innocent its origin. He ought to have examined his life, to have known himself, before this, and discovered its harmful nature. An act committed by a mature man under the influences of passion is no less symptomatic. He ought to have foreseen that temptation constantly comes from unsuspected sources in unusual strength ; he ought to have strengthened his Christian purpose till it could resist the unknown as well as the known.

Where, therefore, such acts and habits are found in maturity, though there may indeed be some excuse for them in special cases, they are no less symptoms of real sin—sin generally in the deliberate and known omission of self-examination, or the deliberate and known refusal to strengthen the moral purpose. The priest, once he has discerned these sins, will not hesitate to deal with them according to the

---

[1] See *Summa*, i. 2, qq. 6, 76, 77. Cp. also an early discussion in Clem. Alex., *Strom.* book ii. chaps. 14, 15.

[2] Thus *Summa*, i. 2, q. 6, a. 8 : ' Dicitur ignorantia voluntaria eius quod quis potest scire et debet . . . cum aliquis notitiam quam debet habere non curat acquirere.'

general methods found efficacious for the treatment of sin
—methods we are to consider later. Where, however, the
symptoms occur in childhood, they must be regarded more
as temperamental defects, and treated along the lines laid
down for disorders of that character, each according to its
particular bias.

It will be seen that in the whole of this discussion we
have ignored what to many is a clear test of sinfulness—
the harm that an action or habit causes to others. This introduces another important question : is the gravity of a sin
to be estimated by its danger to the soul committing it, or
by the wrong it does to others ? The latter is no doubt
the common view : the former is equally certainly the
Christian one. We cannot arrive at a working definition
of sin until this point has been cleared up.

We are concerned, let us repeat, with sin in its practical
rather than in its essential character. And so far we have
found its practical importance for the priest to lie in the
obstacles it throws in the path of spiritual progress for
individuals. But it may well be urged that religion is a
social as well as—possibly, even, more than—an individual
possession. May it not be possible that sin should be
regarded more from the point of view of the harm it does
to the Christian community than from that of the harm
it does to the individual who is guilty of it ?

At first sight this would seem most decidedly to be the
standpoint of the New Testament ; and it is one peculiarly
adapted to the temper of the present day. Christian ethics
is concerning itself more and more with the social, as distinct
from the personal, side of morality. Christian duty is seen
to stretch far beyond a man's immediate environment. It
is not enough that he should be prudent, temperate, brave
and just in all his dealings with those of his family and
acquaintance. He must extend his conception of the cardinal
virtues to cover the vaguest relationships into which he
is brought with his fellow-men. Thus he should ensure, as
far as possible, that he buys no article made by sweated
labour ; that he invests his money in no undertaking
suspect of unfair trading ; that he supports no cause

which forwards even desirable ends by questionable means.

There is much in the New Testament which bears out this point of view. Indeed it is at one and the same time one of the most important contributions which the gospel made to the problem of sin, and one of the most valuable legacies it received from the older dispensation. To cause a little one to stumble, to offend a weaker brother, to bring the good name of Christian into disrepute, are rebuked in terms as unsparing as any sin could merit. St. Paul, indeed, is prepared to sacrifice his own soul's welfare—to become anathema from Christ—if by that means he can achieve the redemption of Israel;[1] he is willing to pass over any injustice committed against himself so that a whole community may exercise the virtue of forgiveness.[2] And the missionary spirit of the Church itself has sprung from the consciousness that in the teaching of Christ ' my neighbour ' means not merely *the nearest to me*, but even *the furthest from me*.

Would it be well, then, to discard our view of sin as *that which harms the individual soul* in favour of one which sees in it *that which harms the community*? To do so would safeguard what is indeed a very important element in Christian teaching, but for practical purposes we should gain nothing and lose something. We should gain nothing : for in practice the two definitions are identical. A man cannot endanger his own soul, even in the slightest respect, without causing ultimate loss to the community, little though he or any other may be conscious of it at the moment ; nor can he do harm to the community without real loss to his soul. In either case, effect may not follow closely upon cause, but it will follow no less surely for that. We need not delay to illustrate this principle : so much at least is guaranteed to us, not merely by everyday experience, but also by the doctrine of the solidarity of mankind both in Adam and in Christ.

---

[1] Rom. ix. 3.
[2] 2 Cor. ii. 10. For the general question of the widening social outlook of Christian ethics see R. L. Ottley, *Christian Ideas, &c.*, pp. 259 ff. ｜ T. H. Green, *Prolegomena to Ethics*, book iii. chap. 3, sect. B.

Yet, though the two definitions are identical in extent, we should lose something, for practical purposes, if we estimated sin in the first place by a consideration of the harm done to society at large. For in most cases, where harm is done both to the individual soul and to the community, *it is easier to recognise the former than the latter*. It is easier, for example, to prove that impure thoughts or unworthy motives are detrimental to the individual who harbours them than to show that they injure his neighbours. As Dr. Strong has shown, this is well illustrated by the case of Ananias and Sapphira. ' It was not for producing less than the whole price of their property that Ananias and Sapphira were condemned ; there was no obligation to produce all or any part of it. It was the thought in their hearts, the desire and the conspiracy to deceive, that S. Peter denounced.'[1] Their sin lay in the dishonest motive which conditioned an apparently generous act. Their fellow-Christians would have no difficulty in seeing that the sin of motive was a spiritual disaster to the guilty pair ; it would be more difficult to show that it was the same disaster to the community—although indeed it was. To ordinary eyes the Church had benefited materially by their gift, and had not suffered spiritual loss through their sin. It needed the clearer discernment of the apostle to see that the dishonest thought itself was a danger to the community, ' a breach of the new social order.' It is just because the priest may be lacking in such clear discernment that it is wiser for him to approach the question of sin from the side of its personal, rather than of its communal danger.[2]

We may, as a result of this discussion, accept as satisfactory the working definition of sin with which we started.

---

[1] *Christian Ethics*, p. 226. Dr. Strong's analysis of the incident is not however directed towards the question discussed in the text.

[2] It should be noticed also that sins in which little or no apparent harm is done to the community may be *more* dangerous to the soul than those which produce much harm. Thus *Summa*, i. 2, q. 73, a. 8 : ' Non sequitur quod, si nocumentum maxime habet locum in peccatis quae sunt contra proximum, illa peccata sint gravissima ; quia multo major inordinatio invenitur in peccatis quae sunt contra Deum, et in quibusdam eorum quae sunt contra seipsum.' To St. Thomas it is *inordinatio*—the derangement of the agent's soul—which is the fundamental danger of sin

Sin is any action or habit inhibiting or delaying the soul's progress to perfection, of the danger of which the soul is, or ought to have been conscious. And we may at this point deduce two other conclusions as to sin which have taken a prominent place in moral theology.

(*a*) Sinful habits are more dangerous than sinful actions ; for habit, as we have seen and shall have cause to see again, is a more permanent element in character than sporadic acts. The latter indeed, if repeated, will become habitual and so ingrained ; but at the moment of commission they are less dangerous than the former.

(*b*) It is not when an act has been committed that the danger to the soul begins, but when the thought of it has been favourably accepted in the mind. A lustful thought is as sinful as a lustful act ; a feeling of hate deliberately fostered as deadly as any word or act to which it may give rise.[1] It is from within, from the heart, that danger threatens. The commission of the act suggested by the heart intensifies indeed the wrong done to the agent's personality, for every act helps to stereotype the condition of mind from which it issues ; but we must not on that account minimise the irreparable evil that must come from sinful thoughts continually encouraged. It is neither excuse nor consolation to be able to say, ' I did not do it after all,' so long as one is bound to confess, ' I would have done it if I safely could,' or ' I would have done it had I not been hindered.'

2. *The Biblical Doctrine of Sin*

Hitherto we have examined the character of sin from an empirical point of view—considering it, that is to say, in the light in which it is best known to us, as an impediment to, or even a reversal of, spiritual progress. In this character it shares with temperamental disabilities a place of fundamental importance in the scheme of Christian ethics. The same place is assigned to it in the Bible by the word ἁμαρτία, which implies just the point of view we have adopted—a wandering from the path, a cessation of

---

[1] Matt. v. 22, 28.

progress, even a retracing of one's steps. But the most fundamental element in the Biblical doctrine of sin is one which we have not yet considered.

In several passages in the Old Testament[1] the word 'sin' is mentioned in connection with two other words —*iniquity* ('a-uōn) and *transgression* (pé-sha'). Of these the former has the sense of 'perversion' or 'enormity,' the latter that of 'open rebellion.' The former implies a deliberate misdirection of effort; the latter, a law *and a lawgiver* who is wittingly disobeyed. And here we have the clue to the deepest thought the Bible gives us about sin. Sin is rebellion against a God Whom the Old Testament recognises above all as holy, whilst the New knows Him both as loving and merciful. So familiar is this thought to the Christian mind that it has possibly lost much of its vitality; and it is worth while to consider for a moment what a depth of meaning it contains.

First of all, it elevates sin into something infinitely more terrible even than loss or damage to oneself or the community. Loss to oneself can at least, we hope, be repaired; damage done in a community of which no member is perfect is perhaps not altogether a surprise; but insurrection against One Who has never given us the slightest cause for complaint, for discontent, for anything but gratitude—can anything imaginable be more horrible than that?

How terrible was the impression produced by this aspect of sin upon the minds of priests, prophets, historians, evangelists and apostles alike, can be seen written on every page of the Bible. Sins of inadvertence or ignorance or ceremonial neglect—these can be purged by the ordinances of the law; but the sin 'with an high hand,' the sin in which the sinner deliberately and willingly proclaims himself rebel and outlaw against the greatest of all Kings— for that there can be no hope of forgiveness.[2] Or again, in sin the offence is threefold—against oneself, and against one's neighbour, and against God; but the third offence

---

[1] Exod. xxxiv. 7; Job xxxiv. 37; Ps. xxxii. 1, 2, li. 4, 5; Dan. ix. 5. Cp. on this whole question H. P. Liddon, *Some Elements of Religion*, lect. iv., especially pp. 151 ff   [2] Num. xv. 30.

overshadows so utterly the other two that they are as nothing. It is against God and God only that we sin and do this evil in His sight.[1] Such sin is unnatural; it has the monstrosity of a bride's unfaithfulness to her husband,[2] of a foundling's ingratitude to the foster-parent who has saved it from exposure and nourished it with every luxury.[3] There is a ' note of panic ' in such utterances which rightly emphasises the true horror of sinfulness.

In the New Testament this same unnatural, rebellious character of sin is expressed, but the colouring of the picture is not altogether the same. On the one hand, the ' note of panic,' to employ again Dr. Strong's expressive phrase, has disappeared; there is a marked contrast between ' the furious hatred of evil which breathes in some psalms and in some of the writings of Isaiah ' and ' the almost matter-of-fact way in which St. Peter in his early speeches describes the message he has to deliver.' ' The whole treatment of sin in the New Testament is cooler than in the Old.' [4]

But, Dr. Strong adds, though it is cooler, ' it is no less severe.' We may indeed say that it heightens the horror of the tragedy of sin by adopting the method of the greatest dramatists. The Old Testament has sounded the depths of horror in language whose passion cannot be surpassed. The New Testament intensifies it by a series of commonplace, everyday comparisons infinitely pathetic in their simplicity; just as at the emotional crisis of the greatest tragedies the passion breaks into some childish, simple phrase more poignant than the most terrible outburst could have been.[5] And so it is suggested that sin resembles ' debt,' or ' disease,' or ' slavery,' or ' pollution,' or ' homelessness,' or ' darkness '; that it has the coldness of death itself; that its callousness is nothing but a second Calvary.[6] These trivial unemotional

---

[1] Ps. li. 4; cp. 2. Sam. xii. 13 (David's confession).
[2] Hos. iii.   [3] Ezek. xvi. 1-34.   [4] Strong, *op. cit.* p. 216.
[5] Cp. the ' Cover her face: mine eyes dazzle: she died young,' of Ferdinand in *The Duchess of Malfi*; Macduff's ' He has no children '; Lear's ' Art cold ? I am cold myself '; Ophelia's ' snatches of old tunes '; &c.
[6] See Matt. vi. 12, xviii. 23; Mark ii. 17; John viii. 34. Cp. Rom. vi. 16, vii. 14; Mark vii. 23; Eph. ii. 1, iv. 18; and Heb. vi. 6.

phrases are more replete with meaning than the highest
rhetoric ; for they emphasise what is the most horrible fact
of all about this horrible thing—that it has become as
commonplace to us as debt or dirt or darkness.

It is natural enough that the New Testament writers
should have used the only means still open to them to darken
the Old Testament picture of the monstrous and inhuman
character of sin ; for they knew something of the nature
of God which was unknown to the older dispensation. The
person and teaching of Christ had revealed to them God,
not merely in His known character of a holy yet merciful
King, but in the new light of a tender, devoted, self-forgetful
Father. ' Impudent children,' ' a rebellious house,' Ezekiel
had called the people of Israel ; [1] the phrases took on a new
meaning for those who had learnt what the Fatherhood of
God meant to Jesus. And it is supremely moving to notice
that almost all these simple phrases which we have seen
to touch the heart of the New Testament doctrine of sin
we owe to our Lord Himself, Who, though He did no sin,
yet, through His perfect sympathy with the soul of man,
understood its power far better than man himself.

Sin, then, is lawlessness, as St. John tells us ; or rebellion ;
or, in the phrases of later theology, 'a free violation of the
moral law.' [2] Phrases of this kind may convey little to the
modern mind ; but it is of the utmost importance that the
priest should, by every means in his power, keep the truth
they represent alive in the consciousness of his flock. For
if it be true, as we have seen, that no part of the Christian
gospel has so strong an influence upon man's spiritual
progress as the truth of God's infinite tenderness and
compassion, it must be equally true that nothing will wean
men from their sin so much as the knowledge that, in sinning,
they grieve, rebel against, and trample underfoot this
wonderful mercy and love. Other motives, no doubt, will

---

[1] Ezek. ii. 4, 5.
[2] Augustine, *De Duabus An.* 11, 12. Cp. *id., c. Faust.* xxii. 27 :
' Any transgression in deed, word or desire of the eternal law.' For other
Augustinian definitions see T. A. Lacey, *Nature, Miracle and Sin*, pp. 115,
116. Cp. *Summa,* i. 2, q. 72, a. 1 ; q. 109, a. 4 : ' Nihil aliud est peccare
quam transgredi divina mandata,' *et passim.* Cp. also Jas. iv. 17 : ' To
him that knoweth to do good and doeth it not, it is sin ' | and Luke xii. 47.

often be the first to rouse in a man some sense of the degradation of sin—the desire to escape from its shackles for instance, self-respect, the example of a friend, even the fear of consequences. But no motive, in the end, can have so permanent an effect upon the will or so powerfully affect the emotions as the thought of the indignity which sin offers to God.

We need not be distressed, indeed, if converts or penitents fail to exhibit the refined and searching contrition of St. Augustine's 'Confessions' or the 'Imitatio Christi,' or Andrewes' 'Private Prayers.' Nor need we hesitate to stimulate the sense of sin by other means. Indeed, we can do harm by insisting too much upon the truth we are considering among those whose conception of God is too slight for them to grasp it ; harm, both by puzzling and even repelling the strong-minded, and by inducing an unreal and emotional sentiment in the weak. Unseasonable emphasis upon this aspect of sin as disobedience has indeed been one cause of that dangerous tendency to regard Christian morals as no more than compliance with an external code of behaviour, to which allusion has been made in previous chapters. But wherever a Christian soul is seen to be earnestly striving after higher things and sincerely learning to know more of God, there we may be sure that a clear, and if necessary (as in some cases it is necessary) an unimpassioned insistence upon the rebellion and disobedience inherent in the fact of sin, will reap its own reward in a growing purity of spiritual life.

We need not dwell further upon the other contributions of the New Testament to the doctrine of sin—its inwardness ; the special danger of hypocrisy and spiritual pride ; the metaphysical origin ascribed to it by St. Paul ; the danger of relapses. In so far as they touch the immediate problem of the treatment to be applied to sin, they will be discussed in this and the following chapters. Their details in other respects can be gathered from any of the many books which deal fully with the subject.[1] One point, however, which

---

[1] For example, J. Müller, *Christian Doctrine of Sin* (Eng. tr.) ; H. B. Swete, *Forgiveness of Sins* ; H. R. Tennant, *Origin and Propagation of Sin* ; H. V. S. Eck, *Sin* ; R. Mackintosh, *Christianity and Sin*.

must be discussed as a necessary preliminary to the practical question still remains :—the psychological process by which a sinful act, and still more a sinful habit, comes into being. Of this process the Bible offers more than one searching analysis.

3. *The Psychological Origins of Sinful Acts and Habits*

Any analysis of a psychological process is, as we have seen before, open to the criticism that it makes divisions in the indivisible. But to refrain from inquiry on this account would be to abandon the attempt to understand, not merely the nature of the soul and its actions, but all Nature too. We must recognise frankly that any conclusions that result from analysis are unreal, in so far as they ignore, and are compelled to ignore, the most vital factors of all—the continuity and unity of consciousness.[1] No dissection of the body can discover the principle of life ; and without life the body is an unnatural, we might even say an unreal, phenomenon.

Realising the inadequacy and even the misleading character of analytical investigation of this kind, we may yet persevere in it to attain such measure of truth as it can afford. Our immediate purpose is to discover the stages by which a sinful act comes into being, and by which a repetition of sinful acts will produce a sinful habit. And we must recognise that as far as its cause and mode of production is concerned, a sinful act—one that is to say which is hostile to the spiritual progress of the soul—is no different from any other act. What we have to do is to trace the general laws of consciousness in conformity to which every action comes to the birth.

This has often been done before ;[2] but it is worth while

[1] Cp. L. T. Hobhouse, *Mind in Evolution*, p. 369 : ' The material universe of molecular physics is not the universe as known to sight or touch, only rather more completely known ' ; and see above, p. 3.

[2] See, e.g., T. H. Green, *Prolegomena to Ethics*, book ii. chap. 2 ; G. Stevens, *Psychology of the Christian Soul*, pp. 112–141; and cp. St. Thomas Aquinas, *Opuscula*, lxv. (ed. Rom.) ; *Summa*, i. 2, q. 75, aa. 2, 3 ; *Ductor Dubitantium*, book iv. chap. 1, rule 3 ; Thomas à Kempis, *Imitatio Christi*, book i. chap 13.

to recapitulate the result. The ultimate ground of all action is *instinct*. No word in the whole language is more abused or less understood than this ; Dr. McDougall has collected from various ' cultured writers ' at least a dozen different meanings in which it is employed.[1] Indeed psychologists themselves are not at one as to its connotation. For our purposes, however, it will be enough to define it as *a primary impulse to action accompanied by a definite emotional tone.*[2] Such instincts are fear, hunger and thirst, the maternal emotion, hatred, the sexual impulse and the like. The discussion of their number and identity (if indeed they can be so distinguished in thought as to be severally enumerated) will occupy us at a later stage.

Every action is the result of the awakening of one or more of these instincts. This awakening of an instinct, its change from a dormant to an active force, is not itself without cause. It is a reaction to stimulus—to some change of environment which ultimately, if not immediately, affects consciousness. Fear, for example, is not aroused unless some object of fear is presented to the mind. Even if it be presented only by memory or imagination, it may be traced back to some event in the past which first brought the instinct into operation. The unreasoning terrors of a child in the dark are due perhaps to the unwise threatenings of its nurse, or, if to nothing more, to the transition from a normal condition of light and society to the abnormal one of darkness and loneliness.

The stimulus, then, may be perceived in the immediate environment of the present, or recalled from some environment of the past. In either case we may say that it emerges into consciousness as the result of a *perception*, an act of awareness, which partakes at all events in some degree of the nature of intellectual cognition. And this leads to a conclusion even more important for the theologian than for the psychologist. To the latter, the instincts are obviously natural endowments whose proper function is the preservation of the species. The perception or awareness of the

---

[1] W. McDougall, *Social Psychology*, pp. 21, 22.

[2] *Ibid.* pp. 29, 42, 47, &c. ; and for a full discussion of *instinct* see the same book, chaps. i–vi and supplementary chap. ii.

individual presents him with some change in his environment, and the appropriate instinct is aroused to stimulate
him to action which shall bring him into harmony with this
change.   The body grows weak through want of food ; the
instinct of hunger is aroused to lead it to eat.   The approach
of something inimical endangers its safety ; the instincts
of fear or pugnacity or both impel it to flight or to resistance.

The theologian sees something more fundamental and
penetrating even than this.   He sees that no instinct, *however
sinful be the actions that result from it,* can be in essence evil.[1]
Sin enters with some later stage of the action; it is not present
at its birth.   Our instincts are God-given, and their function
in life is beneficent ; they lead first of all to the preservation
of the body, but later, with the development of the spiritual
consciousness, to the salvation of the soul.   Sin may be
due to human weakness and depravity ; it is not due to
complete pollution of life at its very source.   Sin is 'the
corruption of the circumstances of virtue.' [2]

The instinct once awakened in personality is not without
effect in its most distant regions.   Personality, we need
hardly repeat, is essentially one ; no change that enters
into it can fail to influence every element in its composition.
It is true that some instincts result in immediate actions
in which we cannot trace the operation of mind or will, sometimes not even that of feeling.   Where these are not habitudes
(that is, the result of repeated conscious action in the past)
we must class them as pure reflexes, or *impulsive* actions,
without moral importance except that, perhaps, they *should
have been* inhibited in the interests of the general well-being
of the soul.   Such reflex actions are, for example, the
emission of tears, or of a cry, at a sudden spasm of pain ;
the various actions which go to make up the process of
mastication and the like.   It is not necessary for his moral
well-being that the individual should always have these
under control, though, wherever they are susceptible of
control and are not purely physiological, it is his duty to

---

[1] *Summa,* i. 2, q. 24, a. 1 ; cp. Chrysostom, *In Ep. ad Rom. Hom.*
xiii., on Rom. vii. 14.

[2] *Summa,* ii. 2, q. 53, a. 2 ; cp. H. Rashdall, *Theory of Good and Evil,*
vol. ii. p. 73.

be able to control them, and that without hesitation, if his moral consciousness calls for it.

Where, however, the action under consideration can be regarded as a considered or deliberate one, the effect of the excitation of the basal instinct can be traced both in the intellectual and the emotional sphere. In the intellectual sphere there is gradually formed an *idea* of the gratification of the instinct ; thus the idea of eating food presents itself to the hungry man, whatever the stimulus which aroused the instinct may have been.[1] Nor is this the end of intellectual activity in the matter. The possibility and advisability of the action in question are canvassed ; in many cases its moral rightness is considered as well ; and even though it may have been found to be impossible, inadvisable, or morally wrong, the mind may yet go on to revolve the various conceivable steps by which it could be brought into effect.

Meanwhile an emotional process is at work. By definition, as we have seen, every instinct is accompanied by a distinct emotional tone. In proportion as the idea is fostered in the mind, so the emotion connected with the possibility

---

[1] It is to be observed that an instinct may be excited by any one of many different stimuli—thus the instinct of *hunger* may arise from a painful physiological sensation due to lack of food, or to the sight of food, or to a recognition of the fact that an accustomed meal-time has arrived. With the widening of experience and development of consciousness the number and variety of the stimuli, or perceptions, to which a given instinct will react, are steadily increased. Moral indignation, for example, is a habit of mind based upon the *instinct of repulsion* when roused by distressing or revolting facts of a moral order. These facts, however, do not arouse any such instinct in a child ; his experience has not as yet led him to an *awareness* of their repellent nature. *How* it comes about that instincts which primarily (it would appear) react to physical perceptions ultimately react to intellectual or moral ones, is a problem which no materialistic psychology has been able to solve ; to the theologian, who regards man's spiritual environment as being as real, if not more real, than his physical one, the difficulty is less acute. From this point of view, every natural endowment, including not least the instincts, has a part to play in relation to spiritual as in relation to natural phenomena ; and instincts which do not react, in a fully developed personality, to due spiritual stimulus are symptoms of some far-reaching atrophy or defect of character.

For a psychological attempt to explain this phenomenon (the response of primary instincts in a matured personality to the social, moral and religious sentiments), see McDougall, *op. cit.* pp. 31–40, and chaps. vi., vii. and viii.

of its realisation develops and deepens. There may indeed be conflicting emotions ; in some of its aspects the proposed action may attract, in others it may repel ; just as there may be conflicting thoughts about it—the thought of its advisability in some respects conflicting with the thought of its inadvisability in others. This is the stage of emotional or of intellectual *conflict*. With respect to the vast majority of actions this conflict may be so slight as to be negligible ; [1] in the case of others it presents a long and painful struggle.

In this struggle there enters, or should enter, another factor : that of the *will*, the formed purpose of the man's life. This may be strong enough to dominate all other influences ; it may be weak, yet strong enough to get the mastery when reinforced by intellectual considerations or by emotional concurrence. Or finally it may be so weak as to fail to take control. For a time the struggle may continue ; only now it is a moral, not an intellectual or an emotional one. In this state of instability the soul will remain until at last the intricate complex of cross-currents cuts out a single channel, and the personality is balanced or harmonised either for, or against, the contemplated act.

If the final balance is in accord with the general tenor of the man's will, or moral purpose, the result may fairly be called a victory of will over passion. If the result is opposed to what has hitherto been the tenor of the will, it is a victory of passion over will. Yet, in this latter case the action is no less *voluntary* than in the former one : the will, in accepting defeat, has incorporated the solicitations

---

[1] All conscious action presents as concomitant parts of the process the same four elements : the stimulus, the awakened instinct, the emotional colouring, and the action of the intelligence. But in the vast majority of cases neither of the latter factors obtrude themselves upon consciousness. Thus the simple act of getting up to close the window, for example, has an emotional context—a feeling of discomfort due to the draught, let us say ; and an intellectual context—the process of reasoning from which we conclude that to shut the window will be to exclude the draught. There may even be an emotional struggle—the discomfort of the open window being countered by a disinclination for rising from the chair ; and an intellectual one, the possibility of the draught coming from some other source being weighed against the possibility of its coming from the window. Yet the man who says ' I have just shut the window,' will in all probability have the vaguest possible recollection only of the complicated phases which preceded the act in consciousness.

of the victorious passion into itself—its general tenor for the future is no longer the same as it has been, for it has admitted the satisfaction of the passion in question, partially or entirely, as a legitimate factor in the complex of motives which go to make up the man's purpose in life. The will has been *weakened* in so far as it has admitted into itself an element which hitherto it had regarded as discordant with itself.

It is here that we see the importance of the fundamental contention of moral theology—that the soul can most surely be led to virtuous actions by the continued orientation of desire, intellect and will to the service of God. If the intellect judges according to no other criterion than that of God's greater glory ; if the desires have all been subordinated to the single desire of serving Him ; if the will to serve is both strong and unswerving—then there can be no fear that the soul will be out of harmony with itself, or that its harmony will lead to any action that might hinder its spiritual achievement by weakening, or rendering less virtuous, its will. It is only where one or more of these factors are still directed to something other than the service of God that moral struggle occurs ; only where such discordant elements prove stronger and more enduring than those which make for goodness, that we need look for sin.

As a concrete example of such a process issuing in a sinful act, we may select the melodramatic incident—the exchange of the children in infancy—which determines the plot of 'Evelina.' Fantastic as the story is, it is yet redeemed by its exceptionally faithful psychology. ' The deceit which [my nurse] practised,' writes the heroine to her guardian, ' was suggested to her by a conversation she overheard in which my unhappy mother besought you that, if her child survived her, you would take the sole charge of its education. . . . Her own child was then in her arms, and she could not forbear wishing it were possible to give *her* the fortune which seemed so little valued for me. This wish once raised was not easily suppressed ; on the contrary what at first appeared a mere idle desire, in a short time seemed a feasible scheme.' [1]

[1] Fanny Burney, *Evelina*, letter 79.

Here the various elements are all strongly marked. The
stimulus, which in conformity with theological usage we
may henceforward call the *occasion*, was a suggestion overheard by chance. The instinct aroused was that of maternal
emotion, recognised by all psychologists as one of the most
fundamental and primary of all human endowments. We
see the intellectual process at work, developing a mere fancy
into a ' feasible scheme ' ; as well as the emotional one, in
which a passing wish becomes something not ' easily suppressed.' At this point the process is complete ; the woman
seems to have no moral purpose strong enough even to
interfere, far less to inhibit. A favourable opportunity is
found ; and the sin is committed.

So far, then, we find five definite elements combined in
one process : the occasion, the instinct, an intellectual
process issuing in a clearly articulated idea, an emotional
one culminating in a passion or craving, and the will, or
moral purpose, which in the case of a sinful act is overcome
by the other influences at work. We have already noticed
how indulgence in an emotion gives it added strength, and
assent to an idea or train of thought tends to standardise
it for the mind ; it is easy, therefore, to estimate the
psychological consequences of such a process. The emotions
associated with the action will be intensified ; the idea of
it strengthened ; the practical reasoning by which its
commission is thought out, the excuses by which it is
to be justified, will all be ready to hand ; and the power
of the will to resist will by just so much be weakened. In
each recurring instance the moral struggle is less than
before ; in the end it becomes negligible. By such stages
a series of sinful acts becomes a sinful habit of soul ; the
instinct has only to be stimulated in circumstances favourable to the commission of the act, and the latter will
inevitably be repeated.

The practical conclusions resulting from this analysis
we must leave until the next chapter, when we consider
the treatment of sin. But we may well pause for a moment
to notice how clearly the process we have been tracing
is pictured in the Bible. Two passages in particular
stand out as emphasising in all their fullness the various

stages which lead up to sinful acts and habits—the description of the Fall in the third chapter of Genesis ; and
St. Paul's analysis of his own spiritual condition before
his conversion (Rom. vii.).[1]

The first of these, as we should expect, is the simplest ;
but it lacks none of the essentials.   There is the occasion—
the tree with its fruit, and the serpent to make his
treacherous suggestion.   The instinct aroused is perhaps
that of cupidity—the desire of possession ; perhaps merely
of natural hunger.   We see the intellectual process in the
growth of the idea ; the acceptance of the serpent's argument
' Ye shall not surely die.'   The craving is put before us
in the strongest terms :   the woman sees that the tree is
good for food, and pleasant to the eyes, and a tree to be
desired to make one wise.   Yet her will is not defeated
at the first onslaught of temptation, though it does not
resist long.   ' God hath said,' she replies to the tempter,
' Ye shall not eat of it.'   But she makes no other protest,
and the sin is committed.

St. Paul's account is more involved and rhetorical, and
carries the process further to its natural issue in habitual
sinfulness.   For him the instinct of cupidity is aroused
by a suggestion of the law—' for I had not known lust,
except the law had said, Thou shalt not covet.'   From
this simple occasion springs a riot of craving and passionate
desire :   ' Sin, taking occasion by the commandment,
wrought in me all manner of concupiscence.'   Again, with
a variation of the same phrase, he expresses the gradual
compliance of the intellect : ' Sin, taking occasion by the
commandment, deceived me '—' for all sin,' as one com-
mentator [2] says, ' is committed under a deception as to the
satisfaction to be found in it ; the excuse to be made for
it ; and the probability of punishment.'

So far, then, both desire and intellect have consented
to the sinful suggestion.   To them is opposed the man's
moral purpose : ' What I would I do not, but what I
hate, that I do.'   ' To will is present with me, but to work
that which is good is not.'   ' The good that I would I do
not, but the evil I would not, that I do.'   The moral purpose

---

[1] Notice also Jas. i. 14, 15.　　　　[2] Vaughan, *ad loc.*

is there, but it is not strong enough to counter the sinister influences. St. Paul's description of his final state is not altogether clear. His own estimate of his condition is more pessimistic than would be that of an observer acquainted with the facts. ' Here is a man,' the observer would say, ' fighting a hard fight with temptation. Perhaps he is conscious no longer of any desire to be righteous ; his desires are wholly sinful. Perhaps too his mind cannot persuade him that there is anything to be gained by continuing the struggle. Yet he does not give up ; time after time he falls, but returns to the fight again ; his will remains to him—his moral purpose, his moral self-respect, we may almost call it. He will not give in finally because he has never willingly given in yet—he continues the fight in sheer obstinacy of character. For such a man there is still hope.'

St. Paul takes a gloomier view. He sees that, apart from some new power in the field, the fight can have only one issue ; will, self-respect, stubbornness—call it what you wish—cannot survive unaided for ever. With each fall it becomes weaker—identifies itself a little more with the unclean thing. He has come to the last gasp of the battle ; he is all but a broken and defeated man. And so in his account he anticipates the inevitable finale : ' I am dead,' ' I am fleshly, sold under sin.' We have to disentangle in his account the sentences which refer respectively to each of these two steps in the process : the penultimate, in which his will still resists ; the ultimate, in which its resistance is broken. The latter, in strict fact, has not yet arrived ; but the logic of the fight assures him that it is only momentarily delayed.

The ambiguities of this account are therefore attributable to the fact that St. Paul is contemplating, with a kind of moral second-sight, two pictures at once. The first is the picture of himself still struggling ; the second of himself no longer struggling, but wholly submissive to a habit of sin. It is with the latter picture in mind that he uses such a phrase as ' I see that in myself, that is in my flesh, dwelleth no good thing '—a phrase impossible to a theology which definitely opposed the Gnostic and

Manichæan suggestion that the flesh is wholly evil, unless it refers to a condition of complete surrender to sin. So, too, the words τὰ παθήματα τῶν ἁμαρτιῶν—the *motions*, or *instincts* of sin—can only be attributed to a state of soul so wholly void of its original tendencies to good that every instinct is *bound* to produce a sin. And although his personification of sin is doubtless no mere rhetorical exaggeration, but the expression of genuine belief in a spirit of evil capable of entering the soul and taking possession, yet the sentence, ' It is no longer I but sin that worketh in me,' must, like the others, refer to a state of degradation in which the idea of personality conveys no longer any meaning ; the ' self '—the self which God made for a good end—is no more. There is no longer in the sum of character any tendency to good ; and without such a tendency to good true selfhood, personality, is an impossibility. Whatever it is that remains is at best an unreal mockery of the soul which God made in the beginning. The soul is no longer human ; it is in a sense more real even than that in which Augustine used the words, a *massa peccatorum*.

This, then, gives us a glimpse of the final state of desperate and hopeless habit to which the constant repetition of sin, *even through continual moral struggle*, may bring a man. If such a state ultimately supervenes, he may well be spoken of as *dead* ; his personality, in any sense in which the word is understood by us, has ceased to exist.[1] Happily such a state of complete degradation is very rare. Few have so completely lost every trace of their original tendency towards good that there is nothing left to which appeal can be made ; that ' their entire purpose, of its own accord, is directed towards evil.'[2] But with respect to particular sins the thing is not so uncommon. Men are to be found whose moral consciousness with reference to this or that factor in their life is dead ; who pursue some evil end with entire callousness as to its implications. There are cases where affection turns to hate, or disappointment breeds revenge, which approximate

---

[1] To this state St. Thomas gives the name of *malitia*. See *Summa*, i. 2, q. 78 ; and *infra*, p. 265.

[2] *Summa*, i. 2, q. 78, a. 3.

nearly, if not absolutely, to this condition. Such cases, it is clear, are outside the reach of ordinary treatment. The priest can do something by stimulating the spiritual life in other directions, in the hope that its influence will revivify that part of conscience which has suffered atrophy; beyond this he can only pray the Holy Spirit to repair what by human means is irreparable, and wait for God's grace to bring about a moral miracle.

CHAPTER XI

THE TREATMENT OF SIN

1. *Mortal and Venial Sin*

MORAL theology recognises certain *distinctions* or classifications of sin, of which four are essential, the remainder accidental. The four essential ones correspond to four questions which the priest must put to himself with reference to any spiritual disorder which he would attempt to heal. These four distinctions are respectively : the distinction between *original* and *personal* sin ; that between *formal* and *material* ; that between *habitual* and *actual* ; and that between *mortal* and *venial*.[1]

The first three of these have in fact been discussed in the previous chapter, and we need only recapitulate their character briefly ; the fourth remains as a distinction of crucial importance for our purpose, whose true bearing is to many Christians far from clear.

(*a*) *Original and personal.* Without entering upon the metaphysical problem brought up by this distinction, we may regard it simply as one marking the difference between inherited and acquired tendencies injurious to

---

[1] See *Summa*, i. 2, qq. 72, 73, 81, 82, &c. ; W. W. Williams, *Moral Theology of the Sacrament of Penance*, p. 175 ; W. W. Webb, *Cure of Souls*, p. 73. Among the accidental or non-essential distinctions we may notice : sins of *commission* and *omission* ; sins of *malice*, *infirmity* (overwhelming and sudden passion) and *ignorance* (culpable) ; sins of *deliberation* and of *inadvertence* ; sins of *thought*, *word* and *deed* ; sins *against God*, *against neighbours*, *against oneself* ; sins *carnal* and sins *spiritual* ; and—two interesting classifications used by Bishop Andrewes—sins *in luxuries* and sins *in necessities*, and sins ' *with the cord* ' and sins ' *with the cart-rope.*' Many of these distinctions are, of course, cross-classifications. Their principal value lies (*a*) in helping to estimate the gravity of sin, and (*b*) in providing simple guidance for the individual Christian in self-examination and confession.

the soul; in other words, between temperamental disabilities and sinful disabilities proper. This point we have already considered.[1]

(*b*) *Formal and material.* This corresponds, as we have seen, to the distinction we drew between sinful acts and habits deliberately committed or contracted by the sinner with full knowledge of their real character, and those of whose danger he *ought to have* been conscious, but in fact was not. In the latter case the true sin—the real problem to be handled—lies not in the act or habit itself, but in the *culpable* and *vincible* ignorance which caused it.

(*c*) *Habitual and actual.* Here the priest will ask himself : Have I to deal with an isolated act of sin, or with a habit already stereotyped or in process of formation ? The latter case is obviously one of greater gravity than the former.

It is clear that in every case in which the priest contemplates action for the spiritual welfare of an individual soul, he must have found the answer to these three questions. It is no less important also that he should have reached a conclusion upon the fourth question, which we must now consider, *Is the sin mortal or venial ?*

The distinction between mortal and venial sin has its origin in the verses 1 John v. 16, 17 : ' If any man see his brother sin a sin not unto death, he shall ask ; and He shall give him life, for those who sin not unto death. There is a sin unto death ; I say not that he should ask concerning that. All unrighteousness is sin ; and there is a sin not unto death.' But this distinction between a graver and

---

[1] On the relation between the doctrine of *original sin* and modern theories of heredity and environment, see the works mentioned *supra*, p. 232 ; C. C. J. Webb, *Problems in the Relation of God to Man*, pp. 115–29 ; T. B. Strong, *Manual of Theology*, pp. 236–256 ; F. J. Hall, *Evolution and the Fall* ; J. R. Bernard, article ' Fall ' in Hastings' *Dictionary of the Bible*, vol. ii. The theory of heredity cannot fairly be said to deal with all the facts of which the doctrine of original sin offers an explanation. The modern doctrine, in effect, substitutes the idea of *temptation* for that of *original sin*, and so tends to destroy the conception of *equality* in sinful tendencies which is at the root of the traditional Christian teaching, and is fully borne out by the experience of the mature religious consciousness. Nor does the modern doctrine insist, as does the Catholic one, upon the necessity of grace *for all* if they are to be restored to righteousness.

a lighter form of sin is not confined to St. John. We find it also in Jeremiah (vii. 26 and xvi. 12), and in our Lord's own words : ' Every sin and blasphemy shall be forgiven to men, but the blasphemy of the Spirit shall not be forgiven to them. And whosoever shall speak a word against the Son of Man, it shall be forgiven him ; but whosoever shall speak against the Holy Ghost it shall not be forgiven him, either in this world or in the world to come' (Matt. xii. 31, 32; cp. Mark iii. 28, 29 ; Luke xii. 10). So too our Lord's answer to Pilate, though it does not explicitly refer to any *unforgivable* sin, certainly contemplates *degrees of sinfulness* : ' Thou couldest not have power over Me if it had not been given thee from above. Therefore he that delivered Me to thee hath the greater sin ' (John xix. 11). We may notice also that three passages in the Epistle to the Hebrews suggest (though in none of the three cases is the meaning perfectly clear) the possibility of unforgivable sin.[1]

If we look at sin from the strictly theological point of view as an offence, or rebellion against God, this distinction is a very difficult one to understand. Where there is rebellion against an all-loving Father there can surely be no advantage in, no justification for, a ' nicely-calculated less or more.' In every case, however trivial, the offence is incalculable ; St. James's words say no more than the truth : ' Whoso keepeth the whole law yet offendeth in one point, is guilty of the whole.' [2] Infinite harm may be done by minimising the wickedness of the slightest sin.[3] Nothing short of absolute purity is befitting for the Christian ; he has no right to regard even the slightest decline from the ideal as being of small account. To do so is the surest way of warping and stultifying his conscience ; once teach him that certain sins are not serious, and he will soon come to think that none are.

---

[1] Heb. vi. 4–6, x. 26, xii. 17. See commentaries *ad locc.*

[2] Jas ii. 10. Cp. R. C. Trench, *On the Study of Words*, lect. 3, on this passage and the word ' integrity.'

[3] Hence Sanderson speaks of the classification of sins into mortal and venial as ' putida illa distinctio, quo velut fermento totam theologiae moralis massam foede corruperunt [Casuistae] ' (*De Juramenti Obligatione*, praelect. iii. § 15). Jeremy Taylor is equally emphatic (*Unum Necessarium*, chap. 3).

There is, then, a point of view from which the distinction we are considering must be regarded as unreal ; and not merely unreal but dangerous. From the point of view of God, so to say, it is unreal ; from the point of view of the sinner himself, it is dangerous. There is, however, the third point of view : that of the priest whose business it is to try and repair the damages caused by sin to human souls. And from this point of view the distinction between mortal and venial sin is both real and valuable.

It needs little discussion to see that, whilst the offence against God is infinite, and so equal, in all sins, the danger to the sinner himself may be very different. In some cases an act or habit, though deleterious to his spiritual progress, will only take effect slowly ; there will be time in which corrective influences may be brought into play ; the urgency is slight. In other cases the habit has obtained so tyrannical a grip upon the soul—a passion has become so intense—an act has been committed of set purpose and in cold blood so outrageous to the moral sense—that immediate and drastic steps must be taken to repair the damage. The danger to the soul is urgent ; spiritual progress as matters stand is impossible.

The nature of these drastic steps we are about to consider in detail ; for the moment we need notice two points only about them. First of all, they are, as we shall see, of that type of corrective which is bound to result in some mutilation of personality. The man may be saved, indeed, but he will suffer loss.[1] Remedies of this character are indicated in the Sermon on the Mount : ' If thy right eye offend thee, pluck it out and cast it from thee. For it is profitable for thee that one of thy members should perish, and not that thy whole body should be cast into hell. And if thy right hand offend thee, cut it off and cast it from thee : for it is profitable for thee that one of thy members should perish, and not that thy whole body should be cast into hell.'[2] It is profitable, that is true, but it is only a second best ; the best thing of all, if it may be, is that there shall be no mutilation of personality—that the spiritual life shall be complete.

[1] 1 Cor. iii. 15.   [2] Matt. v. 29, 30.

S

In the second place, if the soul is in imminent spiritual peril—if the act committed or habit contracted is of such a character as to inhibit all spiritual progress, or even to introduce real danger of backsliding—it can scarcely be restored without a very definite appeal to conscience. Penitence and amendment must be urged upon the sinner ; a special effort of attention and will demanded of him to remove the obstacle he has put in his own path, or to make up for the ground he has lost. Such a course is a very necessary, yet often a very dangerous one. It can scarcely be carried to a successful issue without drawing the sinner's attention to the heinousness of his sin itself ; and this is, in part at all events, to concentrate attention upon the idea of the sin. We have seen in a previous chapter the influence which attention and ideas have upon character. There are sins—especially those connected with the more passionate instincts : sins of hatred, of lustful thought and the like—in which *any* dwelling upon the idea of the sin is certain to enhance its hold upon the imagination and to inflame the emotions which surround it ; to produce a result, in fact, the very opposite of the desired one. That is the reason why pamphlets and addresses on the question of purity should be the work only of experts in dealing with souls. They run the risk of sowing the seeds of evil—of fostering its vitality instead of eradicating its growth.

Yet there are cases in which no other course seems open except such a direct appeal to conscience, with its necessary exposition of the hideousness of the sin in question. But because of the risk involved in such a course, as well as for the other reason already considered, the priest will naturally hesitate to adopt drastic means unless he is well assured that no other way is possible. He will prefer to use calm and gradual methods of healing rather than violent, destructive, and dangerous ones. And to this end it is important for him to know what type of sin is amenable to the former, and what type can only be attacked by the latter method. It is to help him to such a decision that the distinction between venial and mortal sin is of value.

'Venial sin' may be taken to denote sin in which the danger to the soul is not immediate or urgent, and which therefore admits of treatment by gradual and innocuous means. ' Mortal sin ' is sin in which the danger is great and urgent, and against which *every* means of treatment, gradual or sudden, harmless or dangerous, must be employed, in spite of the risks involved. This distinction between the two accords with that usually accepted in moral theology. Mortal sin, by turning the soul away from God, deprives it of its contact with Him, and so of grace, and of the right to eternal happiness ; venial sin leaves these privileges untouched.[1] ' There is a sin unto death,' said one of the masters of the spiritual life in our own time,[2] ' not by virtue of its criminality but because it is such as to separate us from the action of the body of Christ.'

It has indeed been suggested that the conception of mortal sin would be more easily grasped if it were spoken of as *mortiferous*—as *leading directly to spiritual death*.[3] That at least is its essential character, the distinction by which it is separated from venial sin. But this distinction is of little use for our purposes unless we know as well by what means to recognise mortal sin. The ' Summa ' gives us three distinguishing characteristics of mortal sin,[4] though it mentions numerous other points which affect the question of the gravity of sin. The three decisive ones, however, are these :—

(*a*) The sin in question must be one causing *grave injury* to an individual, to the Christian community, or to God and His purposes. Nor need this injury be *overt* : thus impure

---

[1] *Summa*, i. 2, q. 72, a. 5 ; q. 73, a. 2 ; q. 88 ; q. 89, a. 1.

[2] Fr. Benson, in *Report of the Fulham Conference on Confession and Absolution*, p. 87. See also B. F. Westcott, *Commentary on the Epistles of St. John*, additional note, pp. 209–214.

[3] The substitution of the idea of *mortiferous* for *mortal* solves what is otherwise a perplexing logical problem : how is it possible, if mortal sin deprives the soul of God's grace, for the sinner ever to repent at all ? Repentance is the work of grace, and grace is *ex hypothesi* impossible in such a condition. St. Thomas met this difficulty by two rather artificial devices : (*a*) the theory that *attrition*, though it ' cannot become contrition ' (*Summa*, Suppl. q. 1, a. 3), is a sufficient disposition to secure forgiveness (e.g. in baptism—*Sent.* iv. d. 6, q. 1, a. 3 ; q. 3 ; and see *supra*, p. 65)—from this line of thought developed the later distinction between *attritio naturalis* and *attritio formidolosa* ; (*b*) that remission of mortal sin is only possible after a new infusion of grace (*Summa*, iii. q. 87, a. 2).

[4] *Summa*, i. 2, q. 72, a. 5 ; q. 77, a. 8 ; q. 88, aa. 2, 6 ; q. 89, aa. 3, 5, 6.

thoughts are a form of mortal sin, as being violently opposed to the very nature of God.

(b) The sinner *must be fully aware* of this evil character and consequences of his sin.

(c) Though aware of its character and consequences he must have sinned *with absolute deliberateness and intention.*

Any sinful act or habit therefore, which is known to be gravely at variance with the moral purpose of life, and yet which is deliberately committed or persisted in, is mortal ; its danger to the soul is infinite and imminent. That this is so follows from the very nature of the case. Such a sin represents a deliberate attempt to turn the desires and will away from God, and to overthrow every principle of right reason. If committed, still more if persisted in, it must form a complete barrier to spiritual progress.

It may be urged that sin of this character is rare ; it is sad to have to admit—as any priest of experience is bound to admit—that so far from being rare it is not uncommon Cases where conscience is thus deliberately violated— particularly in the matter of dishonesty, personal gain, hatred, and ill-temper, and what is more definitely called ' immorality '—with practically no attempt at inhibition or reformation, and on excuses which admit of no shadow of justification, are of constant occurrence. In such cases it is clearly only a matter of time—and probably of a short time—before the disease which has stultified conscience in one respect will deaden it also in others, and spread to every part of life. Even the man who deliberately neglects devotional practices which he knows from personal experience to be necessary to his soul—prayer and meditation for example—is guilty of mortal sin, perhaps even more so than the flagrantly selfish or immoral person ; for nothing reacts so immediately for ill upon the whole character as the neglect of well-established spiritual habits.

Venial sin, on the other hand, is sin which does not separate from the grace of God—such sin for example as occasional lapses from the truth in trivial matters, occasional neglect of the duties of religion, occasional pieces of self-indulgence. It is not to be thought, however, that venial sin is wholly without danger. It may easily develop

into mortal.[1] In venial sin the purpose for which the sin
is committed is usually no more than the gratification of
a passing impulse ; but it is always possible that repetition
will make it the final purpose of life.   Or again, venial sin
may lead to mortal sin by suggestion—' as an idle word
will lead to fornication.'[2]   Still we may recognise that the
danger in venial sin is not immediate.   There is time for
treatment by gradual and safe means ; but if such treatment
fails to eradicate the sin, it will by degrees become mortal,
and the more abrupt methods may have to be employed.

Certain other circumstances are noticed by St. Thomas
as affecting the gravity of sin.[3]   We need only consider
them briefly.   *The gravity of the injury inflicted*, for example,
affects the gravity of the sin, other things being equal ; thus
' murder is graver than theft.'   *Spiritual sin is graver than
fleshly sin*, both because it cuts more directly at the root
of goodness, and because less excuse can be found for it in
violence of temptation.   *The relationship of the sinner to
the person sinned against* may enter in as a factor.   A sin
against God, or a parent or benefactor, is graver than one
against someone from whom injury has been received ; a
sin against a monarch is graver than one against a private
person, because the sin affects more people.   So, too, *the
status of the sinner* influences the gravity of the sin.   One
who has received great gifts from God, other things being
equal, is a greater sinner than those less fortunate than
himself ; or one who sins in a position of responsibility or
privilege, ' both because of the example he gives and because
of the scandal he causes.'

Many interesting points are raised by the above summary
of the circumstances which aggravate sin.   We might notice
especially the emphasis upon sin against government—a
peculiarly modern touch, and one that specially requires
recognition at the present day.   But the important fact that
emerges is that there is *no final criterion of mortal and venial
sin*.   The decision in each case must be upon the merits.
The priest must sum up the character and circumstances
of the sinner, and then decide whether or no the danger to

---

[1] *Summa.* i. 2, q. 88, aa. 3, 4, 5.

[2] *Ibid.* a. 2.   [3] *Ibid.* qq. 72, 73.

his soul is sufficient to warrant the employment of extreme measures, with their attendant risks. The considerations indicated will help him to a decision, but they provide no infallible rule. Experience—his own and that of others— careful thought, and the guidance of the Holy Spirit above all, are the only guides upon which he can rely. There are times even when ' reflection can do nothing and resolution must do all '[1]—when, after every effort of consideration has been exhausted, the question remains open ; in these cases he must choose his course with such care as the circumstances permit, and trust to God to overrule his action for good.

2. *The Treatment of Sin*

We may consider the treatment of sin, therefore, under two heads—methods safe but gradual, and methods violent but dangerous. Under the latter we class all courses of action which involve a mutilation of personality, or which adopt the method, so dangerous in the case of the more violent passions, of direct appeal to the conscience. The gradual methods, we have seen, should be applied first in all cases of venial sin—of sin, that is, which does not threaten the soul with imminent danger of spiritual ruin. Only when they fail should sterner measures be tried. In general the latter are to be reserved for cases of mortal sin. In this conclusion we are following the lead of the Church, whose interest in sin was largely disciplinary. Following St. Augustine, theologians have always held that the harm done to the soul by venial sin can be repaired by daily prayer and religious observances ; for mortal sin the severer method of sacramental confession, penance and absolution is necessary.[2]

---

[1] Jane Austen, *Sense and Sensibility*.

[2] Aug., *De Symbolo*, 15 ; *Enchir.* 64, 71 ; *Ad Jerom.* clxvii. 4 ; *Serm.* 56. Cp. Chrysostom, *In Matt. Hom.* xix. 8, xli. 6 ; Gregory, *In Evan₂. Hom.* xxxiv. 5 ; *Summa*, iii. q. 86, a. 2 ; q. 87, aa. 1, 3 ; Suppl. q. 6, aa. 1, 3. The development of this principle in the Church, however, shows a very striking refinement of the Christian consciousness. To Tertullian the ' mortal ' sins for which penance and absolution are *necessary* are of the type which create public scandal (*De Pudic.* 18, 19). To Augustine (*De Fid. et Op.* 19, 26) and Pacian (*Paraen. ad Poen.*) they are of the same

In cases of venial sin, the priest will be content to stimulate the normal spiritual life by the means we have discussed in previous chapters—choosing of course those methods most suitable to the character, age, sex and condition of the sinner. And he will hope that by these means the spiritual life will so be strengthened—mind, desires and will so occupied by the love and service of God—that the sin of which he has observed the symptoms, so far from gaining any further hold upon the character in which it has effected a temporary lodgment, will steadily fall into oblivion. For the most part he will use the ordinary opportunities of parochial intercourse to insinuate these counsels, without suggesting that he has any grounds for uneasiness. Except in the case of ' choleric ' temperaments there will usually be no need for him to speak definitely and explicitly to any individual about his sin at all. Where, however, he does so, it will be in an encouraging and kindly manner, deprecating any suggestion that the matter is one of grave spiritual danger, and saying what has to be said merely in the form of a friendly warning.

An appeal to the sentiment of self-respect, or honourable (as distinct from sinful) pride, often works wonders. ' Self-conceit,' says Anthony Trollope of one of his heroes,[1] ' was not his greatest danger ; had he possessed more of it he might have been a less agreeable man, but his course before him might on that account have been safer.' Even in desperate cases, in cases of mortal sin, there may be a saving grace in pride ; far more so in venial. ' The conscience of many a man, of many a kingdom, has been

type, though different in essence, being the three sins *par excellence* of the early Church, fornication, apostasy (idolatry) and murder (Acts xv. 29), which Tertullian, at all events, had regarded as irremissible on earth (*De Pudic. loc. cit.* ; cp. *Adv. Marcion*, iv. 9). It is only in later centuries that inward wickedness rather than outward scandal becomes the test of ' mortal ' sin. Cp. *infra*, p. 265, n. 3. On the decree of the Lateran Council, and its interpretation by the Council of Trent and later Roman Catholic authorities, see F. von. Hügel, *Mystical Element of Religion*, vol. i. pp. 120, 121 ; and cp. J. Gury, *Compendium*, vol. ii. § 457. But on the *advisability* of confession in all cases see St. Thomas Aquinas, *Sent.* iv d. 17, q. 2, a. 1 ; q. 3, ad. 8.

[1] Mark Robarts in *Framley Parsonage*.

reached only through their pride. Pride is the last nerve which comfort and habit leave quick ; and when summons to a man's better nature fails, it is still possible in most cases to touch his pride with the presentation of the facts of his decadence. . . . The nerve of pride was touched in the prodigal : " How many hired servants of my father have enough and to spare, while I perish with hunger." ' [1]

Cases continually occur in which the initiative is taken by the sinner himself, and the priest is consulted, either in the confessional or in a less formal manner, as to some weakness or fall of a trivial character. Here, of course, he may with safety and advantage go further than in the other case, and suggest a definite rule of life or religious exercise as a corrective for the sin ; for he has the acknowledged good-will of the sinner on his side. Intercession for any whom one dislikes or despises ; the practice of thanksgiving if or when inclined to depression ; simple meditation and acts of recollection for those who forget God in the press of daily affairs ; apology for trivial wrongs inflicted ; special almsgiving in cases of self-indulgence, or slight and harmless abstention from pleasures for a time—all these may be prescribed, as occasion offers, as remedies efficacious in the case of the various sins mentioned.

The treatment of venial sins, therefore, presents no real difficulties ; it demands of the priest merely tact in dealing with the sinner, and a certain ready ingenuity in devising remedies appropriate to the different kind of sins that come up for treatment. Experience and sympathy, guided and strengthened by the Holy Spirit, will give him all he needs.

It is very different with mortal sin. Here the director's responsibilities are far greater. A false step may produce the very result he wishes to avoid ; hesitation or moral cowardice may be every bit as disastrous. He has to act boldly and at once, yet he has to act with the skill of an expert ; for it is unlikely that he will have a second opportunity if he wastes the first. A sinner to whose conscience he has appealed in vain will hardly offer him a second chance. It is essential therefore, in cases of this

---

[1] Geo. Adam Smith, *Book of the Twelve Prophets*, chap. 22.

kind, to disentangle among the complex of evil influences
in the sinful soul any which above the others is a cause
of danger ; to plan carefully the remedy to be proposed ;
and finally to appeal to the sinner with all the earnestness
and emphasis at command, on that one head alone. It is
idle to accuse a man of many vices ; if it does not rouse
his antipathy, it may touch his heart, but most probably
with despair rather than hope. ' Disregard the lighter
sins,' is St. Gregory's wise advice, 'and concentrate upon
removing the graver.' [1]

What practical steps, then, can be urged upon a man
in the grip of mortal sin ? First of all, and above all,
enhanced devotion—or it may be renewal of devotion—
to the practices which promote spiritual progress. In
many cases such a revival of the spiritual life will be impossible without an act of confession and the grace of
absolution as a preliminary. Here we are faced by the
peculiar difficulty of the English Church : that to the vast
majority of her children confession, in the sacramental
sense, is not a part of the normal fibre of religion at all.
Two observations are necessary on this head. First of
all, experience shows that if the priest's appeal to conscience
has been successful—if it has enlisted the sinner's willing
co-operation in an attempt to eradicate the sin—less difficulty than might have been expected will be encountered
in the attempt to reconcile him to an act of confession.
In the second place, if his religious history is such that
he can hardly be brought at once to see the need of confession, there is at least one other method which will often
take its place effectively. Such sanctity surrounds the
Holy Communion in the English mind, that to a non-
Catholic Churchman an act of special preparation for its
reception, with the definite intention of seeking in it a
medicine for sin, will often have the psychological effect
of confession, penance and absolution. He can be urged
to examine his conscience more carefully than has been
his usual custom, to confess his sin explicitly to God,
asking earnestly for forgiveness and grace to persevere,
and to prepare some special resolution of amendment

[1] *De Past. Cur.* iii. **38.**

of life and reparation to offer up at the altar. Opinions may differ as to how far this can be a satisfactory substitute for confession; at least we may say that where, through the strength of inherited prejudice, the latter cannot at once be conscientiously adopted by the sinner, the other method is open to him, and by God's mercy will be very far from unavailing.

A conscientious man harassed by mortal sin has usually a not unnatural reluctance towards receiving the Holy Communion, even though at the same time he is struggling hard against his sin. This is especially the case with young men in the grip of youthful passions. A growing irregularity of attendance at the Eucharist may therefore be not merely a symptom of serious sin, but also a sign of an awakened conscience. Yet such reluctance to receive the sacrament, though natural and laudable, is wholly misdirected. So long as the struggle against temptation continues, so long the Eucharist will be the greatest force the Christian can have upon his side. If it be neglected, the danger of ultimate submission to sin is increased tenfold. 'I who always sin, should always seek this medicine.' [1]

The maintenance at all cost of the full spiritual life, restored to grace by confession and absolution, and sustained by the Eucharist as by all other means of religious progress, must be the first step in countering deadly sin. But even so it is the peculiar nature of such sin that the penitent is still afraid of it. He fears the recurrence of temptation in even more insidious and violent forms; he has a growing despair of ever achieving immunity from it. The spiritual life develops only slowly, especially when weakened by continued sinfulness; temptation is strong and urgent; the struggle is a weary one. The insidious suggestion that after all indulgence in the sin in question is compatible with outward decency, with a certain degree of religious life, penetrates into the mind. Such are the usual concomitants of mortal sin. It is in these cases that the violent and dangerous remedies we have spoken of are necessary; and we have reached a point at which they must be considered in detail.

[1] [Ambrose] *De Sacramentis*, iv. 6.

It is here that the analysis of the stages by which sin develops is of value. The principal factors which enter into such a development were seen, in the last chapter, to be a basal instinct, the occasions which stimulate it, the idea of its gratification, the passions inflamed by it, and the successive acts which go to form a habit. Some of these at least are susceptible of drastic treatment, though the treatment in each case is surrounded with pitfalls. But among the drastic methods which may be adopted we must notice the following :—

(a) *Break the habit.*[1]

In cases of venial sin a man may be weaned from his habit gently and by gradual degrees. In cases of mortal sin the habit must be broken once for all. It is scarcely necessary to emphasise the extraordinary difficulty often met with in such an attempt. Only a supreme effort of will on the part of the sinner is competent to effect it. Hence in advising the step—and it often has to be advised— the priest must take certain precautions. An attempt to break a sinful habit which ends in failure is a disaster to be avoided at all costs. It may lead to despair, abandonment of the struggle, and callousness. It may be the mother of hypocrisy, leading the sinner either to dissimulate his real condition from the priest whose help he has sought, or to run from one adviser or confessor to another so that none may guess the urgency of his case.

To minimise this danger, therefore, anything in the form of heroic resolutions must be discouraged.[2] It will be task enough for the sinner to break the habit alone, without undertaking special acts of mortification or penance in addition. His will is already enfeebled : it must not attempt anything beyond its strength. Again, he must beware both of the danger of failure in the task he has undertaken, and of the danger of success. The danger of failure is very real. A habit which has taken strong hold upon character cannot be thrown off in a moment ;

---

[1] This question is commonly treated in ascetic theology under the heading of *Relapses.* See W. W. Williams, *op. cit.* p. 150; Scaramelli, *op cit.* Treat. i. §§ 313, 433 ; Schieler-Heuser, *op. cit.* pp. 448–459, 521–536.
[2] Cp. A. Chandler, *Ara Coeli*, p. 54.

occasional relapses must be expected. It is important that the penitent should be alive to this fact; otherwise failure to achieve his purpose at once will produce the despair of which we have already spoken. Still more real is the danger of temporary success. Under the stimulus of a genuine penitence and a renewed desire for holiness the habit may indeed be broken for a time; optimism and carelessness will set in; the soul will be off its guard against the temptation, and a recurrence will lead to a fall worse than the former one. These possibilities must be put before the sinner clearly and fairly, yet without pessimism; he must be encouraged to make the attempt, but warned of the danger of possible failure.

(*b*) *Remove the occasion.*

Occasions of sin are usually classified under the three following headings.[1] They may be *free* or *necessary* (' free ' being those which the sinner himself creates : ' necessary ' those created by his condition or environment). They may be *proximate* (that is to say, leading directly to the sin through an immediate stimulus of the instinct), or *remote*—leading to it through various stages; as gambling may lead to dishonesty; intoxication to immorality; envy to hatred; or wit to mockery and contempt. Lastly, they may be *continual* or *interrupted* (occasional).

The rules with regard to them may be deduced from the classification. ' Free ' occasions of known sin must of course be given up. ' Proximate ' and ' continual ' occasions must be given up unless they are also ' necessary.' Both ' remote ' and ' interrupted ' occasions are better given up; wherever there is any obvious danger of their becoming, through the sinner's weakness, proximate and continual, they *must* be given up.

The real difficulty comes with ' necessary ' occasions. A man's business, his family life, even his religion, may expose him to continual temptations of the greatest danger to him. Few problems with which the missioner or confessor

---

[1] W. W. Williams, *op. cit.* p. 144; Schieler-Heuser, *op. cit.* pp. 488-518. There is a practical little discussion in Gaume, *Advice on Hearing Confession*, chap. i. art. 3, § 67. Cp. also Jeremy Taylor's ' Eleven Rules for obtaining Temperance,' *Holy Living*, chap. ii. sect. 2.

has to deal are harder or more painful than this one. It may be possible for him, by an appeal to others, to mitigate the severity of the temptation—to effect some change in the man's environment which will give him at least temporary relief. No opportunity of this kind should be left untouched. It may be best to allow him to bow down in the house of Rimmon for a time ; this course is possible in cases where the moral purpose of the tempted man offers hope of ultimate strength to resist, in spite of the continuance and danger of present temptation.

But extreme cases occur in which the sinner must at all costs be removed to an environment less plentiful in occasions of sin. Wherever the priest finds it necessary to urge such a removal, which may involve a complete change of employment, or a break-up of the home, it is clear that his responsibility is not at an end until he himself, alone or with help, has found a new environment for the sinner in which conditions will be more favourable. A man whose employer insists, for example, upon his using dishonest methods in business cannot simply be advised to give up his work and trust in Providence ; the priest who interprets God's will to him in this sense must also, to the utmost of his ability, attempt to be God's mediator to him in other respects—to co-operate with God in providing for him an environment more hopeful than his former one. Anything less than this would be a cruel and inhuman neglect of the responsibilities of the priesthood.

Setting apart these extreme cases, however, it must be noticed that it is just in the giving up of occasions of sin that there occurs most frequently the mutilation of personality of which we have previously spoken. For occasions of sin are occasions also of virtue ; and to cut them off is to remove the soul from opportunities of realising its full possibilities and developing its strength. They are also occasions of experience ; and experience, particularly experience of temptation, is the most powerful factor in making for sympathy. It is generally those who have led most sheltered lives who are least able to understand the dangers and temptations of others and consequently to help them when they require it. It follows then that, *if a soul can be strengthened to resist temptation, it should not be removed from temptation.* To do so will result in spiritual loss ; and in spiritual loss of a specially regrettable kind— the loss, namely, of sympathy for, and power to help, others who find themselves tempted.

The removal of temptations, of occasions of sin, involves another and even more insidious danger. It is never possible to guard against every form of stimulus ; sooner or later, however closely a life has been sheltered, the normal temptations of human nature will assail it. It is true that during the sheltered period the spiritual life may have so been strengthened as to make resistance more possible to temptation when it comes. But usually, it must be admitted, such a result does not happen ; and we may find the reason for it in what we have previously learnt as to the character of the spiritual life. That life, as we have constantly seen, demands as one of the factors in its growth the true alignment of the mind with the will of God—the mind, that is, must be able to recognise in any given case of temptation what is and what is not sinful. *But it cannot do this without some previous knowledge of what the temptation involves :* it must have considered the temptation in question, or some other nearly akin to it, before the actual danger arises.

For this reason it is psychologically necessary to give to a developing mind not merely a clear conception as to what right is, but also a clear conception of what wrong is. The negative form of the commandments is a necessary one : the growing boy or girl must learn the nature of the sins that must be avoided, as well as of the virtues that are to be acquired. The emphasis on the latter factor, as has previously been shown, must be far greater than that upon the former ; but both are necessary. The mistake made by those who would remove the occasions of sin from childhood is too often that, in their anxiety to do so, they destroy also the very means by which the mind may hereafter recognise and so avoid sinful suggestions. Ignorance of the character of sin may indeed be innocency, but it is the very reverse of spiritual strength ; it is one of the most fertile causes of sin.

The removal of occasions of sin, therefore, is to be

deprecated, unless absolutely necessary—in any case where it will lessen experience, sympathy, and the knowledge of the character of temptation. In such a sense the removal of occasions is emphatically one of the remedies against sin which we have characterised as drastic and dangerous, and only to be employed where no other course seems to offer any certainty of success.

(c) *Correct the idea.*

No sin takes hold upon personality without some excuse or justification in the mind. This excuse is a part, and an important part, in the vivid ' idea ' of the sin which we found to be a factor in its growth. The sinner is *deceived*, in St. Paul's language ; he tells himself that whilst for other people or in other circumstances the action he contemplates would be culpable, for himself, conditioned as he is, it is blameless.

Few factors are more important in the first commission of a sin than this one. The sinner persuades himself first of all of the innocence of his proposed action, then even of its laudability. Readers of ' Framley Parsonage ' will remember the sophistry by which Mark Robarts argued himself into a course of action which he knew to be morally blameworthy. ' I refused at first,' he wrote to his wife, ' but everybody here said that my doing so would be so strange ; and then they all wanted to know my reason. When I came to render it I did not know what reason I had to give. The Bishop is going, and he thought it very odd that I should not go also, seeing I was asked. . . . I think I should have been wrong to stand out when so much was said about it. I should have been seeming to take upon myself to sit in judgment upon the Duke. I doubt if there be a single clergyman in the diocese, under fifty years of age, who would have refused the invitation under such circumstances.' [1]

Common as argument of this kind is in justifying the first commission of a sin, it is even commoner as an excuse for a relapse. The converted drunkard who breaks his pledge, William James reminds us,[2] has always a perfectly good reason for doing so ' just this once '—it is Christmas, or someone's birthday, or he needs something to keep out

---

[1] Anthony Trollope, *Framley Parsonage*, chap. 4.
[2] *Principles of Psychology*, vol. ii. p. 565.

the cold. There is, therefore, another method of combating sin—that of correcting the distorted ideas under the influence of which it has been committed. Two steps are necessary. First of all the sin must be represented to the sinner in its real character as an offence against God, against man, against his own soul ; the wall of make-believe with which the mind has surrounded it must be broken down. Then, it must be insisted, no excuse will ever justify a sin which is recognised as such. Once a rule has been made, under wise guidance and in a spirit of penitence and prayer, no argument whatever (unless perhaps of overwhelming cogency, and in a matter of life and death) should be allowed to interfere with its maintenance. It is in matters such as these that the appeal to self-respect, which has already been considered, may help to maintain the sanctity of rules as against passing excuses for their breach.

The danger inherent in this method was alluded to on an earlier page. It lies in the fact that argument about the sin must inevitably heighten the idea of the sin. However carefully reproof or advice is phrased, it is always possible that a chance word may start a train of evil imagination of the most dangerous kind. This is more particularly the case with sins of youth and passion ; and it is therefore in dealing with them that argument should most sparingly be used, and direct allusion to the details of the sin most sedulously avoided.

(d) *Inhibit the emotions.*

Once more, an appeal may be made to the sinner for a special effort of will to restrain the emotions surrounding the idea of the sin, and (as a necessary preliminary) to exclude the idea itself from the mind. Everything that has been said as to the difficulty of breaking habits applies here with even greater force ; for a habit of feeling or of thought is more deep-rooted even than one of action. Indeed we may say with Professor Welton[1] : ' There can be no such thing as *breaking* a habit. All habituation is a determination of the direction of a part of life. We cannot cut out a piece of life ; we can only change its form.' This is more true even of internal than of external habits ; they are practically

[1] *Psychology of Education*, p. 182.

ineradicable. But they *can* be temporarily inhibited, both
by direct action of the will, and by the immediate substitution for them of pleasurable and harmless—or better
still, of virtuous—interests. The latter method is indeed
an ideal one ; the difficulty lies in finding an alternative
sufficiently absorbing to exclude the more passionate
emotions which surround the idea of vice. In the case of
mortal sin this is usually impossible ; a direct appeal must
be made to the will for an act of temporary inhibition which
will allow the harmless or beneficent emotion time to take
root in the soul.

It is clear that any such violent inhibition of feeling
is unnatural, and must involve danger to the soul. The
emotion which has been expelled from consciousness will
gain added strength and vehemence in the subconscious
region, and may either break out in overwhelming force,
or be the parent of some other excess of character, or even
finally overthrow reason itself. The undue mortifications
to which ascetics have sometimes been addicted have
almost always issued in one of these three results. Either
they have led to disastrous and irretrievable relapses,
or to some abnormal morbidity of character very far from
the true Christian ideal, or to a condition bordering upon
lunacy itself. Anything more than a limited and temporary
inhibition of feeling has always been condemned by responsible theologians. Thus St. Thomas urges that self-
mortification should only be employed ' within the measure
of reason.' ' Tame the emotions but do not extinguish
nature : remember the words of the Apostle, " Present your
bodies as a living sacrifice " ; to which he adds immediately
" which is your *reasonable* service." ' [1]

So far, then, we have found that none of the methods
suggested by experience for dealing with mortal sin—sin
that has become an imminent danger to spiritual health—
can be regarded as altogether satisfactory. They demand
an immense exertion of will—an exertion of will of which
the enfeebled soul may be almost if not quite incapable ;
they have their own peculiar dangers which may involve

---

[1] *Quodl.* v. a. 18. See Scaramelli, *op. cit.* Treat. ii. § 54. Cp. *Summa*,
ii. 2, q. 88, a. 2, ad 3 ; q. 147, a. 1, ad 2.

T

results as disastrous as the sin they are designed to cure ; and, it may be added, at the best they ensure only a transient security. For, as we have seen, there lies behind every sin an instinct in which it had its root ; and so long as the instinct survives, how can any man be safe ?

3. *Redirection of Instincts. The Seven Capital Sins*

The answer to this question is one in which both theologian and psychologist concur with the testimony of everyday experience. Drastic methods of dealing with sin we have seen to avail in so far as they secure a measure of time, a breathing space, during which the attention of the soul may be diverted to other and harmless employments. Any such employments will be of value, but more especially those which not merely do not impede but actually promote the spiritual life ; and among these most of all those which—if only they can be discovered— *will give a new outlet or sphere of activity to the very instinct which lay at the root of the sin concerned.* If we can once ' divert ' the instincts at fault ' with some laudable employment, and take off their edge with inadvertency ' there is every hope that the disease of the soul which took its rise from them will be fully and finally cured—' for the faculties of a man cannot at the same time with any sharpness attend to two objects.' [1]

To this method that shrewd observer of character, W. E. H. Lecky, gave the significant name of the *moral safety-valve*. ' There are elements in human nature,' he wrote, ' which many moralists might wish to be absent, as they are very easily turned in the direction of vice, but which at the same time are inherent in our being, and if rightly understood are essential elements of human progress. . . The true policy of these things is to find for them a healthy, useful, or at least harmless sphere of action. In the chemistry of character they may ally themselves with the most heroic as well as with the worst parts of our nature ; and the same passion for excitement which in one man will take the form of ruinous vice,

---

[1] Jeremy Taylor, *Holy Living*, chap. ii. sect. 1.

in another may lead to brilliant enterprise, while in a third it may be turned with no great difficulty into channels which are very innocent.' [1]

Lecky proceeds to illustrate his thesis with examples of an everyday character, which must appeal to the common sense of every reader. This doctrine of the ' moral safety-valve,' or, as we may prefer to call it, the ' redirection of instinct,' is indeed fundamental in the renewal of character. No other method open to human choice offers so good a hope of effecting permanent change for the better. In order to put it into practice something must be known of the number and nature of the primary instincts, the sins to which each is most likely to give rise, and the innocent or beneficent channels into which it is capable of being diverted.

Moral theology recognises [2] a list of seven ' capital' or ' root' sins (not, as so often called, ' deadly' [3] sins) which derive their name from the fact that all other sins originate in one or other of them.[4] The seven, as is well known, are pride or vainglory, gluttony, sloth,[5] covetousness, anger, lust and envy. Each of these is the ' parent' of many others—pride, for example, of presumption, hypocrisy, obstinacy, quarrelsomeness and disobedience ; gluttony

---

[1] *Map of Life*, p. 264. Cp. the admirable treatment of this subject as a whole by J. A. Hadfield in *The Spirit*, pp. 96-102.

[2] *Summa*, i. 2, q. 84, a. 4. Gregory's *Moralia in Job* is the classical exposition of the subject. See especially book xxxi. chap. 45.

[3] Much confusion has been caused by the application of the name *deadly* to the capital sins. Indeed the practice robs both ' mortal' and ' capital' sin of any real meaning ; for *all* sin, mortal or venial, is traceable to a ' capital' sin ; and capital sins can express themselves in venial forms. The idea of ' mortal' and that of ' capital' sin must be kept wholly apart for either of them to have practical value. The confusion probably arose from Tertullian, who gives (*Adv. Marcion.* iv. 9 ; cp. *De Pudicit.* 18, 19) a list of ' seven deadly sins,' by which he meant what Augustine calls *crimina*—i.e. open or scandalous sins for which public penance was necessary, even if they did not involve lifelong excommunication. This is a conception differing both from that of mortal (in the strict sense) and capital sin, though it has affinities with both. The confusion presumably arose from the use of the mystic number seven in each case.

[4] Though it would appear that St. Thomas also recognised *malitia* (the state of formed sinful habit) as a cause of sin distinct from the capital vices. See the whole discussion in W. H. V. Reade, *Moral System of Dante's Inferno*, chaps. 13 and 15.

[5] *Tristitia* in *Summa, loc. cit.*—usually *acedia*.

T 2

of drunkenness, vain joy (with consequent weakening of love to God), impurity, selfishness, and love of ease.[1] The list is of great antiquity, and has caused a great deal of misunderstanding and confusion, for the sins which comprise it are of very varying degrees of heinousness. But it is important to notice that in one of its earliest appearances in theology the seven[2] are spoken of not as *sins* but as λογισμοί—the ' hidden motions of the soul out of which all kinds of sin arise.'[3] This gives us a clue to the real bearing of the catalogue. It is an attempt to enumerate, in theological rather than psychological language, and from the point of view of experience rather than from that of scientific investigation, *those of the primary instincts which are most likely to give rise to sin*. And, on comparison with the conclusions of present-day psychology, we must confess that it is not at all an unsuccessful attempt.

Psychological writers are not indeed altogether in agreement as to the precise identity of those impulses to action which may fairly be regarded as primary instincts. We may, however, select the following as a typical list[4] : hunger and thirst, pugnacity, self-assertion (sometimes technically known as ' positive self-feeling '), the sexual instinct, acquisitiveness, self-preservation (fear), gregariousness, curiosity, constructiveness, the tender emotions (and particularly the maternal emotion), and self-abasement (or ' negative self-feeling '). Of this list it is perfectly clear that the first five correspond quite

---

[1] It may be of interest to continue the list of sins to which each of the seven respectively is ' parent ' :—

Sloth is the parent of hatred of spiritual things, weakness in prayer, dullness of spirit (*acedia*), moral cowardice, despair.

Covetousness : of fear of loss, anxiety, worldly sorrow, callousness, dishonesty, uncharitableness.

Anger : of suspicion, ingratitude, resentment, mental agitation, rancour, &c.

Lust : of blindness of mind, hardness of heart, inconstancy, cruelty.

Envy : of falsehood, calumny, evil interpretation, contempt.

[2] The list in question actually contains *eight* sins. See T. B. Strong, *Christian Ethics*, p. 260.

[3] So too they are often spoken of as *radices*—*roots* of sin.

[4] J. Welton, *Psychology of Education*, p. 76 ff. The order of enumeration in the text is not however Dr. Welton's. Cp. W. McDougall, *Social Psychology*, chap. 2.

definitely to five of the capital sins—to gluttony, anger, pride, lust, and covetousness respectively. Envy, a sixth sin, has no definite parallel in the list of instincts; Dr. Welton, however, only refuses it a place among them because he regards it as a combination of self-assertion and pugnacity.[1] It might equally well, or even better, be considered as the resultant of acquisitiveness and pugnacity.

The only one of the capital sins, therefore, which cannot be said to be represented at all in the list of instincts is sloth. And even sloth we might consider to be represented by ' negative self-feeling '—the tendency *not* to assert or exert oneself. On the other hand, there are numerous instincts which have no parallel in the list of capital sins. Of these we must fairly admit that fear must be regarded as a capital sin ; its omission is possibly due to a desire to keep within the limits of the mystic number seven. The remainder are not instincts which lend themselves readily to sin of any serious kind ; they are not specifically *self-regarding*, and sin may be said to begin with self-regard.[2]

We conclude, then, that there is little to choose between the list of capital sins and that of self-regarding instincts as a working basis for the redirection of instincts. Every sin can be traced back to a capital sin, or better to a primary instinct, as its source ; and the work of the priest consists in finding for such an instinct an absorbing, harmless, and if possible beneficial outlet. We might indeed spend time over the capital sins, examining the character of each of them, and especially of that mysterious spiritual disorder of sloth by which ' the mind, not being inflamed by any burning fervour, is cut off from all desire of the good.'[3] To do so, however, would protract the discussion unduly ; and the subject is fully dealt with in the standard manuals.

---

[1] *Psychology of Education*, p. 85.

[2] Thus Athanasius (*Contra Gentes*, 3) describes the aversion of man from God as beginning in self-regard (ἑαυτοὺς κατανοεῖν ἤρξαντο). Cp. Augustine, *De Civ. Dei*, book xiv. chaps. 3, 8 ; *Confessions*, book iii. chap. 8 : sin is wrong self-love.

[3] Gregory, *De Past. Cur.* iii. admon. 16. For a full treatment of sloth (*acedia*) see F. Paget, *Spirit of Discipline*, chap. 1.

It remains for us to consider the practical application of the doctrine of the redirection of instincts.

The first step, then, is to discover which instinct lies at the root of any given spiritual disorder. Lying, for example, may be traced back either to pride, to envy, or to fear, as its source ; drunkenness to gluttony, sloth, or fear, physical or moral ; theft to covetousness, envy, or hatred (anger) ; and so on. Specific sin, even though mortal in character, is to be regarded not merely as a thing to be corrected in itself, but even more as a symptom of a misdirected instinct ; and the instinct concerned must in each case be correctly diagnosed with reference to the particular circumstances of the sin.

The second step is to check the sin in question, both by steady development of the spiritual life, and perhaps, in addition, by one of the drastic means which have been discussed. This, however, should be a measure adopted mainly to gain time ; and the time so gained must be employed in finding and offering to the instinct concerned a new outlet for its activity. Here again the imagination, sympathy and initiative of the priest are called into play. He must envisage for himself the channel in which the instinct will most naturally and readily reassert itself or be absorbed. Self-assertion, for example, may be diverted from evil purposes by opportunities of leadership or organisation ; pugnacity by its enlistment in the cause of the oppressed ; [1] the sexual instinct by the friendship of good women ; [2] sloth (which involves a desire for comfort and quiet) in simple tasks of consoling or amusing others.

Acquisitiveness is a peculiarly difficult instinct to treat, because it is of so eminently selfish a character. Perhaps the best thing that can be said about it is that it is naturally allied to emulation ; and a man whose danger lies in this direction might perhaps be saved from selfishness by being

[1] ' The director will strive to engage those who waste their natural fortitude on vice and worthless objects, to turn it to things supernatural and divine.'—Scaramelli, *op. cit.* Treat. iii. § 120.

[2] In this connection it must not be forgotten that devotion to Our Lady, as the ideal of purity, though capable of over-emphasis, has shown itself in Christian experience to be a real source of moral strength ; and merits greater emphasis than it receives in the Church of England to-day.

invited to exert himself for some good purpose in competition with others.[1] Where, however, acquisitiveness has issued in definite dishonesty or injustice, such redirection of the instinct must of course be accompanied by restoration or restitution wherever possible. Gluttony, again, and in particular drunkenness, is difficult to correct, but it has natural affinities with good-fellowship ; and experience shows that the instinct can as well be gratified in society where over-indulgence is impossible, as in an environment where it is the rule. This at least was the principle which produced such remarkable results when applied in the philanthropic institutes set up in camps at home and abroad during the war ; and clergy who work in industrial centres are well aware that the chief cause of the popularity of the public-house is the unattractiveness of the home. Correct the latter, and the harmless instinct for meat and drink can find its full satisfaction in the domestic circle without fear of over-indulgence and its even graver consequences.

The reader may be left to apply the consequences of this far-reaching principle for himself. One concrete example, however, contributed by a priest who has been led to recognise its importance by parochial experience, will perhaps show how widely it may be applied. It was brought to his notice that one of the boys in his lads' club was perpetually cheating at games, and that the constant repetition of the offence, often only in the most trivial forms, was having a definitely evil effect upon his character. Inquiry seemed to indicate that the instinct at fault was not covetousness—the desire of prizes or gain—but rather self-assertion. What the lad wanted was to be *first* in something. As a remedy against this tendency, it was decided to give him a position of responsibility in the club, in the hope that by this means his aspiration for prominence would be satisfied. The result justified the expectation, and from the moment of his assuming office the boy's dishonesty

---

[1] ' If the director meet with any who are absorbed in amassing wealth and possessions . . . let him endeavour to change the object of this sordid passion and substitute the acquiring of means for relieving the poor and enhancing the splendour of divine worship, and he will soon change them into men of extraordinary piety.'—Scaramelli, *op. cit.* Treat. iii. § 120.

ceased. The instinct had been correctly diagnosed, and the remedy chosen absorbed its energies to the exclusion of the vicious practices to which it had till then been directed.

The instance is trivial enough, but the greater part of pastoral effort is directed to the cure of trivial things. Indeed, their trivial nature often makes them as puzzling and difficult to deal with as the grosser sins. But whether a sin be great or small, venial or mortal, the priest can be assured that in looking for the instinct which causes it, he is adopting the truest and most certain of human means of healing the soul. If even this means often seems to fail, it is because God in His wisdom reserves to Himself some other method of dealing with the sin. Our efforts are only a shadow when compared with His ; if, after the best of our endeavour, the result is still a failure, He is faithful, and His methods do not fail.

BIBLIOGRAPHY OF AUTHORS CONSULTED OR REFERRED TO

AN exhaustive Bibliography has not been attempted. A list of about seven hundred writers on moral and ascetic theology is given in Skinner's *Synopsis*. Shorter lists, mainly of post-Tridentine Roman Catholic writers, will be found in Slater, *Moral Theology*, and W. W. Williams, *Moral Theology of the Sacrament of Penance*. Useful bibliographies are given in Hastings' *Encyclopædia of Religion and Ethics* under the various headings.

Patristic writers are not included. Roman Catholic writers are marked with an asterisk.

I. MORAL THEOLOGY

AQUINAS, ST. THOMAS (Dominican), 1225–1274. *Opera Omnia.* The authoritative edition is the new Roman one, *jussu impensaque Leonis XIII.* That quoted here is the Parma edition, 1852–1873. (English Translation of the *Summa Theologica*, by the Fathers of the English Dominican Province. London. In course of publication.)

ELMENDORF, J. J. *Elements of Moral Theology*, based on the *Summa Theologiae* of St. Thomas Aquinas. 2nd edition. New York. 1902.

*GURY, J. P. (Jesuit), 1801–1886. *Compendium Theologiae Moralis.* Many editions; that quoted here is the 5th German, Ratisbon, 1874. Edition 9 (Rome 1887), annotated by A. Ballerini, is regarded as of high authority.

*LEHMKUHL, A. (Jesuit). *Theologia Moralis.* 11th ed. Friburg, 1910.

READE, W. H. V. *The Moral System of Dante's Inferno.* Oxford, 1909.

*RICKABY, J. (Jesuit). *Aquinas Ethicus.* A translation of the principal portions of the second part of the *Summa Theologica.* London, 1896.

—— *Moral Philosophy.* 4th ed. London, 1918.

SKINNER, J. *Synopsis of Moral and Ascetical Theology.* London, 1882.

*SLATER, T. (Jesuit). *Manual of Moral Theology.* New York, n.d.

—— *Cases of Conscience.* New York, n.d.

2. Penitential Theology

BELTON, F. G. *A Manual for Confessors*. London, 1916.

CARTER, T. T. *The Doctrine of Confession in the Church of England*. London, 1865.

CHURTON, E. T. (Bishop). *The Use of Penitence*. London, 1905.

*GAUME, ABBÉ (tr. E. B. PUSEY). *Advice on Hearing Confession*. Oxford, 1878.

*REUTER, J. (Jesuit), 1690–1762. *Neo-Confessarius*. Edition consulted, Paris, 1850.

*SCHIELER, C. E., and HEUSER, H. J. (Jesuit). *The Theory and Practice of the Confessional*. New York, 1905.

WATKINS, O. D. *A History of Penance*. London, 1920.

WEBB, W. W. (Bishop). *The Cure of Souls*. New York, 1892.

WILLIAMS, W. W. *The Moral Theology of the Sacrament of Penance*. London, 1917.

3. Ascetic Theology and Casuistry

*BAKER, AUGUSTIN (Benedictine), 1575–1641. *Holy Wisdom* (English Translation. London, n.d.)

CHANDLER, A. (Bishop). *Ara Coeli*. 7th ed. London, 1916.

—— *The Cult of the Passing Moment*. 3rd ed. London, 1915.

HALL, JOSEPH (Bishop), 1574–1656. *Resolutions and Decisions of Diverse Practical Cases of Conscience*.

JENKS, DAVID. *A Study of Meditation*. London, 1909.

LAW, WILLIAM, 1686–1761. *A Serious Call to a Devout and Holy Life*.

*LEHODEY, V. (Cistercian). *The Ways of Mental Prayer*. (Eng. Tr. Dublin, 1917.)

*POULAIN, A. (Jesuit). *The Graces of Interior Prayer*. (Eng. Tr. London, 1912.)

SANDERSON, ROBERT (Bishop), 1587–1663. *De Obligatione Conscientiae Praelectiones Decem*.

*SAUDREAU, A. *The Degrees of the Spiritual Life*. (Eng. Tr. London, 1917.)

*SCARAMELLI, J. B. (Jesuit), 1687–1752. *Directorium Asceticum*. (Eng. Tr. 7th ed. London, 1917.)

TAYLOR, JEREMY (Bishop), 1613–1667. *The Rule and Exercises of Holy Living*.

—— *The Rule and Exercises of Holy Dying*.

—— *Ductor Dubitantium*.

—— *Unum Necessarium, or the Doctrine and Practice of Repentance*.

—— *The Golden Grove*.

4. Ethics and Christian Ethics

BUTLER, JOSEPH (Bishop), 1692–1752. *Fifteen Sermons upon Human Nature, &c.*

*DÖLLINGER, I. VON, and REUSCH, H. *Geschichte der Moral-streitigkeiten in der römisch-Katholischen Kirche seit dem sechzehnten Jahrhundert.* Nördlingen, 1889.

DORNER, A. *System of Christian Ethics.* (Eng. Tr. Edinburgh, 1887.)

GREEN, T. H. *Prolegomena to Ethics.* 5th ed. Oxford, 1906.

HALL, T. C. *History of Ethics within Organised Christianity.* London, 1910.

ILLINGWORTH, J. R. *The Christian Character.* London, 1904.

INGE, W. R. *Christian Mysticism.* (Bampton Lectures.) London, 1899.

LECKY, W. H. *History of European Morals.* 1st ed. London, 1869.

—— *The Map of Life.* London, 1899.

MARTENSEN, H. *Christian Ethics.* (Eng. Tr. Edinburgh, 1882.)

OTTLEY, R. L. *Christian Ideas and Ideals.* London, 1909.

RASHDALL, H. *The Theory of Good and Evil.* Oxford, 1907.

—— *Conscience and Christ.* London, 1916.

SIDGWICK, H. *History of Ethics.* London, 1886.

—— *Methods of Ethics.* London, 1913.

SMYTH, NEWMAN. *Christian Ethics.* Edinburgh, 1892.

STRONG, T. B. (Bishop). *Christian Ethics.* (Bampton Lectures.) London, 1897.

UNDERHILL, E. *Mysticism.* London, 1911.

*VON HÜGEL, F. *The Mystical Element of Religion.* London, 1908.

—— *Eternal Life.* Edinburgh, 1912.

5. Psychology and Religious Psychology

COE, G. A. *The Spiritual Life.* New York, 1900.

—— *Psychology of Religion.* Chicago, 1916.

HALL, G. STANLEY. *Adolescence.* New York, 1904.

INGE, W. R. *Faith and its Psychology.* London, 1909.

JAMES, W. *Principles of Psychology.* London, 1890.

—— *Varieties of Religious Experience.* London, 1902.

McDOUGALL, W. *Social Psychology.* 1st ed. London, 1908.

—— *Body and Mind.* London, 1913.

RIBOT, T. *Psychology of the Emotions.* (Eng. Tr. London, 1911.)

SAUNDERS, K. *Adventures of the Christian Soul.* Cambridge, 1916.

STARBUCK, E. *Psychology of Religion.* London, 1914.

WELTON, J. *Psychology of Education.* London, 1909.

INDEX

I. GENERAL

II. TECHNICAL TERMS